The Common Thread

This collection of writings won't provide easy answers to your
question, 'Who is working-class?' But what it will do is challenge
the above caricature. Working-class women are not all Flo Capp,
Hilda Ogden, Vera Duckworth or miners' wives. Some of us live
in seemingly permanent poverty. Some of us have relatively good
jobs and a reasonable standard of living. Many of us have been
denied access to education and resources. Some have overcome
these obstacles, but never without a struggle, without sacrifice
and difficult choices.

We come in all shapes and sizes, nationalities and ages. We're
black and white, Jewish and Gentile, lesbian and heterosexual,
and we live with a range of disabilities, physical and otherwise.
Our experiences and our politics are varied and wide-ranging,
and we speak with many voices – with pride, sorrow, joy and
pain, anger and bitterness, generosity and kindness, resilience,
strength, intelligence, humour, fatalism and revolutionary commitment. We have our differences, and here we celebrate them
and the common thread of class experience that links us.

The Common Thread

Writings by Working-Class Women

edited by

June Burnett, Julie Cotterill, Annette
Kennerley, Phoebe Nathan and
Jeanne Wilding

Mandarin

A Mandarin Paperback

THE COMMON THREAD

First published in Great Britain 1989
by Mandarin Paperbacks
Michelin House, 81 Fulham Road, London sw3 6rb

Mandarin is an imprint of the Octopus Publishing Group

British Library Cataloguing in Publication Data

The Common thread:
    writings by working-class women.
    1. English literature. Women writers,
    1945 – —Anthologies
    I. The Common Thread
    820.8'09287

ISBN 0 7493 0028 0

Photoset by Rowland Phototypesetting Ltd
Bury St Edmunds, Suffolk
Printed and bound in Great Britain
by Cox and Wyman Ltd
Reading, Berks

Contents

The editors' thanks are due to the copyright holders of the following stories for permission to use them in this volume:

'A Day in the Life' and 'To Alice', copyright © 1989 Viv Acious; 'Ground' and 'Holding the Baby', copyright © 1989 Sylvan Agass; 'No Earth Moved, Just The Rear Suspension', copyright © 1989 Jill Aldred; 'Bless This House', copyright © 1989 Pat Angove; 'Women's Aid', copyright © 1989 Sandra Anlin; 'The Bitter Ore', copyright © 1989 Joan Batchelor; 'Where the Houses are Bleak', copyright © 1989 Jennifer Bauer; 'Firecrackers', copyright © 1989 Mary Bird; 'Near the Knuckle', copyright © 1989 Sue Buddin; 'Acquaintance', 'The Daughters', 'Father', 'The Half-Black Woman's Memory Book 1960', 'Night', 'Observation' and 'Vanishing Point', copyright © 1989 June Burnett; 'The Merge', copyright © 1989 Chaucer Cameron; 'Genesis' and 'Paris', copyright © 1989 Miriam Carney; 'Back to the Mispocheh', copyright © 1989 Elizabeth Carola; '18p', copyright © 1989 René Carrick; 'Disturbing the Curtains', copyright © 1989 Della Chapman; 'Arthritis', copyright © 1989 Kay Chell; 'Diary', copyright © 1989 Barbara Collins; 'Weekending', copyright © 1989 Julie Cotterill; 'Power Play', copyright © 1989 Anne Cunningham; 'Last Swim', copyright © 1989 Nan Dalton; 'Co-opting the Platypus' and 'Event on an Andean Mountain', copyright © 1989 Mandy Dee; 'Is There Something In The Coffee?', copyright © 1989 Lizzie Demdyke; 'Curly Cabbages', copyright © 1989 Hania Dolan; 'At Fourteen', copyright © 1989 Dolores; 'The Parting', copyright © 1989 Suzanne Doran; 'Out in the City', copyright © 1989 Sharon Dunham; 'A Wumun's Work', copyright © 1989 Susan Evasdaughter; 'An Elbow in the Consciousness' and 'We Sit And Pick', copyright © 1989 Eve Featherstone; 'Cold Morning', copyright © 1989 Jane Fell; 'Breakdown' and 'Broken Window', copyright © 1989 Marion Finan Hewitt; 'Lizzie' and 'Voices', copyright © 1989 Kitty Fitzgerald; 'The Master' and 'Whose Justice', copyright © 1989 Sally Flood; 'Tea Party', copyright © 1989 Caron Freeborn; 'Two Fragments', copyright © 1987 Janice Galloway; 'Travel and Change', copyright © 1989 Lori Gatford; 'My Own Song', copyright © 1989 Margaret Graham; 'Saying Goodbye to Booba', copyright © 1989 Sandra Grayson; 'To my Father', copyright © 1989 Alison Guinane; 'Apology at 41', 'Dying Breed', 'Menarche', 'My Mother' and 'Today's List', copyright © 1989 Kate Hall; 'The Abortion' and 'The Last Day', copyright © 1989 Janet Hawkins; 'Brenda on Holiday', copyright © 1986 Mary Haylett; 'I Was

Thanks are also due to June Burnett for the illustrations on pages 2, 7, 12, 44, 97, 106, 153, 199, 209 and 236, 270, 280 and 349, and Joanna Gorner for the illustrations on pages 80, 132, 134, 245 and 291.

With thanks to Alice Walker for permission to quote her poem 'Women' which appears in *Revolutionary Petunias and Other Poems*, published by The Women's Press in 1988.

Introduction

This book is for working-class women:

- working-class women who are as clear and passionate about their identity as we in the Common Thread
- working-class women who are angry at the stereotypes that exist, presenting us as loud, inferior, scatty, stupid, more bigoted, more violent, incapable of taking decisions and ultimately without value
- working-class women who have denied their class identity because these stereotypes have made them feel ashamed
- working-class women who don't fit easily into narrow and nineteenth-century definitions, and so have questioned their identity and called themselves classless
- working-class women who, after years of denial, have reclaimed their identity.

This book is ours.

This book is also for middle-class women:

- middle-class women who want to be our friends, and are genuinely seeking definitions – elusive and slippery – so that they can respect our identity and hear our voices
- middle-class women who have ignored us, treated us as tokens, and sought definitions in order to deny our identity
- middle-class women who have spoken for, defined and stereotyped the women 'out there'.

This book will be a learning experience.

And finally, this book is for ideas- and image-makers – academics, sociologists, political leaders, writers, TV producers and film-makers – who show working-class people as inept and brutish, ignorant and inarticulate. Think again!

This collection of writings won't provide easy answers to your question, 'Who is working-class?' But what it will do, is challenge the above caricature. Working-class women are not all Flo Capp, Hilda Ogden, Vera Duckworth or miners' wives. Some of us live in seemingly permanent poverty. Some of us have relatively good jobs and a reasonable standard of living. Many of us have been denied access to education and resources. Some have overcome these obstacles, but never without a struggle, without sacrifice and difficult choices.

We come in all shapes and sizes, nationalities and ages. We're black and white, Jewish and Gentile, lesbian and heterosexual, and we live with a range of disabilities, physical and otherwise. Our experiences and our politics are varied and wide-ranging, and we speak with many voices – with pride, sorrow, joy and pain, anger and bitterness, generosity and kindness, resilience, strength, intelligence, humour, fatalism and revolutionary commitment. We have our differences, and here we celebrate them and the common thread of class experience that links us.

Class, like money, is considered by many to be 'not nice to talk about', and it's usually the people with most to protect who refuse

Her despair grew, contribution 4000 still eluded her!

to acknowledge class as an issue. This is done in a variety of ways: by the media, arts and literature, which persist in galloping and largely unchallenged classism; by a political assumption that our oppression as women overrides any other; by liberals who insist that we're all middle-class now; by a smug redefinition of history which claims that anyone with a job these days – from managing directors, surgeons and Margaret Thatcher, to clerks, typists, cleaners and dinner-ladies – is working-class; by a catch-all and Marxist definition of working-class, that embraces everyone without capital. As Anne Phillips points out in 'Divided Loyalties' (Virago Press, 1987), this definition might be useful in identifying an important basis of economic power, but it doesn't, in the end, satisfy, and it evades our sense of ourselves and the world in which we live. In such ways, class is dismissed. The list goes on. This book is filled with the experiences, feelings and politics of working-class women who know otherwise. It demonstrates that our lives have nothing to do with the relentless stereotypes we're fed by television programme-makers. In her poem 'Power Play', for instance, Anne Cunningham, '. . . knows our gains have always been denied and we are called stupid/thick/rough/dirty/loud/ugly' – but she fiercely proclaims her strength: 'I am big/loud/working-class lesbian mother woman fighter.' In Section Six especially, we find a celebration of our class – our ability as storytellers, demonstrated by Janice Galloway's 'Two Fragments' and Sarah Hunter's 'The Witchery of the Ocean', for example, as well as pieces that demonstrate our spirit, strength and pride.

And it answers the media boys who consider the lives of the rich and powerful, middle-class and 'intellectual' the only ones of any interest and importance. It is rare that working-class women have significant storylines developed around them. Instead, they occupy the sidelines or back-of-stage, as waitresses, servants, relatively passive roles, there to service the leading players or provide comic relief. Many of our contributors have looked back on their lives and the lives of women close to them, and their stories are far from irrelevant or boring. Mary Legg's 'Memoirs of Theresa' recalls time in service from the servant's point of view. 'Lizzie', by Kitty Fitzgerald, and 'Saying Goodbye to Booba', by Sandra Grayson, paint colourful portraits of their formidable grandmothers – fascinating women with sharply contrasting lives. 'Shirley', by Sue Vodden, and 'Little Memories of a Lancashire Childhood', by Nickie Roberts, peer into the more recent past, revealing the preoccupations of a London adolescent and a child's adventures on the streets of a northern English town. 'I feel myself drawn to remembering child-hood . . .' says Nickie, 'not through nostalgia so much as the desire to establish a sense of history.'

For many years it has been unacceptable for working–class women to put class on the feminist agenda. It's seen as divisive, and wandering from the main point. Socialist feminists, always with an eye on male approval, sit discussing how to reach 'ordinary women', working-class women 'out there', whilst ignoring those of us who are 'in there'. After all, if you've managed to find your way to a feminist meeting and can articulate your opinions, then you can't possibly be working-class – or so goes the middle-class myth. Other schools of feminism simply get defensive, or look the other way when class is mentioned, seeing economic class as a mere 'male concept', and thereby disposing of the day-to-day reality of our lives. Working-class women have been silenced by these assumptions – many of us almost began to believe them. But here, particularly in Section Seven, and at Common Thread readings, we have working-class women who have long been able to put a name to their oppressions, and have fought them.

There have even been a few books published in this country which have tried to reclaim our place in feminist and political history. For example, *Life As We Have Known It* (Virago Press, 1977), describes the lives of women in the hugely successful co-operative movement, and *One Hand Tied Behind Us* (Virago Press, 1978), challenges the myth that the female vote was won by a family of middle-class activists and their equally prominent followers. Ironically, though, it has been from America, where the notion of a classless society is strongest, that some of the most challenging writing by working-class women has come – often from black women, in anthologies like *Home Girls* (Kitchen Table: Women of Color Press, 1983), and *This Bridge called my Back* (Persephone Press, 1981).

It was unfortunate, but perhaps not surprising, that an analysis of class represented such a very small percentage of the writings we received. As working-class women, we are preoccupied with so much else! But here, we add the voices of a few more politicized working-class women – women active in the women's movement and/or in their everyday struggles. Hania Dolan, in 'Curly Cabbages', looks at how the forces of classism and racism combined to shape her identity; Rozena Maart, in 'Brave Soil', describes the struggles that face black people in South Africa. And Sandra Anlin's story, 'Women's Aid . . .', sees a working-class woman's fight against male violence. 'The Power of Letters and Articles', by Jeanne Wilding, recalls Evelyn Tension's inspiring analysis of class and feminism in *You Don't Need a Degree to Read the Writing on the Wall* (1979), and introduces Marlene Packwood's critical analysis, 'Judy O'Grady and the Colonel's Lady'. In an exchange of letters in 'Working-Class Women's Voice', Maria Noble and Jeanne Wilding voice the experiences, politics and analyses of working-class women within the women's movement.

Class has been the invisible issue for far too long. Sociologists and anthropologists have recorded our lives, as zoologists report on chimpanzees behind bars. Their conclusions are usually misguided, ill-informed, inaccurate and patronizing. This book speaks of working-class women's lives as they are. It is saying that *we* are the experts on working-class life, because *we* are the ones who live it. According to Theresa Verlaine, 'The sociologist . . . sits me on his desk like an executive toy taking me apart and putting me back together again (but never in the right way)'. June Burnett's 'Letter From My Treadmill' finds a working-class woman having to defend her identity to a group of middle-class intellectuals, while Julie Cotterill's 'Weekending' turns the tables on middle-class documentary-makers, examining, from a working-class woman's point of view, the middle classes at leisure.

Popular legend has it that anyone can be middle class if they work hard enough (which is ironic, when you consider the division of labour and distribution of resources and work) – the assumption is, that we all want to be middle-class. Women who have contributed to this book are daring to assert that we are

5

proud of our own values, crafted out of struggle – we don't wish to borrow somebody else's. 'In my silence, I can understand and value my experience, keeping my culture and beliefs from your analytical claws,' says Annette Kennerley in 'About to Speak'.

Working-class women know the terms of 'making it', of 'passing', of being assimilated into the hallowed halls of privilege, and many of us have no wish to make the payments. Amazingly, despite the struggles many of us face, graphically described in the first five sections, we survive, and maintain our sense of humour – as in Kate Hall's 'Dying Breed', which explains the contradictions facing a working-class lesbian with a university education; Josephine Zara's 'The Burning', which tells with ironic wit of coping with appalling poverty; and Sue Buddin's 'Near the Knuckle', which alternately makes us laugh and cringe at the domestic trials of an overworked mother. Our strong sense of identity comes not only as working-class women, but as black women: in 'I Am – Contradictions', Jenneba Sie Jalloh describes '. . . a working-class woman, a black woman, a woman of mixed race, conflicting heritage, a Londoner . . . not English,' and as lesbians such as Jules Haywood, proud and defiant 'On Rotherhithe Tube', or Viv Acious, down-to-earth and full of good humour in 'A Day in the Life of One Lesbian'. The Identity section shows working-class women dealing with issues of disability, age, gender and more.

This book, then, contains the voices of many different working-class women, so when we ask, 'Who is working-class?', perhaps they give the beginnings of a definition. We don't all agree with the sentiments and views expressed, and each piece has been argued over and thought about. The choices we made were far from arbitrary. It's taken about four years to put the collection together. In that time, we've organized a number of open meetings and readings of working-class women's work in different parts of the country, encouraged individual women to write, and the setting up of working-class women's groups, made hundreds of contacts, contributed to other anthologies, written articles,

6

One of CT's founder members seemed preoccupied with the cover design.

participated in conferences and challenged classism in a range of different ways. For all of us in Common Thread, the involvement has, literally, changed our lives.

We spent a year building a group that reflected a broad cross-section of working-class experience, and we struggled with collective working. At the same time, we became familiar with the ins and outs of publishing. Though there've been times when we felt we'd never see the book in the bookshops, what has kept us going apart from the deep and lasting friendships we've developed, has been the knowledge that this anthology will help give us, and other working-class women, a positive sense of our identity.

The collective has never been static, and, until this last year, had twelve or so core members. For all sorts of reasons, as the book went to press, we were down to only five. These were June Burnett, Julie Cotterill, Annette Kennerley, Phoebe Nathan and Jeanne Wilding. But we count among those who made this book possible all those working-class women who've participated in readings, who've been in the collective for however long, who've shared their experiences with us, who've read and commented on hundreds of pieces sent in for the book, who've helped us with the film discussions; and women at feminist publishers who have encouraged us – Sylvan Agass, Jill Aldred, Jan Allain, Sandra Anlin, Linda Bean, Jackie Bennett, Chaucer Cameron, Dolores Choudhury, Siobhan Cleary, Anne Cunningham, Carole and Suzie Emmett, Eve Featherstone, Sally Flood, Tricia Fox, Joanne Gorner, Amy Hall, Kate Hall, Bernadette Halpin, Cec Holland, Joan Howard, Misha Illahi, Isobel Irvine, Jenneba Sie Jalloh, Jackie Kay, Cathy Loader, Suzannah Lopez, Gladys McGee, Dee Morson, Maggie Nicholls, Joyce Nixon, Lucille Newman, Elaine Okuro, Lucy O'Leary, Sola Oyeleye, Maud Sulter, Sue Vodden, Theresa Verlaine, Rita Williams, Kerilyn Wood, Josephine Zara, Christine, Dee, Dot, Julie Mellor for our logo, Leonora, Sheila, and others too numerous to list, plus the women who trusted us with their work. This book is a testament to the strength, commitment and creativity of all those women.

The book was partially subsidized by GLA, the Eleanor Rathbone Trust and Rowntrees, and we also thank Hackney Council, Haringey Arts Council, the Sarah Robbins Trust, West Midlands Arts and several anonymous donors for their financial assistance; for practical help, our child-minders, Women and Manual Trades, Homeless Action, Tindelmanor, Wesley House, IFSU and Cultural Partnerships; and for invaluable help on the film for Channel 4*, our film-maker, Audrey

* The Common Thread was concerned to define and determine images of working-class women in the film for Channel 4. For all sorts of reasons, our film-maker could not guarantee the group this degree of control or even an all-woman crew, so we reluctantly decided not to go ahead with the film.

Droisen, and assistant commissioning editor, Caroline Spry.
And finally, for her confidence in us and her patience, respect
and advice throughout, we thank our editor at Mandarin, Elsbeth
Lindner.

Julie Cotterill and Jeanne Wilding
for The Common Thread
March 1988

IDENTITY

Identity means different things to the individual women represented in these pages – whether they're young or old, black or white, with or without children, able-bodied or disabled, heterosexual or lesbian, Irish, Jewish or a combination of races, cultures and abilities. One thing remains constant – their class pride, as the producers of wealth and creators of diversity in our world.

Identity is the cornerstone of a woman's morale. It's the key to her self-worth and confidence. Her sense of herself is her strength and the last thing she gives up.

Those of us who can recall the recent history of our times, remember the stoicism of the Jewish women in the ghettos of Poland. They reared their children in the face of oppression, arbitrary punishment and selection for death. They held onto their identity as a race with dignity as they boiled clothes to prevent the spread of disease, or stood naked with their children in snow, waiting for annihilation.

And now, the women of South Africa sing their songs of protest despite whips and bullets. They face detentions without trial. A precious son or daughter of only eight can be questioned as a state enemy. They take buses from the townships to the designated white areas where they work. State controls enforce their poverty. African women always sang their soul's freedom at the funerals of their sons and daughters. Now their voices have been temporarily silenced, but their soul sings on. They share identity with millions – a wave that cannot be soaked up by the blotting paper of indifference.

This wave will become a flood.

And in this collection of writings are black women who know they have to struggle that much harder than their white sisters to hold on to, or reclaim, their identity. Historical events show clearly enough that their identity has been wrested from them, and their culture devalued. Here, too, is an Irish woman who passionately asserts the values she treasures in the face of poverty

I think poor Mary's having an identity crisis. She asked me if she was working-class or middle-class. I sorted her though. I told her she was a poet.

and gross materialism. And the mother who bravely secures a place for study so that she can begin her own 'growing' now that her children have done theirs. We read of women with disabilities, whose words leap unimpeded from the page, crushing isolation and the crude stereotyping of an able-bodied world. A woman struggles with the class-hatred of childhood and her pride in Jewish culture. One woman describes herself as a list of mundane tasks and positive accomplishments. And lesbians recognize their own hopes and dreams for freedom reflected in the eyes of another woman, on the tube and in the city.

All are a powerful cluster of voices gathering strength, like a ride on a roller-coaster. The contributions provide a mixture of the poignant and the amusing. Each is a personal voyage of discovery, by women who hold their identity with pride.

12

We stand amongst millions in common humanity, yet our voices are unique.

June Burnett

Christine Hyde Do I Dare?

Do I dare
to say what I think
in an action or word
not normally me
at the risk of upsetting someone
and let words come out
as clear as water runs
and do I
really need
a plug of certainty
so what
if I'm not certain
what have I to lose
only words
that will reflect on me as
my own circles on the surface
circling me
in regret
pleasure
honesty
some kind of hope
and expression.
I do dare,
I do,
to open my mouth
and talk.

Jenneba Sie Jalloh
Who's English, Who Cares?

'Your English is very good,'
        said my mini–cab driver,
    On my way to a party,
        which was more or less over.

'Well . . . thank you,'
        I said,
searching for words which sounded
                quite casual.

What can one say
    in one's only tongue?
(Spoken since birth,
        written on pages, written in verse)

What can one say
(After 21 years of speaking it fluently?)
        But . . .
Say something stupid.
Look stunned.

The ignorance encountered,
        every day of your life,
            when asked . . . by old women,
'How do you manage the cold?
when you come from somewhere
so hot and so nice.'
(Does she mean my mother's womb?)

What else do I know, but
this language I speak,
        first memories
            fond recollections
                familiar streets.

The ignorance,
      the questions,
            the rudeness,
                  the vibes . . .
Insist on reminding us that
      something in England's
            multi-cultural society,
just isn't quite right.

Our country? We belong to?
      No, not just yet.
Our task,
      in our new home,
(through option, or force, or no other choice)
            is TO SURVIVE.

Theresa Verlaine The Sociologist

The sociologist
looks down on me
through a vast microscope
of mis–understanding
non–understanding.

He sits me on his desk
like an executive toy
taking me apart
and putting me back together again
(but never in the right way).

He writes books about me
sends love–letters
and hate–mail
puts me on a pedestal
then crashes it down.

Meanwhile
he's making lots of money
from the stories of women
such as I.

Then
when he has finished exorcising his guilt
at my expense
he turns his back
and waits,
SILENT
as I clean his house.

Theresa Verlaine For Phil Lynott

If I . . .
. . . had grown up in the Dublin that my mother knew
I would have stalked the streets
with shoeless feet
and mixed with orphans.

I would have run away
from the musty cloistered oppression
of dark corridors
And danced down O'Connell Street with my satchel
bursting from the catechism
of false and bigoted dreams
that blew in the face of innocence.

I would have scrounged pennies
from rich men in coffee shops
– and their painted women
(who didn't mind paying the price of your absence
from their material guilt).

And dancing . . .
. . . I would continue across the bridge
across the 'Liffey water'
and the winds of change that roamed the streets
tainted with the sighs of souls
such as mine.

I would have danced
into the arms of popstars
like those which I now see from a far distance
and across a decade
and maybe . . .
. . . I might have changed history
earlier than I will.

June Burnett The Daughters

My blood cries out
as daughter by dark daughter
seeks a place
in this forbidding land
where arid acceptance
accompanies a sneer.
A tinted reminder
a brazen, unashamed hint
of collective guilt.
Your rich rain runs down my hair
like beads on a Moorish curtain,
flows into my pursed lips
like a waterspout.
I am diluted by softening drops
rinsed, not cathedral white,
but yellow, as the dust I dwelled upon
in my Motherland.
Cradle of the race of daughters.

Once, I was nourished, and proud,
but you, my brothers,
took me from my own vineyard
to tend yours.
My grapes were neglected
and withered on the bough.
Daughter by dark daughter
you purchased my labour,
and my virginity.
My ever–paling skin
a prize.
Generation by generation,
daughter by dark daughter.
My blood cries out:
    'I am black, but I am beautiful
Oh ye daughters of Jerusalem.
As the tents of Kedar, as the
Curtains of Solomon.'

Elizabeth Carola
Back to the Mishpocheh* – reflections on a working–class Jewish childhood

---

At two, I remember my father carrying me along the steamy corridor, saying hurriedly, 'We'll go down the back stairs to avoid the *mishpocheh* on the landings.' He was tense and anxious. 'Sitting about in their *shmates, kvetching* away. *Mishpocheh.*' He spat the word with disgust. I didn't know what 'mish-bush-ahs' were, but some of the older women down the corridor had kind faces, winked and gave me candy, their guttural, Slavic intonation rich and low. If only *some* of them were *mishpocheh*, I reasoned, I might then be freed to trust, like, talk to, some of the others.

The next time we came face to face with some of the older people, I tore away from my father's hand and asked nervously,

* Mishpocheh is a Yiddish word for peasants, folk.

'Are *you* mish-bush-ahs?' I was pulled quickly away, and told off. I had breached the unspoken cardinal gap between us and Them.

For a long time, I didn't think of myself as working-class. I knew I wasn't middle-class. But I also knew, or thought I knew, that I wasn't Them. Working-class was Them – the retired clothing-industry workers I grew up surrounded by in the Union housing projects, who my parents taught me to fear and despise and politely avoid.

But recently, on a trip back to New York, walking up the street, my street, I looked round those projects, the familiar complex of twelve brick tower blocks particularizing, focusing, as I neared mine. Inside, I looked round the cinderblock foyer and at the pensioners playing cards in the lobby, as they have for twenty-eight years, since the projects were built. I smelled the slow, musty smell of the lift until it stopped at 5, and smelled the ancient over-boiled chicken in the corridor, before stopping at the right numbered door to the flat where I grew up, where my father still lives. And I felt with a certainty, for the first time, that I *was* them, they *were* me, that this is where I come from.

The International Ladies Garment Workers' Union built those projects in the late 1950s, as housing for the workers in the garment trade, south of Times Square. In the early 1960s, there were a few openings for working families not in the textile trade, and my parents got one of these when I was three. The flats were small and close, but considered a step above the city welfare housing they were moving from.

Now, when I think of class, I think about poverty and its ripples down through the generations.

I think about the cycle of carelessness, bitterness, dislocation, despair. (Where does it start? In my family, did it start on the *shtetl* in Poland? Did it start with my grandmothers, exhausted, bearing child after child after child? Can I stop it?)

I think of my father's family – all eight of his brothers and sisters dying one by one, of poverty, helplessness, terror, loneliness, despair. They didn't make it. I think of my mother's relatives, on the other side of the river in cumbling Hoboken, who did. Not 'make it' in the conventional sense of making it into the middle class or the professions, but who work contentedly in department stores and dry-cleaning shops and sit around on *Shabbes*, uproarious, and tell inane, anti-Semitic and racist jokes; who, comic, perfunctory, slap napkins on their head to bless the candles on Friday night and then rush out to the Chinese for Pork Lo Mein. They made it, in the sense that they retain the will to live.

When I think of class, I think of what makes you make it, and what doesn't. I think of the division between the states of 'survivor' and 'casualty', and I think of the circumstances that push people over the edge, from one place to the other.

I think of my parents' weariness, their desperation.

Most of all, I think of the life-force.

I see my mother – newly a mother, still a kid – standing at the window of the flat in the old projects, looking down at the East River. The water is cold and choppy, stretching down, out to New York Harbour and then widening to Lower Manhattan Bay, the industrial skyline of Queens, grey and solid, on the other side. She is furious. There is never enough. Never enough time, choices, money, food, freedom. The little bundle on the day-bed beside her starts to scream. Again. Interminable. Maternal love, she thinks grimly. They tell you babies are life, but they are death. Death to time, choices, FREEDOM. She knows what the baby wants, but she can't. She can't. Her back twitches with the memory of her mother's touch, a brief, gruff, daily tenderness as she got handed her chunk of bread each night before soup. First because she was youngest. As a child she had always wanted to be eldest, because then she'd be last in the queue and maybe get more. More bread, more of a hug. The nightly chunk of bread with its lump of margarine in the centre. Never spread out over the bread ('You can eat it like it is,' snapped her mother when she asked for a knife). Never spread out into her life. Never enough. Tears well up, the river blurs. 'Stop it, this instant!' she screams at the baby, turning from the window. *Enough*.

What is the point at which you say, *enough*, and pull yourself out? My father never did – and was broken.

For twenty years, all through my childhood, my father worked in a small film lab, whose output was mostly pornography. He processed and cleaned the film. Twenty years of dip and dry and cut and splice. Twenty years of those pictures, a focused point of light in the darkroom. What this ended up doing to his head is another story. But as a child, I didn't know exactly what he did. All I knew was that he hated his job, hated his fellow workers, and would be home from his nightshift, swinging his empty coke bottle, every night at 12:25.

And each night I would programme myself to wake up at about 12:15. I'd lie in bed listening for the tone of the slammed door. When it was furious or miserable, I turned over and went back to sleep. When merely exhausted or resigned, I got out of bed and ran to greet him.

And each night – exhausted, resigned or kindly, depending on the evening's ravages – he would kiss me and say, 'What are you doing up, this time of night?' While he washed, I got out his midnight snack, the same every night: a can of beer, chunk of cheese and raw onion. I would sit across from him while he moodily ate, quiet, glad he was home. And every night, when he was finished, he'd slam down his beer can, mellowed by the alcohol, groan humorously, expostulate in Yiddish, tell me to go to bed.

At 12:05 every night he left his lab in Times Square to walk the ten streets down to the projects, swinging his brown-paper lunch bag. Inside of it was hidden his talisman, an empty coke bottle. 'See, if anything happened, I just break the top against the nearest building, like *this* – and look what I'd have.' He'd show me the jagged edge with a boyish pride. 'They'd be crazy to get near *this*.' Charm, amulet, or merely good deterrent, I don't know, but he never got attacked, though we lived in a high-crime precinct, a definite knife/gun zone. It's worked for me, too.

My mother had her tricks, too, teaching in the South Bronx. Make sure to see Them before They see you. And when you see Them – gesturing slowly, deliberately, she would slide her hand into her raincoat pocket and cup it into an imaginary shape with an imaginary trigger, never taking her eyes off a potential attacker – when you see Them, you out-psyche them. The best defense is a good offense.

My parents were obsessed with Them. Potential attackers on the street, the lumpen colleagues they were forced to work with, but most of all the neighbours. *They* didn't have anything to do with *us*. *They* read the *Daily News* – *we* read the *New York Times*. *They* listened to Frank Sinatra – *we* listened to Verdi. *They* were the huddled masses, not even bothering to yearn to breathe free – *we* were an island of culture. My parents were not happy with their condition and never gave up trying to pretend it was otherwise, building elaborate barriers between 'us' and everything around 'us'.

As a child, it didn't occur to me that in an urban housing project, no family is an island, that the workers above and below and down the corridors from us, by the very conditions of their lives, couldn't have been totally disconnected from us. No, I believed my parents, and thought *we* were different.

'We' were and 'we' weren't. Certainly, through being told and believing you're different, you become so. But now I need to go back, back to the *mishpocheh* and, for the first time, affirm my sameness to them. On a class level, on a basic human level. Because all of it – the miles of dense brick, the *schmoozing* in the corridor, the vitality and tension and life of the city, as well as the prison-like silent staircases, the dust and the alienation, fear and 'dreams deferred' – is where I come from.

Barbara Ponton
Some Women of Marrakesh

Grieve for your sisters of Marrakesh, cocooned
in a niche of wide, white walls,
unseen by alien men, and precious
only for the membrane.

But on your street
lives Betty Grey, typing the day
in tall, glass towers.

Snug at night, she stretches hours
with one who mostly fails to see
her needs behind her mystery.

She has no saint
to burden with strayed ecstasy,
no woman
who purports to be a sister,
who dances for her;
comprehends the pain.

Jennifer Bauer
Where the Houses are Bleak

She looked at the alarm clock. Ten minutes past five. Why could
she never sleep more than four or five hours without waking up?
It had been after midnight before her mind had slipped away to
oblivion; and now she was back again, in reality. There would be
no more real sleep until it was time for her to get up. She dozed
fitfully, looking at the alarm clock every ten or fifteen minutes. At
some point, her mind slithered away to complete unconscious-
ness, and the shrill ring of the alarm jerked her back. She felt the
nervousness in the pit of her stomach. Time to get up. Time to
face the day. She wanted to pull the cover over her head, sleep,
and never, never get up. Grey daylight was breaking through into
the room, and she saw the hated thing from the corner of her eye.
The wheelchair. She nudged Mike gently, the nerves in the pit of
her stomach tightening, bracing herself for the ugly, early-
morning ritual.

'Mike, time to get up.'

'In a minute,' he mumbled, and carried on snoring. She always
left this to the last minute. Experience had taught her to do so.
Mike wouldn't lift an eyelid until the last second, except to look at
his watch. To disturb him a second earlier than necessary meant
risking his anger, which was too much to take at this time of the
morning. She waited, feeling the nervousness growing. She

needed his help before she could get into that hated thing. And she had to get into it by seven, so that she had plenty of time to get Mark's breakfast and get him ready for school. Her disabled body made her dependent on Mike. Put her at the mercy of his moods. If she hadn't needed him to help her get up, he could have slept on, as far as she was concerned. Be late for work, for all she cared. But she couldn't let Mark down. She couldn't let Mark be late for school. He depended on her. Desperately, she prodded Mike.

'Get up, Mike, it's getting late . . .'

'For Chrissakes, leave me alone . . .'

She needed Mike and hated her dependence.

It was not her fault she couldn't walk. It was not her fault that she was totally paralysed from the waist down. Mike had been driving. He had been drunk. It was an accident, everyone said. Particularly his family. Nobody's fault, yes, but she had to carry the consequences. No one was to blame. Fine. But the consequences were hers to cope with for the rest of her life.

Everything took such a long time. She needed him to help her from her stomach position on to her back. Adjust the bed so that she could sit. She needed him for her daily bath. He helped her into the bathtub and back out again. Then she could cope alone. Emptying her bladder with a catheter. Getting dressed. It all needed time. So much time. Particularly getting dressed. Heavy, dead limbs which rolled around aimlessly, no longer following orders from the brain.

'Mike!'

Suddenly he jumped out of bed, his eyes blazing.

'I heard you the first time. You're a bloody pest, you know that?'

The same every morning.

'Mike, I'm sorry, it's getting late and . . .'

Her voice was thin and anxious. She felt herself flinch under his aggressive eye.

To be a woman. A lot is said about being a woman these days. To be 'physically handicapped'. Sometimes things are said about that, too. The 'handicapped' are strange creatures in a zoo; to be laughed at, admired and pitied. They do not form a part of Real Life. To be a woman and disabled. Does the woman's lot suddenly stop because of the disability? Does the disability stop the woman being a woman and turn her into a creature to be laughed at? Are there any advantages to be gained for the woman by being disabled? Do household drudgery and responsibility for child-rearing suddenly disappear with the disability? Does she become a waited-upon, cossetted, fussed-over, alien creature, because she is now disabled? For we all know the disabled are cossetted, fussed over and spoiled. Do all female duties and routine vanish with the disability and allow her to stare through a window all day and do nothing at all? Does she lose her female-ness, and do the consequent destiny and duties of woman vanish as a result of her new status as she is clicked into a slot marked 'Physically Handicapped'? Does she stop wanting job satisfac-tion, an escape from the traditional role, self-realization? Can she, in a bad marriage, get out, get divorced, become independent, make a new life for herself? Can she find herself? Or do all these now-acknowledged female aims and desires stop when the dis-ability sets in? Being now incontinent and having to wear nappies for the rest of her life, can she contemplate having any more children, even if it is physically possible?

The woman in our story, spends her day doing all the house-work she is physically capable of. Taking far longer than the average able-bodied woman would need. She needs time during the day to cope with her disability. She is exhausted by far less work than would exhaust an able-bodied woman of her age. The restrictions of incontinence mean that she cannot just get the housework done, get a shopping bag, close the door behind her and escape for a while. Mean that she cannot cope with a job outside the home. Mean that, very probably, employers would not accept her if she could. Mean she must stay in a bad marriage, for she is much more dependent on the man than the average non-disabled woman. Mean that, as she is still capable, she must nevertheless wash, iron, cook, sweep floors and clean up behind the family. Mean the worst of both worlds. And every day she needs a mac, for she never knows when it will rain. If anything were to happen which she could not cope with, such as falling out of the wheelchair, how would she get to a phone?

Her days are narrow and dark, even when the sun shines. For she hardly ever goes out. And she still needs a mac.

Sharon Dunham Out in the City

Whatever happens to me and you,
remember us together,
against the background
of raised eyebrows,
pointed fingers,
dagger looks,
accusing stares,
together feeling stronger,
arms wrapped round each other
at bus stops, on tube trains,
shopping precincts, cafés,
flirting with danger,
inviting those who felt
threatened by us,
to threaten us,
verbally, physically,
with their insecurity.

Whatever happens to me and you,
remember us together,
being true to our sexuality
out of defiance,
perhaps, even,
out of love?

Jules Haywood Rotherhithe Tube

Smack, normality hits me right between the eyes –
    a family, pushchair, and skin the colour of newspaper print.
Can feel their heads move as if at a tennis match when I walk by.
Is it my tough, fast legs that they look at?
Or maybe my height of ten feet tall!

Maybe the neon-light which flashes 'no men here' large and
    bright above my head.
Can they see perhaps, so clearly, that my body moves to the heat
    of another woman's?
Or simply, you know that I don't relate to what you stand for?
I'm in transit, between one lesbian zone and another.
Yes, plotted, tea-potted, and squatted.
In various parts of this grey, cold, hard, bleak landscape
are dykes, tens, hundreds, thousands, millions of us,
pushing up like sunflowers in cement cracks.
I saw one of us on the tube the other day,
    looking guarded, like the first day at school.
In her eyes, clear, alive and burning was a light,
    glowing and filling the whole carriage.

Barbara Collins Diary

Week 1
He's going to try and get the kids away from me – I know it. He
doesn't understand. How can he? His life is rigid, disciplined –
even loving had to be analysed. If only I could explain the
gentleness of loving another woman. The joy in our likeness.
The pleasure in touching a soft, rounded body instead of impersonal, muscular, hardness. And understanding shared, female
experiences.

Week 2
Saw my solicitor – a woman. Hoped perhaps there'd be understanding. I must admit, she tried not to sound prejudiced, but
failed miserably. She kept referring to 'your friend' in a controlled
voice that sounded as though she might be sick if she let go.

His affidavit swears I am 'unsuitable' to be in charge of my three
children. They will be subject to 'immoral influences'.

What am I going to do?

Week 3
He's been talking to the children, saying how disgusting I am.
How can that be? I'm only loving someone. Someone who loves

me and the children and grieves, too, at everyone's anger. If she moves out temporarily it won't solve anything, because he is convinced I have 'unnatural tendencies'. Anyway, WHY SHOULD SHE MOVE OUT? Fuck the system which makes people become artificial in order to live within its rules. I WON'T.

Week 4
I'm looking out at the garden while I write. I wish spring was in the air instead of autumn. I feel a sapping of my spirit. I am frightened.

Week 5
How can a man who doesn't know me or my children sit in judgement and decide my future? That's what court comes down to. And this man, who won't even recognize me if he passes me in the street, took my children away from me. How can this person, who is a nobody, play God and judge me guilty of the crime of loving?

I can't think straight at the moment. I'm sure I'll know what to do.

There'll be something I can do . . . something.

Dolores At Fourteen

I was going to be married off,
at 14,
to a man I didn't know,
                in India.
An arranged marriage,
so I arranged to play truant,
and ran off to a wild pop festival
        ran off to a world of sex and drugs and rock and roll.
Danced in front of thousands
met the band and DJ's
and got photographed (fame!)
and I knew I'd be a star before long,
singing and dancing.

But dreams are just dreams, and
I came down to earth with a wallop
when the police appeared
and so it was back to school
             and my strange uneven world
coloured white
coloured brown
and my dad's dreams of me,

             London girl gets degree
             and marries, to settle down
             to the Indian way of life.
But it didn't happen that way –
He died, an alcoholic,
and so saris and ceremonies and the unknown hot yellow
             brown land
        disappeared from view,
but it was never forgotten.
I often wonder
what might have happened,
what would they have made of me,
In Chittagong,
             a half-Indian half-German
             London-born.
A wild-haired and colourful young dancer,
too English,
too independent,
to be tied down.
Well, I kept my hair long and black
for years, until one day,
a friend cut it
and it was as if a whole part of me
had gone,
        forever – like the prospect of that marriage.
And in its place
grew strength
and confidence,
no more being pulled by my hair,
this way or that.
I still know,

it's still there for me.
when I want it.
And I know what I want.

Tina Wildebeest Whiteness

Whiteness –
whatever that may be,
tried to impose
its supremacy
on an African child
born in the mild,
though hostile climes
of post-war England.

Schooling –
fifteen years denied
my natural sense
of racial pride,
to be of 'mixed race'
was a form of disgrace,
in the hostile climes
of post-war England.

Adolescence –
brought growing pain
and a desperate need
to feel whole again,
one personality
split into three,
in the hostile climes
of post-war England.

Womanhood –
whatever that may be,
yet another struggle
for liberty,

I've seen through the lies
and learned to DESPISE
the hostile climes
of post-war England.

Rozena Maart Don't Move

The land was black and alien
they entered
white as snow
they stood and looked
amid the breeze
that echoed them to go

They came and went
and came and went
and came to claim
and stay

They looked
and stared
at us all bare
who danced for them to go

Our eyes met theirs
our spears declined
O God of sun and
moon we prayed

Our sun was gone
our moon astray
our children screaming at the day
that pretended
not to be
but be
within the realm of a
white reality

Three hundred years
I'm told went by
Three mournful hundred years
of fights and claims
of our domains
that sunk into their chains

The links are beaten and battered
the metal stands and fights
my sons and daughters
they don't stare
because the land
they say
is black.

Sunday 1 September
Day of the Athlone march to Pollsmor prison –
Release Mandela Campaign.

Lesley Summers Private Memoirs

1st entry

They – the Americans – regard me as a curious freak of nature. Looking like I do, I should speak with the guttural deep voice of the ghetto black from North Omaha, not with a 'cultured' English accent. They look at me, whisper among themselves, and then look again, and I look back, knowing what they are thinking and laughing at their confusion, but not outwardly of course – got to keep a stiff upper lip.

I'm still regarded with just a little suspicion. Don't all English girls look like the lass off the Ovaltine tin, hair the colour of ripe corn, framing piercing blue eyes that twinkle from under long golden lashes? Surely, I jest with them, I've spent long long hours locked away somewhere, where the sun never shines, practising my accent.

Last night was a prime example; you know, they just couldn't believe that I was there in that club, they looked, looked again, some sniggered, some just gaped openly, but still they didn't believe a black girl in their rock and roll club, tapping her feet, and getting up to dance to Billy Idol with one of them, a white girl with golden hair and smiling eyes.

'Don't take any notice,' Kathy had said, laughing. 'You know Omaha is the backwoods, most of the guys in here are rednecks anyway, they'll get over it.'

And they did, but their poor confusion was hilarious: 'What brings you here? Don't you know, there are loads of clubs over in the north of town that play funk and disco?'

'Yea, I know. I don't like funk and disco, I like rock, always have, hard core, heavy rock, chewing-glass-and-spitting-it-out music, you know, AC/DC . . .'

'Wow, man, you're cool, what's England like? I've always wanted to go there.'

Later, we ate breakfast at Denny's. That's the thing to do here, you know, go out and get wasted and then head for the nearest diner and eat scrambled eggs, sausage patties, hash browns and English muffins. I had to smile when I read 'English muffins'. The nearest thing we have to a muffin is a crumpet, and these things they served up resembled nothing less than a crumpet. Still, it was different. I went to use the toilet – 'rest room, if you don't mind,' – and some seven foot black guy with Michael Jackson hair and bright red trousers grabbed my arm.

'Hey, sister, you shore lookin' nice tanite. Hmm. Hmmm . . .'

I laughed, embarrassed and unsure what to do. I'm not used to this 'bull in the ring' approach, and don't like it. It seems cheap, somehow.

'Don't let 'em talk to you like that, then,' said Kathy, shovelling a fork-full of eggs into her mouth and dropping some onto her blouse.

How do you explain to somebody how totally alienated it makes you feel, to have your first conversation in ages with someone the same colour as you, only to discover that they make you feel just as uncomfortable and out of place as it would a member of the Ku Klux Klan? You don't feel like a traitor because you are what you are, what others have made you, yet you feel ill at ease, belonging neither to one side nor the other, but instead just hanging somewhere in limbo, waiting for somebody to come up with the answer for you, because the question is too complex for you to sort out alone.

When I was confronted by the same leering guy again, as we were leaving, you would have thought I'd hit him in the face with a cricket bat by the way he looked at me when I told him autocratically, 'Don't call me "sister", because I'm not, and, furthermore, if I do look like a fox, I certainly don't need the likes of you to confirm that fact for me!'

'Great!' Kathy had said. 'You're learning.'

Yes, I was, and I didn't like what I was discovering.

Stereotyping a person wasn't my idea of progressive thinking, but this is what was happening, has been happening since my arrival two months ago.

Maybe I did come here with too many high-blown ideas, I read too many Horner and Onstott novels, I think. They paint such an idyllic picture of the old South.

Of course, according to them, I would be nothing more than a Mulatto – I'd immediately gone to find the dictionary and looked up this word that the Americans had invented for people like me, and wasn't too amazed to discover that it was a purely racist term, meaning someone of mixed blood – one white parent, one black – or, as they so quaintly put it, 'half human'.

Yet, despite the fact that I would have been regarded as part-animal, I'd have been given an easy job in the pre-Civil War days. I would have helped out in Lucretia Borgia's immense kitchen by day, and, if my hair was not too kinky and I really looked more human than animal – not losing sight of the fact, though, that I had tainted black blood and therefore was never to be totally trusted – I may even have had the supreme honour of being the Master's bed-wench by night: Oh, delight of delights!

Of course, I could never hope to be present at the Octroon's Ball or Quadroon's Ball in New Orleans' French quarter, that was reserved exclusively for wenches with one-fourth and one-eighth black blood respectively, but those were the breaks.

When I read these novels, it never ceased to amaze me that someone who was only one-eighth black could be 'detected', anyway.

Anyway, enough of last night. Today awaits, only one more

long hour before I must present myself at the 42nd and Fort Street Police Station for my Driving Test; wish me luck . . .

2nd entry

Incredible! I still can't believe it now, even though I'm looking at the little green and white plastic card that carries my photo, making me look about four shades darker than I ever was, even after the inferno that passes for an American summer. I don't know whether to laugh or cry, really. I have passed my test, but in so doing, have somehow lost a chunk of my pride, a small ounce of my courage, that before has always enabled me to confront any situation, unafraid to be challenged.

The test was simplicity in itself. Of course, I had a few hectic moments when, momentarily, my heart stopped beating, as just for a split second I suffered a time-warp and thought I was back on the roads of England, and driving on the wrong side. But it passed as quickly as it came, and the young black policewoman nodded understandingly and didn't hold it against me.

It was while we were sitting in the car beside the station that the real hassle began.

It was a bright sunny morning, I could see Old Glory blowing gently in the wind from the flagpole of the store opposite – there are flags everywhere here, even outside ordinary people's homes. An old white pick-up, blotches of rust blatantly emblazoned across the wings, hood and bonnet, the obligatory wild and ungroomed Siberian husky pacing the floorboards at the back, groaned by, the driver leaning out and spitting slowly and deliberately onto the tarmac road as he passed.

The policewoman turned, and for a moment I saw anger in her eyes, helplessness, then it was gone. I didn't say anything, what could anyone have said?

'Well, I'm happy to tell you that you've passed,' she said, beginning to write on a large legal-size form.

'Great! I've passed, I've passed!' I whooped, genuinely overcome with excitement and relief.

'Yep, you sure have. Now, I need a few particulars . . . full name . . . ?'

'Lesley Susan Summers.'

'Date of birth?'

'30 May 1966.'

'Race?'

'English.'

She paused in her writing. 'No. I said race, not nationality.'

'But that is my race!' I replied, never before having been confronted with the question and at first not realizing its implications.

'Well, here in the States, race and nationality are two totally different ball games.'

'But that is my race, I'm English.'

'Look, this is America. Here, look, see my driver's licence, it has race, that's what this little "B" stands for under that column – Black.'

'But I'm not black, I'm mixed.'

'We don't recognize mixed as being a race,' she replied, turning to look at me. Was she angry again? I didn't know and, truth be known, was beginning to feel just a little irritated myself.

'But I am mixed,' I persisted. 'My mother's white, my father black – mixed.'

'Listen, lady, you got three choices; Black, White or Other. That's it, finnito!'

'But I'm not black and I'm not white. What's "Other", anyway?' I asked, the frustration beginning to show in my voice.

'Other is Other; Indian, Hispanic, Mexican . . . you know . . . Other.'

'Well, obviously I'm not Other either . . . damn . . . I'm mixed!'

'Listen to me, I've already had a shit of a day, I got half-a-dozen other people in there, all ready to take me for what could be my last ride on the roads ever, and I haven't got the time to bullshit around with you, you make up your mind what you are in the next sixty seconds or you've failed. It's as simple as that!'

'But you can't say that,' I gasped, not believing my ears.

'I just said it!' She smiled falsely, lit a cigarette and looked pointedly at her watch.

'But how can you sit there and tell me that after twenty years I don't exist?'

'Fifty seconds . . .'

'But it's not fair, I'm mixed blood, mixed, a bit of both; what you're saying is I must deny one side of my heritage in order to conform to a stupid law.'

'Thirty seconds . . .' She stubbed out her cigarette angrily, sending a shower of red ash over the dashboard.

I needed my licence. Buses were few and far between in this neck of the woods and I still had the better part of two years before I graduated from college with my associate's degree. I needed transport – desperately – but I also needed time to think.

I had just been told that I didn't exist, and here, in America of all places, the country that proudly displayed its motif, 'equality for all mankind' around the globe.

Time was running out, and I knew it. I glanced sideways at the woman beside me, her mouth set in grim determination and her anger now obvious. What did she feel, why was she so mad at me, was it because I was mixed? Because she thought my stay in this country was going to be more pleasant for me than for her because I had some white blood? I didn't know.

What I did know, though, was that the American police were highly suspicious of anyone black at the best of times. You saw them approaching a car with a black driver with much more caution than they would employ had the occupant been the same colour as themselves.

Their hands would be so close to their holsters that any sudden panic on their part and they would have blown their own balls away. As far as they were concerned, I was black, and to present them with a licence that said 'w' would have been asking for trouble.

She was reaching for the door, now . . .

'Black . . .' I said meekly, not being able to bring myself to look at her. Out of the corner of my eyes I saw her shoulders slump as relief passed through her body. She swung herself back into the car and took a deep breath, before entering the letter into the appropriate information box. All the joy that, minutes ago, had been mine disappeared in a puff of smoke. I felt hurt, embarrassed, like a traitor to my mother, but above all mad, very mad.

'Go back into the station and wait in Room D, they'll call you when they're ready to take your photo.'

She got out of the car and, without a backward glance, disappeared into the building, leaving me sitting there dazed.

Later, formalities completed and heading for the door, she stopped me. I didn't want to talk to her, but she stood in front of me, blocking my path, I had no option.

'I don't make the rules, you know,' she said gently, all the fight gone from her, her eyes reflecting things I had never before even considered I would have to deal with.

I nodded.

'You did the right thing, you can't pass for white, and you're obviously not Hispanic, either.'

'I've never tried to pass for white!' I snapped, pulling myself up to my full height.

For the first time since it had all begun, I understood, or thought I did anyway, why she acted as she had done. She had felt a kindred spirit with me at first, relaxed, two lost souls together, but my hesitation to acknowledge I felt black, was black, hurt her. It was like my telling the guy in the diner I wasn't his sister. To them, solidarity was all they had, it was what made life bearable, knowing that they all shared the injustices together.

'Take care . . . and thanks,' I said, emotion filling my voice, and aware that people were beginning to look.

She tried to smile but didn't quite succeed and, instead, turned away and hurried down the corridor. I watched her go, wondering if I had got my message, my confusion across to her. Just when I thought that I had failed, she glanced back over her shoulder and smiled at me; I smiled back and raised my hand in salute. The test was over.

Julie Noble Diary Extract

Sunday August 12th

Who needs boys, anyway? Yesterday, as me, Judy and Pam were riding along Ferndale Moor, we could see into Bransdale, to the High Wold. Across the Howardian hills to the Blakey pub on the Bilsdale moor. The wind whistled across us, making the horses think they were tired after galloping three miles or so to the 'Trig' point on the top. Excitement keeps them, and us, going.

As I will write to Mum: Mum, it's not for me to write as if I were Fay Weldon, but what you said the other night is true. I can't jump my time. Time is holding me down, but it is pushing me on, too. Age is saying 'Steady on, enjoy your life as a teenager should, find friends, develop properly,' but my mentality is saying, 'Oh, get on quick, into the safe retreat of your mother's older, more mature, world. Why learn the hard way when you are welcomed into the folds of security. Let your mother take care of you.'

Oh, yes, we all have our problems. Just *that* is what life is about. You'll be happy when you've mastered them, proud, like after a crossword puzzle. Oh, girl, you've got a lot to learn, but the jigsaw's only beginning to take shape. The outline appears.

When I go to the next world, I will leave my books behind me. My diaries will not last long, with the threat of nuclear war over us, and will not be anything special, like the diaries of Anne Frank or Samuel Pepys. Mine will be special only to me and my mother, and maybe no one else.

The light is fading now and the night draws in. Auntie Edna is coming in, and I must close. Yes, she has shouted. Bye!

Kate Hall Today's List

Today
I have been
Lover
Tenant
Employee
Therapist
Dog owner
Customer
Friend
Mother
Dancer
Writer
A member

of a working–class
women's group
and
The wrong number.

Not necessarily
in that order.

Edith Stanton Mum's Career

I announce to my family that, in future, I am claiming time off
from domestic chores to read and write, in preparation for an O
level in English! 'Mum's Career' has long been a source of
merriment, and notes left on the table or cooker are referred to as
'Mum's literary efforts', without any action being taken on their
contents.

Now I am in earnest. Other mothers belong to clubs, play
bridge, golf, bingo. This Mum wants to read to some purpose.
The hour between the children's tea and preparation of Father's
dinner shall be devoted to Keats, or Hardy, or Macbeth. I shall go
into the lounge, away from television noise. My books are
already in there. 'MUM! Is something boiling over on the stove?'
Perhaps the kitchen is the best place to be, after all; I can keep an
eye on the pans at the same time. 'MUM! Just come and look at this
man . . . quickly, before he goes . . . isn't he the man who was
in —— last year?' I protest that this is an unnecessary interruption,
that when the interrupter was doing his homework, I kept quiet
for him.

Pop fan teenager enters the kitchen to put a crease in his
trousers. He is accompanied by his transistor radio, but assures
me he will only be a minute. Would I clear the table for him? The
pop music will not disturb my studies, he says; other people have
it on constantly, and they manage. He did all his homework with
a background of pop music, and look how many O levels he got!

I explain that concentration is less easy at my age, and I need
quiet. He says I'll get used to it. This interesting discourse
continues until Father's key is heard in the lock. Never mind,

there will still be an hour after dinner before bedtime. I sit with Father, keeping him company whilst he eats his dinner.

The pop fan, by this time, is in the bathroom, along with his transistor. The other member of the household is quiet and self-contained. Peace reigns. This, then, is the quiet hour. But first I must know whether Father needs a sympathetic ear. 'What sort of a day did you have? Have you seen anybody interesting?' There is no response at this tired-and-hungry stage. He will be full of news at midnight. I will postpone the washing-up and get to my books now.

'MUM! Will you get our John out of the bathroom? I want to wash my hair!' I sit on the top stair and add a prolonged pleading and knocking to the cacophony of canned pop and running water, without result. I am joined by the quiet one, and later by Father, and together we shout and knock until we outdo the pop singer and the bathroom door opens . . . There are still the pots and pans to wash, and the cooker to clean. I am too tired, now, to care what the poet meant.

Jenneba Sie Jalloh Superior Equality

Show me a religion
which calls me equal
and I will follow.

You tell me that you are superior to me
that God granted you that superiority
in the Bible, in the Quran, in the Torah

You ask me to believe
you ask me, another human being,
another heart, another soul,
with as much pride as you
to believe that I am inferior to you

Are we not to believe that all people
regardless of colour, nationality, religion
are created equally?

You ask me to believe this
and I do believe.
But you, my brother, you
also ask me to believe that you
are superior to me in some way,
your sister, your black sister

If you can find space in your mind,
your soul for this
if you can justify this inequality in your heart
then the white man who has been preaching his superiority
    over you for so long
cannot be condemned by you
and you are no better than him.
It cannot be both, brother.
Either we are all equal under the eyes of God
or equality does not exist.

If you believe that you should have authority over me
and that I should be obedient to you
then you should not preach equality to the white oppressor
because you yourself do not understand oppression,
and you are my oppressor, brother

If I am to fight alongside you
then you must see me as your equal
or I will be forced to fight against you for my rights

I want to fight with you. See me as I am,
your comrade, your sister, your equal
I AM WE.

Mandy Dee
Co-opting The Platypus
(Identity Crisis)

Two elements of the unusual
produce the purely eccentric;
that tame constrained novelty
of which normality is fond.
More aspects of diversity
is perversity; so wrong.

Some humans must make
themselves 'original'.
Almost too many parts
of my individuality
simply occurred in me,
till I longed to find other lives
as diverse, complete, unique.
Thus Platypus, splashypus
swimming in the billabong
the scientists state
you are living all wrong.

Not bearing your milk-fed young
furry water mamminal
you lay eggs in the warm earth
so that through the millennia
your offspring have been
swimming, on and on.

Obviously evolution's song
has reproduced you as a minor aberration.
You cannot live long.
We're momentarily interested,
but then your species can be gone.

Shocking unscientific assemblage –
considered by many, 'Quaintly peculiar,'
innocent of my literary invention
platypus glorious!
In the quiet of the billabong
swim on, swim on!

They celebrated their differences in no uncertain terms.

REMINISCENCES
. . . writing our own history

'We were poor – but we were happy!' This is just one of the stereotypes of working-class people. And for some of us, it may be true. But for most working-class women, past experience is punctuated by hardship and struggle, by the constant battle to make ends meet. This shared experience affects and influences our beliefs and values, giving us a very different outlook on life and on achievement from our more privileged sisters.

Our memories of the past are often tinged with bitterness and resentment at the conditions which have caused unhappiness and suffering in our family lives. Many of the pieces in this section recall our acute embarrassment and unhappiness as children about our homes and family; many express sadness and anger at the suffering of our parents, particularly our mothers. And yet many of the memories are also tender, humorous and hopeful. They are stories of survival and bravery, of strength and courage in overcoming what is usually a difficult start in life.

The work in this section reflects the wide variety of our experiences and backgrounds which unite us as working-class women. We are writing our own history – a history that has been largely ignored or misrepresented. Rarely has it been told by our own voices, in our own words. It is important for us to be able to talk about our backgrounds and our experiences – about ourselves – without being labelled as 'whingeing women'. Perhaps it's hard for people who have enjoyed a privileged upbringing to acknowledge that for others the past has often meant an uphill struggle, and for some it's involved a series of heartaches and tragedies.

This difficulty in accepting our different histories often takes the form of ridicule – like the old Monty Python sketch in which people with pantomime Northern accents compete with stories about how underprivileged they were as kids, making jokes about real hardship with lines such as, 'We lived in a shoebox in the middle of the road'. Perhaps the discomfort stems from guilt, but the desire to silence us and the demand that we forget our past experiences are a dangerous form of censorship.

Our history is rich and varied – it is also as interesting and valid as anyone's biography, but it is rarely written and recorded. This section attempts to make a small beginning in that direction – to give space to working-class women to talk about our history and our lives.

Annette Kennerley

Nickie Roberts
Little Memories of a Lancashire Childhood

We played in the streets.

The world was grey: grey stone terraced houses, grey factory smoke, grey slate lavatory roofs, worn grey flagged pavements and cobbles. We skipped across the flags, avoiding the cracks, chanting:

> 'If you stand on a nick,
> You'll marry a brick
> And a spider'll come to your wedding . . .'

Not long ago, I took my husband, a middle-class Southerner, to see *Whistle Down the Wind*, a film 'they' made round Burnley, with loads of us scruffy kids as extras – dead authentic, we were – and our rough, bare Lancashire country as a backdrop. Steve couldn't get over it; he said afterwards that it was like seeing film footage of Poland, like being back in the nineteenth century. Watching it myself, after all this time, I tended to ignore the 'charming', adult-fantasy plot – a bunch of local children find a murderer in a barn and believe he's Jesus, as if we would – and the presence of 'stars'; I just saw us lot in our gabardines and wellies, with bare, scabby knees, lank hair and expressionless faces.

It took me back, that film, and got me thinking about the past. The older I get, the more I feel myself drawn to remembering

46

childhood; not through nostalgia so much as the desire to establish a sense of history: my own history.

I loved the streets; they were freedom. I had lots of adventures there, with my friends. We split into gangs and huddled on coalshed roof-tops, plotting campaigns against one another in frenzied whispers. I beat Malcolm Johns to a jelly when he said I had to be Maid Marion, a girl couldn't be Robin Hood. I showed him different.

I wanted to be a boy. Not because I wanted a willy, or any such Freudian rubbish – on the contrary, I thought boys' dicks were daft; they reminded me of small worms or teapot spouts, and they looked to me as if they could get in the way of a good rough game. No, I wanted to be a boy because you could be Robin Hood, the Lone Ranger, Black Arrow, William Tell, Flash Gordon, and the rest, without a big battle beforehand. And boys weren't called in by their mums to wash up or dry up, tidy this, tidy that. It made me sick, being a girl.

My mum worked in the cotton-shed, as a tackler. This was highly skilled work, almost always done by men, but Mum stuck up for herself and told the bosses she was as good as any man – which she was. Her greatest triumph was when one sceptical boss, who'd given her a week's trial to begin with, *begged* her to stay on when she put in her notice a few years later.

'You're the best tackler we've ever had,' he finally admitted, but she still went.

I used to listen for her coming home from work every night. We lived behind the railway, and to get to our terrace you had to go down the narrow ginnel beside the army barracks. When the mill-women, including my mum, came through that ginnel, they sounded like a platoon on horseback, their clogs made such a racket. I can still hear the ghost of it in my head, echoing. The very cobbles of our terrace seemed to vibrate. Then the women would appear behind the railings at the top of the grass bank, arm-in-arm, laughing, their woollen headscarves done up like turbans. Looking back now, I sometimes wonder what the hell they could find to laugh at, the conditions of their lives were so bad, even when they were supposed to have 'never had it so good'. Everything was still a struggle – work, worry, worry . . . endless work.

47

Sometimes I was forced to go to the mill to see Mum; an adventure, in a way. I liked getting all the attention from her workmates! But at the same time, I couldn't get away from there fast enough. To begin with, the building looked like a grim Victorian prison, or lunatic asylum, from the outside. Somehow, just looking at it made you feel that life was meant to be terrible, and don't you forget it. Inside, it got worse. The noise hit you right away: a solid-packed wall of noise that made you want to physically cower. How can I describe it? Like being run over by a train, you thought your brain would burst, you couldn't hear yourself *scream*.

They worked eight-hour shifts a day in that racket.

The light was poor and there was no air; you breathed the hot raw cotton fibres. They tasted sickly-sweet, like candy-floss. I hate candy-floss. All around, like giant, clacking people-traps, were the looms. 'Loom' was the right word for them; they loomed, as if they were just waiting for you to fall into them. And workers did get injured, even killed by them. Mum told me about a man, a reacher-in, who got his hair caught in the loom-belt; he was *scalped*. There were tales of people's arms getting pulled off, trapped whilst the machinery was still going.

'You've to keep a sharp look-out,' Mum used to say.

A sweeper got snared up by the wicked loom-belt and yanked right round the shafting . . . killed, dead.

I was terrified by these stories, scared for my mum. Nowadays, I feel anger, a cold, uncoiled anger deep inside, at the thought of her stuck in that place all those years. I recently tried to say how I felt to a middle-class young woman, feminist, but it was useless; she had no idea. I cried, 'Don't you see? It's like bloody pit-ponies, except it was my own mother.' Why waste my breath on somebody who tells me 'class doesn't count for much anyway'?

I think of how Mum and her mates laughed and talked and joked; inventing their own Lancashire mill-language – signing and lip-reading – to overcome the Bad Noise. What it boils down to, is the fact that they managed to communicate with each other; they stayed human even under the most inhuman conditions. That's what is important to me.

Dad's ambition was to get on; his big dream was to someday run his own business and no longer be a wage-slave, except to himself. He wanted a better life for his family than the one he'd had as a child – horror stories of the workhouse and being sent out to pick up dogends off the street for his father.

Dad and Mum loved each other and always worked as a team; their motto was, work hard all the way and you would better yourself and your circumstances.

It was Dad who taught me that the clouds were closer than the sky. 'Nearer than you think,' he told me one morning as he was walking me to infant school. He told me that the stars at night were really suns, that one day people would fly to the moon and back. I peppered him with questions, and he would listen, answer, and explain.

In those days, Dad was a projectionist at the Palace, in Burnley centre. Once, he painted the entire ceiling of the cinema single-handed; I could hardly believe it because it was so *high*: a great, vaulting dome with gold cusps and candelabra and cherubs, and all sorts of fiddly things. For years afterwards I would gaze at that ceiling with pride, missing half the film. Later, when I learned at school about Michelangelo and the roof of the Sistine Chapel, I thought, so what?

'My daddy painted the Palace ceiling, and *he* didn't have any assistants,' I told everybody. I still feel a bit like that about it.

As for school itself, I hated it. Right from the start I thought it was a cruel and barbaric thing to do: shut up children, small people, in horrible buildings with mean, posh grown-ups who hated you. I never thought of school as anything other than punishment; a perpetual torment, and I envied our dog, Duke, who could lollop around on his back and have his tummy tickled, whilst I got told to 'Get cracking, you're gunna be late . . .' Our Duke didn't have to go to school and he was only a dog, so why should *I* have to, if humans were meant to be so superior? was how I figured it. Duke could go out and play in the beloved streets, on the rekky; he was *free*. I didn't think it was fair.

I passed the 11-plus because my Uncle Douggy said I hadn't a cat-in-Hell's chance. (Uncle Douggy was always taking the piss, out of everybody and everything. If you said, 'What's for tea?' he would reply, 'Shit-wi-sugar', then roar with laughter at his own wit.) When the results were given – all 4A passed – they let us go home early to tell our parents. Mum was ill in bed at the time. I ran like the wind, shouting, 'I've passed! I've passed!' at all the neighbours, who laughed at me, as well they might.

Mum said, 'Fetch my purse off the mantelpiece.' She gave me a whole pound note. I bought tubes of Smarties and emptied them on to the rug by the fire. I played with them for ages, running my fingers through them, letting some dribble through my hands, scooping them up. I was mesmerized by all the bright colours. They were my jewels. After some time I ate the lot and was sick.

Mum would say to me, 'You're neither use nor ornament', because I did not help with the housework. I had to be literally forced into doing it. Looking back now, I think I was disgusting for not pulling my weight, but I can understand my reluctance. Housework is slavery, unless, of course, you're rich; then you don't do any.

Ours was a big family on both sides, Mum's and Dad's. I had hundreds of cousins. Mum's family were Irish and, like most Irish families in the North of England, ours was very close-knit. All the aunties and uncles were forever in and out of each other's houses, laughing and arguing, and us kids went along too, squabbling or having a laugh, just like the grown-ups. Grandma Kainey ruled the roost, from the best armchair of whichever house she happened to be in at the time. She was small, bunched up and frail-looking except for her face, which was set like a warrior's. She had a glare that could shrivel you up, and I've never met anybody yet who could match her ferocious scorn. She was particularly good at bringing you down to basics. I remember one time when Dad spent eight pounds – a lot of money then – on a pink marbled toilet seat, which he fixed onto the toilet himself. All day long he kept flitting up stairs to admire it, and coming down again with a big proud grin on his face. Grandma Kainey came by and was shown the beautiful new toilet seat, but made no comment. Later, though, she went up by herself, so we all sat waiting, 'on pins' as Mum would say, for her reaction; but when Grandma came back her face was sourer than ever, and she shook her head at poor Dad.

'Eight quid for a piss,' she said, in her most withering voice. 'You must be bloody mental.'

When she and Grandad came to Blackpool for a week's holiday with us, she went straight out to bingo and won herself a sturdy shopping-trolley. Every day after that she wheeled her empty trolley down the Arcades then wheeled it back again, full, three hours later. Up and down the Prom she went, with that fixed, hit-me-and-I'll-hit-you-back-harder expression on her face, unchanging. She won more stuff in that week than she'd have been able to afford the whole year round on the pension. I sometimes think she made herself win through sheer intimidation, daring the universe to defy her. Besides, as Dad said, 'God help Blackpool if she'd lost.'

Grandad Kainey was entirely another kettle of fish. He was one of the gentlest people that ever existed: small, wiry, with a craggy face and smiling blue eyes. Tender eyes. Mum told me he used to be a glass blower when she was a child.

'He were fantastic to watch . . . he made the most beautiful swans. You need great strength and a good set of lungs.'

Whenever Grandad Kainey saw me he would say, 'Ant she grown? She's a little cracker. And what long legs.'

It annoyed me a bit, because the one thing I wanted was to be tall, and I never grew above five foot one. To Grandad, though, I guess I looked tall.

'I'm champion,' he would say, when asked about his health. And he would sit quietly with his pipe, sending up patient and serene little puffs of smoke, 'puh . . . puh . . . puh . . . puh . . . ,' whilst the world went on around him. If there'd been a family row or scandal, he would remove the pipe from his mouth just long enough to shake his head and say 'It's a rum do', then he'd clamp it firmly between his lips again and settle.

My grandad loved all living, growing things; best of all he loved working on his allotment. He grew the tiniest, sweetest new potatoes you ever saw.

'Just look at that,' Mum would say, rubbing them gently between fingers and thumb. 'You don't even need to put these under the tap.'

After his 'retirement', Grandad Kainey worked part-time at the hospital near us; he would wheel his bike up the ginnel to our house. At Xmas and family do's he had a few drinks and would then sing old Irish songs he thought he'd forgotten. His cap would slide to the back of his head, making him look like a cheeky leprechaun, and his face went pink, 'like a baby's arse,' Grandma said. He'd sing and dance, then quietly fall asleep. When he died,

51

in 1977, Grandad Kainey possessed a tin of tobacco and thirty-five pence.

I loved them both, Grandma and Grandad, each in their own special way.

Cousin Barbara was closest to me in age; closest, too, in terms of friendship. We were always sleeping over at each other's house. One night in my bed at Cornwall Terrace, we saw an angel coming from the cuckoo clock. She shone brightly in a steady beam of golden light. Barbara and I ducked beneath the eiderdown, and when we peeped out again, the angel was gone. We definitely saw her.

Our Barbara was completely different to me, especially in the housework department. 'She's a Big Lift,' Auntie Doreen was forever telling my mum, who would then fix me with a terrible glare. I could've strangled Auntie Doreen! But it was true, Barbara was always cleaning, scrubbing, polishing, even whiting the doorstep . . .

'She's right houseproud,' Auntie Doreen said, over and over again. This became a sore subject in our house, right till the very day I left. 'Our Barbara does this . . . Our Barbara does that . . .' There were times when I hated the dreaded phrase 'Our Baaahbara', it rang balefully, accusingly, in my ear, like a litany. But I loved Barbara like my own flesh; she was like a big sister, even though we grew apart as we grew older. She was my favourite cousin.

At junior school, my best friend was a girl called Karen. She had thick, golden-brown hair, blue eyes, and skinny limbs. We went swimming and climbing and 'adventuring' together. We argued and fought a lot, too, and spent much of our friendship not speaking to each other. We had lots of big dreams . . .

I played a rotten trick on her once – I gave her a Pal butty, pretending it was corned beef. When she'd finished the lot, I revealed my wicked deed. She turned green and ran home; her mum told my mum and I got a good hiding, which was fair enough.

Karen and I practised kissing and wrote long love letters to Richard Chamberlain, in Hollywood. To our delight, we got a reply from his fan club: 'Richard was pleased to hear from you and hopes you're working hard at school' – plus a glossy photo. I wrote back, informing him that I was 'coming to California to see you next summer, please send me some money.' This seemed reasonable to me, since he had loads of money and I didn't; besides, 'You should start as you mean to go on,' as Mum was always saying.

I was nine or so when Mum told me the facts of life. I remember the occasion well. She was ironing and I was watching 'Popeye'. Suddenly she went, 'Turn the television off,' in a weird voice. I thought, 'Oh-oh' and slunk over to do as I was told, my brain flapping all the while, like some crazy index-file: What have I done? What's she found out? Then, to my amazement, she started going on about Mummies, Daddies and seeds. I didn't know what the hell she meant. She kept ironing one of Dad's shirts, madly.

I listened patiently till she got to the bit about the seed leaving Daddy's willy to go to Mummy's winkle, then I couldn't stop myself. I said, 'Does it jump?' and Mum laughed her head off for about five minutes, tears poured down her face. Eventually she pulled herself together long enough to give me the sordid details. By the time she'd finished, Dad's shirt was stiffer than the ironing board. I was fed-up about missing 'Popeye' although, at the same time, I couldn't wait to tell Karen; I ran down our backstreet as if released from a trap, but when I got to Karen's house and told her, in great excited gulps, where babies came from, she burst into tears and said 'I'm getting mine from the hospital.' There was just no getting through to her . . .

'Remember this date,' said the headline in the paper. 'This day will go down in world history . . .'

Well, all right, I thought, and dutifully recorded it in my *Penelope Diary*. I took everything literally, in those days. I believed there was something special and important about the date: the paper said so, so it must be true. Which is why, to this day, 2 January 1959 is firmly engraved upon my memory, although I haven't a clue what happened on it. I think childhood is punctuated with small mysteries like this; mine certainly was, anyway. Adults were to blame. It was the same with the business of the wall next to the bus-stop in Colne Road; the one that had the following advert painted all the way down it in big black letters:

'HAVE YOUR HAIR
PERMANENTLY WAVED
& KEEP SMILING
IN THE RAIN'

Why, I wondered, should ladies with curly hair feel happier about getting wet than ladies with straight hair? It puzzled me for years, that advert; I could only conclude that grown-up people were very strange indeed.

Liza Rymer Mam's Gone

Age Nine
walking home from school,
nothing's altered
nothing new.
In the house
big sister crying,
arms outstretched
and reaching, reaching.
Mam's gone, she said,
go get your things
a clean nightie
and anything else
you want to bring.
Age Nine,
and life goes on the same
for friends
and others
too numerous to name.
We caught the bus.
I had no choice.
The whims of adults,
I had no voice.
Fait accompli
that's what it was.
No time to feel
a sense of loss

Or think of Dad
after a hard day's work
in the empty house
where shadows lurk.
Age Nine
strange bed
laying down to sleep,
thinking
don't make promises
you can't keep.

Margaret Graham My Own Song

The past is a part of the journey, but there can be no turning back, whatever may have been lost upon the way. Looking back, half remembering, it seems a pleasant place to have been.

My first memories are fragmented, like magic lantern slides which I once watched as a child, in a darkened room. Then my mind's eye, like the camera, progresses to silent movies, followed by the talkies.

It is a colourful scene: soft lights above the rows of beds. Perhaps I'm the only one awake, because the ward is quiet. The next scene is a garden, near a building. I am alone. There are rose bushes and the sun shines weakly above the bare branches of the trees. This was in the hospital grounds, about February or March, when I was recovering from Scarlet Fever.

It was about 1927, when the streets were busy with people. I was standing in the middle of the street, at the back of the house. A group of women stood watching. A neighbour bent down to speak to me. She came so close that her spectacles frightened me; I began to cry. Strangely enough, this turned out to be quite a nice photograph of a chubby three or four-year-old girl, with fair, curly hair. The photo was taken by a professional photographer, who must have set up his equipment there, in the road.

In the spring, my sisters took me to the woods, which still hugged the city. We filled our arms with bluebells, then I wandered off into a grassy place.

Another time, I walked across the street, by myself, to call at the house opposite. The young couple there were pleased to see me. I think the lady had not been well. After a while they spoke together, then the young man smiled at me, hurried upstairs and brought down a pram and lots of picture cards, which he gave to me. I wheeled the pram proudly across the road.

My Aunt Beatrice, who lived with us, gave the doll to my sister, Clara, who was about eight years old.

I watched as she paraded it round with her, then later I found it lying in its little green dress, abandoned on the sofa. It was the first doll that I remember – there were to be others, but I don't think I ever played with them.

I looked at my father one day, as he was stropping his razor. He had black, wavy hair and nice blue eyes. He smiled on Sundays. One Sunday morning, he took me to the bowling green on the outskirts of the city. We walked with his friend, along the gleaming path beside the grass.

Our front window had starched collars and cuffs displayed in it, because Mom took in laundry. The room had a counter, behind which there were shelves. I used to play in there, or just twirl around until I felt giddy – a funny feeling. Mom often told me to be quiet. One dismal day, I looked for a long time through the front window. About this time, the couple who gave me the doll moved away and went to live in Kent.

I do not remember the days leading up to the next memory. One morning Mom was standing by the bed, saying that I had to go away. I became upset, saying that I did not want to go.

'It's all right,' she said, then. 'You're going to see Mrs Robertson in Kent.' I sat up in bed eagerly. Soon afterwards I was carried out of the house, past a line of silent children, to an ambulance. Once inside, I tried not to cough, thinking that if I sounded better, they might take me back home. The ambulance man asked gently, 'Do you want to cough?' I said I didn't, and managed to hold it in. At the hospital they were waiting for us. I was put into a cot, then a doctor put a needle into my leg – I cried out! Later on, my hair was washed with something that smelled awful. The time passed.

Mom and Dad came to see me one day. This was to be their only visit. I had diphtheria, and parents were only allowed to see their children if they were on a list of those seriously ill, for this was a fever hospital. My mother, who was wearing a white gown, asked me why I only had one pillow. 'The other children have three,' she said, looking around the ward. After she had gone, I tried to think how I could get more pillows.

It was night-time and I was now in bed on the other side of the ward. I looked down at my legs and wished they would grow. The children were talking together. Where, they wondered, did the children keep going to – the ones who kept leaving the ward? An older boy said that these children were put into something – he described its shape with his hands. I thought he must mean a cage. I did not understand, but felt frightened.

Once, at night-time, I looked down the ward to see a large Christmas tree. The only lights were those glowing in the darkness, above the tree. Nurses and young men were dancing dreamily together. Perhaps they were playing a song called 'Together', which Mom said reminded her of this time. I remember when the nurses brought in a box of oranges which they shared out between us. Mom told me later on that these were sent from my friends in Kent.

Some days, a lovely smell of yeast from the nearby brewery would fill the ward. Birds, too, ventured in through the open windows, alighting on the shining tables, on which lots of daffodils were displayed. I began to take an interest in meal-times, wondering what the pudding might be; hoping it was custard.

The ward filled up so that, as I was so much better, my sheets and pillows were taken to a black Victorian couch in the centre of the ward. This was not soft like the settees of today. I made a half-hearted complaint. Later, I grumbled that I was lying on some crumbs. The sheets were straightened, the pillows plumped, but there I stayed!

There came a day when the sun blazed through the windows. A nurse brought a little outfit for me to wear. These are the first clothes that I remember, because it was such a great day. They seem so small as I picture them now: a beige pleated skirt, a lightweight brown jumper and navy-blue knickers. When I got up, my joy knew no bounds.

I have no recollection of leaving the hospital when I was better, but I do remember getting home. There were some young children waiting for me in a room; lots of presents, too, of which I only recall a box of orange and lemon slices. I must have seemed like a stranger to them, for I was taller, very thin, and my hair was darker, with not a curl in sight. Later on, boys would shout after me in the street, 'Sparrer legs'. This hurt me. It was an accurate description, though, because years later I came across an old photo: there I was, standing to attention on my sparrow legs.

Jesse Locke The Orphanage

The orphanage stood in its own grounds, housing some three hundred girls, a full staff of residential teachers, a Sister, Nurse, Matron, 'Mother' for each individual cottage, Head Gardener, Governess, Boilerman. The cottages were for the children aged from two years of age, up to twelve, with a continuation house for the fourteen and fifteen age group. The school predominated at the bottom of the long stretch of lawn, with its full-chiming, hourly clock, school bell. The church, C of E, was at the entrance to the home. Its stained-glass windows were once destroyed when a heavy oak tree crashed into its side during a bad storm. Vegetables, fruit, plants, flowers, were grown extensively for the use of the 'Co-operative society', providing every known item for the storehouse and kitchens.

The large laundry would have soda, starch, blue, and everything was done by the girls' hands, working at large boilers, washing, rinsing, mangling, ironing. Girls learned sewing, making every item of garment, knitting stockings, in the well-conducted Sewing Room. We had Fire Drills: hoses, buckets, net for jumping from 'high bedroom windows' at every practice; ladders we scaled to fetch down our trapped person (using the fireman's lift) 'over the shoulder'. We girls emptied the cottage dustbins by wheelbarrow, two taking the part of lifting. Only fire ash went into them, true, other than perhaps a broken cup or plate. All vegetable waste the gardener took care of. His chickens' eggs were only for certain staff. We girls never tasted eggs. Only once a year, Easter Day, provided by the Co-op stores, I think. I can call myself a Working-Class Woman.

'The Infirmary', where we sick girls were treated daily, was so familiar, as well I remember, as a child. My first look inside the ward filled me with terror at seeing an aged person sitting in a wooden armchair wearing a mask over her mouth, the dark, piercing eyes trying to smile, her cough almost muffled. She, I learned at a later date, was a 'retained nurse' who died from T.B. (consumption). I turned my eye to the bright, warm fire, its guard was topped with a brass rail which glinted in the pale sunlight, like burnished gold. Here, I myself spent many months, treated too often for a chest complaint. Summer saw me out on the grass taking in air for my lungs. Even at the age of four years I remember the clothes I wore – a white cotton dress with bonnet to match. White button-up buckskin boots. I started infant school. Well do I remember the teacher, she taught us about the ocean, with a tray of sand, while the sea was blue chalk. Sometimes she would let us have water to make rivers. We all wore pinafores.

We had many beautiful warm summers. Our lessons were a treat for us, if we were allowed to take them outside the classroom. I would be fascinated by the small planes flying high up in the blue sky, the feathery clouds moving gently with a southerly breeze, the butterflies, and the feel of the cool grass on my legs. This is but a short piece of happiness from my young age. The story unfolds in less favourable aspects, as we girls never knew adolescence, or teenage wording. A Woman, you were, at fifteen years of age. We were old before we were young.

Mary Legg Memoirs of Theresa

My birthplace now bears no resemblance to the town I knew. Where I was born stands a huge shopping arcade, displaying every kind of fare. Gone is the little corner shop where we could receive credit until father brought home his pittance from the steelworks.

On Friday we could have luxuries, which slowly receded, and were reduced to the minimum by Thursday. The meagre dwellings, with black grates, kettles on the hob and tin baths hanging in the sculleries, were the homes of these poorly paid steelworkers.

My mother's favourite occupation was making 'clip' mats. These were floor coverings made with strips of brightly coloured, cast-off clothing prodded into a pattern of hessian squares. These were in demand, especially at Christmas, and the festivities were made brighter with the pin-money she had earned. Monday morning brought a visit from the rent man, and the regularity of payment was assured by the local pawnbroker, Mr Habergam. Suits and shoes, handed in on Monday and retrieved on Friday, happened with the regularity of a pendulum swinging in a clock. Another 'benefactor' was the street money lender, Mrs Lane – her home was the brightest, her pinny the newest, and her clients the unhappiest.

Death was an impersonal affair. My mother was always at hand to help, and would collect a flower donation from friends and neighbours, accompanied by Aunt Becky with a little black bag. It seems, now, a strange coincidence that there was always sufficient small change for them to have a rare visit to the picture house. My first experience of death was peeping from my Aunt Becky's window in the same road, to see the pathetic pilgrimage of my father and mother following two tiny white coffins, which, I later learned, contained the remains of a twin brother and sister I never knew. I had been taken to my aunt's house to be spared this sad spectacle.

I made my first step towards independence in the outside world as a scullery maid at the stately home of a mill owner. On the first day, I arrived with my carrier-bag, walked up the drive and pressed the bell on the imposing door. Instantly, as if a huge walking-stick had been hooked around my neck, I was transmitted to a side entrance. I learned afterwards that staff had never to be seen at this entrance.

I was interviewed by a housekeeper, and informed that I could not be addressed as Mary because this happened to be the name of my mistress. So, for my first sojurn I answered to the name Theresa, which was my confirmation name.

What wonderment this residence held for me, with quiet rooms, nurseries, drawing-rooms and sewing-rooms. A huge rack, covered with bells and attached to the kitchen, summonsed a pretty black and white parlourmaid to dance attendance in the appropriate quarter.

I found myself constantly in hot water – caviar put aside as an obnoxious substance, horseradish emptied into the pigswill (giving the pigs an unquenchable thirst for days) and the final, unforgivable sin was sticking my finger in a trifle when the temptation to sample it became too much to bear. I peeled potatoes, washed dishes, and made a nuisance of myself until the chores of the late dinners were over. Each morning I was awakened by the housekeeper hammering the stairs with a poker (alarm clocks can't have been invented). My first chore was to clean the huge, sooty grate and sweep up the dead beetles, a task which so repulsed me, it was taken over by a kindly gardener by the name of Harland.

The day arrived when I was allowed to join the parlourmaid for a peep at the world 'upstairs'. The guest-rooms had gowns and slippers at the ready; fruit, milk and fairy cakes at the side of each bed. A huge dining table stood in the great hall with a sideboard bearing tempting delicacies, gleaming tableware and silver cutlery. The huge dinner gong, when struck, caused me to disappear like a wizard's apprentice in a stage act.

I began to miss my home and parents, so I tended my notice and duly received an invitation to talk with the mistress (my namesake). I was awestricken as I entered her drawing-room, and I noticed her tiara most of all. On being asked my reason for leaving, with the candour of a fourteen-year-old, I reeled off my complaints – method of awakening, hour of duties, lack of off-duty. The housekeeper was sent for and I was offered a rise of one shilling weekly and given the information that a local country dance was taking place that evening, and the mistress had given me a pair of dancing shoes and a ticket to the dance.

I enjoyed the evening and found that my beetling friend, the gardener, was also a musician in the band. My life afterwards with the housekeeper was not rosy, as I had given the mistress information that she was constantly taking naps. So one day I caught the bus in the village square and did a 'flit', leaving behind a pair of wellies. When I arrived home, what a welcoming sight was the clip mat with the remnants of my old red skirt and green jumper.

I ventured into romantic dreams, and recall my first crush on a rather plain, spotty-faced youth who, I learned over the teenage grapevine, was partial to coconut macaroons. I bought these confections as bait, but found that as soon as he'd eaten them he disappeared, and I was left high, dry and forlorn.

At the age of eighteen, I followed the trends of three-point dresses, valencia hats and, for a short while, bells on garters. At this time I loved dancing, and my regular Saturday night dance was the height of enjoyment for me. One evening a good-looking musician wanted to make my acquaintance. I was rather shy and lacking in confidence, and peeping at the bandsman, noticed that my admirer was flirting with all the girls, so I decided that it was an unkind hoax. However, this was not so, for as I slowly made my way to the exit at the close of the evening, I heard a huge whistle and frantic efforts being made by the young man to carry his instruments across the hall before I disappeared.

He escorted me home, and I shared the carrying of his instrument cases. Within a year I was sharing his life, and in later years we produced a full ensemble with our musical family, and carrying cases was part of my life. I couldn't understand why my father cried the whole of my wedding day, as if I was being interned, but in later life I had the same reaction, at the weddings of my many offspring.

Sue Vodden Shirley

I fell for Shirley in a big way. We didn't do sexy things together like I had with Jennifer and Christine, or the two sisters, Sandra and Carol, from around the policemen's flats. It was different with Shirley.

When I first noticed her, I mean noticed her like when something happens, we weren't in the same class. Classes didn't mix. There were the odd friendships between Class 1 and Class 2, and 2 and 3, and 3 and 4, but nothing ever happened between Classes 1 and 4. I was in Class 1. We were all white and thought to be the bright ones – not very bright, though. Because it was a fact that Secondary School children were all of average or below average intelligence. Class 4 had mostly Greek girls, one Chinese girl, and a few others that were never paid much attention. Shirley was in Class 2. The first time I remember noticing her was in the hall during a dinner-break. I was about twelve. Some girls were doing a show, miming to pop records. I don't think the teachers were involved, because something about it felt really exciting. Shirley was John Lennon and she had a cardboard cut-out guitar. Wow! She was magnificent.

After this time, I was demoted to Class 2. Oh, the shame of it! They told my mum it was my maths. I was 'not doing as well as expected'. My new form teacher, being a maths teacher, would give me a little extra attention and help me along. It was all lies. I didn't like maths and I couldn't stand the maths teacher. They thought I was bad, not a good influence on my classmates; 'insolent' was the word they used, and my demotion was a punishment and a lesson to others. The maths teacher also taught P.E. and told me she voted Conservative. I nearly socked her one once, and she spent two years trying to get me thrown out of the school.

Class 2 wasn't a scholarly form. It was a typing, office practice, keep-out-of and get-into trouble class. Shirley and I became good buddies, and after minor, then major, feuds with the old Class 1 crowd, I was sort of sent to Coventry. They seemed to be pissed off that me and Shirley were going places – Highbury Corner bus-stop, Sunday afternoon pictures and hurrying past Nan's Café so we could be seen by the Little Highbury. The Little Highbury were Mods – followers, relatives, protégés of the Big Highbury, who were followers, relatives, protégés of the Big Big Highbury. Me and Shirl dressed nearly identical, tight grey flannel pencil skirts past the knee, with a fan pleat at the back, white tights, hush-puppies, white cricket cardigans edged with a red and blue stripe, and where I had a navy crew-neck, imitation-orlon jumper, Shirl had a pink one.

I was in love with Shirley at the time, but I was being too grown-up and into boys to notice. Our aim in life was to walk past Highbury Corner roundabout and be seen, then to progress from being seen, to be spoken of, talked to, touched, kissed, fallen in love with. Part of the fantasy was some heavy petting, but we never spoke very much about that bit. Apart from boys, I'm not sure that me and Shirl talked about much at all. At some point we were noticed, winked at from the tops of buses, turned round at from the backs of scooters. It was so exciting, things were really mounting up. Someone would be falling in love with me soon, I knew it, and then it happened. I was spoken to, going past Nan's Café. It was good-looking Owen Smith: 'Hey, Ginge!' My belly went over. 'Have you got ginger hairs on your minge? Ha! Ha! Ha!'

Annette Kennerley
I Dream of Dralon . . .

I've always hated Crimplene. Okay, so it was crease-resistant – one of the seven wonders of the Sixties – along with cling-film, the mini-skirt, packet soup, BBC 2, walking on the moon, Beatle breath and decimal currency. But I wonder, would Jean Shrimpton have been seen dead in a Crimplene mini-dress, or the USA have staked a Crimplene flag on the moon?

I used to dread my dad coming home from the mill with an ominous bundle under his arm – a perk of the job. As the polythene unfolded, an oily smell crept around the living room and out would spring an end-of-roll mass of bubbling, untreated Crimplene – yard after yard of vibrant colours, sometimes (horror of horrors) patterned in lurid Paisley, rough and unyielding to the touch. And no matter how skilled my mother was at the treadle machine, and no matter how many Comfort-filled washes it was lovingly treated to, it never lost its shock to the senses – nor its odour of old car engines.

Melting instantly on contact with a hot iron, it was impossible to smooth out the lumps and bumps that grew on it. I dreaded a new outfit – the untameable Crimplene would transfer the sleek seams of an A-line dress to a dozen caterpillars, marching head to toe. And my greatest sacrifice to fashion was to suffer the abrasive ordeal of wearing the Crimplene inside out, in a vain attempt to disguise and transform its outward appearance.

It even used to scratch the plastic on my dolls' arms – and Cindy in Crimplene never managed to achieve a glamorous effect. One year, our whole three-piece-suite got a new covering – textured turquoise Crimplene, complete with all-over eruptions that left your legs patterned for hours. Being totally non-absorbent, it wasn't even usable as a floor cloth, and it scratched instead of polished, if used as a duster. Waterproof was perhaps its only claim – no doubt due to the light coating of oil. Maybe some bright entrepreneur could have made a fortune from patenting the Crimplene umbrella.

Nowadays, I do not seek the silk of human kindness, nor a slumber in satin sheets, nor even to slip my feet into blessed cotton socks. But oh, give me a Dralon sofa any day; let me sink into a Polyester-filled duvet dream, and cling to my hundred per cent Acrylic sweater in the winter months. Terylene, Viscose, Bri-Nylon, man-made fibres, fake fur and fuzzy felt. Shower me with these! But please, God, deliver me from Crimplene.

Phoebe Nathan I Remember

When I was a child, I remember going to the baker's for a penny loaf of bread. Sometimes there would be a piece on top to make up the weight. I always ate this before I got home and it always tasted fresh and nice.

I remember big vans, who called at the wet fish shops with huge blocks of solid ice that the men would unload. When they weren't looking, we would run up and chip pieces off. The men would see us and shout: 'Clear off, you bloody kids'. We'd run away to the troughs that were built on the side of the pavement and contained water for the horses, and we would splash each other.

I remember the gas mantels that were so flimsy they nearly always broke when lit with a match. And when you eventually did light them, they nearly always went out when lowered. There was no pressing a switch then.

I remember my aunt asking me to go to the pub. She gave me a jug and fourpence and told me to ask the man for a pint of stout. She lived until she was ninety. I wonder if it was due to the stout!

I remember helping on a fish stall outside the Mile End station. I believe it's still there, but the prices aren't the same! We would sell kippers for a penny per pair, and middle-of-skate for twopence. We would work until nine or ten o'clock at night.

I remember the Saturday night treats to the local 'flea-pit', where we sat on wooden benches and listened to the piano, and watched the silent films: Pearl White relentlessly being tied up on railway lines. And as the train appeared around the corner, the words would flash up on the screen, 'Continued Next Week'. As well as all this, there would be two cartoons and Pathe news. All for twopence!

I remember the nurse coming to school and looking for 'nits'. If she found them, they'd chop all your hair off. I dreaded it ever happening to me. It never did. After school we'd play hopscotch in the street, leaving our chalk marks on the pavement. Or we would play with big wooden hoops, pushing them along with a stick.

I remember going to see my granny. She'd say, 'What's the news?' and I'd reply, 'I'll tell you for a penny.' She had a big old stove and fireplace where you put the coal in the top. If pieces fell out onto the hearth when the fire was poked, it was caught in the fender. Hers was a big brass one. If I owned that now, I'd be rich!

I remember lots of things. I remember my working-class upbringing and the hardships we endured. But above all, I remember being happy (and a bit mischievous!)

Della Chapman
From 'Disturbing the Curtains'

On my way upstairs, I stop to look out of the landing window and see the back gardens of the neighbouring houses and, beyond them, the railway bridge. Returning downstairs, I look out of the window at the blank-faced houses on the other side of the road, identical to the house I am in, the home of my childhood, a council house, something, I sense from my parents, that was nothing to be proud of, but they were not ashamed of it either.

At the windows my mother has lightly-gathered net curtains, as well as the heavy curtains that are drawn across at night. These are patterned with large pink and dark-red cabbage roses all over. She is very fond of them, and every time she closes the curtains across and I am there, she tells me, 'Lovely curtains, these, they're not to go to just anybody when I die, and I don't want people just throwing them out and not caring.' She tells me that the white net curtains are filthy, but they look snowy-white to me. Net curtains, gathered evenly on a taut spring, only went half-way up when I was a child, covering the bottom half of the window. My mother hated to take them down to wash them, exposing the intimacies of family life to curious passers-by. She would make sure it was a good wash-day, but while they were drying, dancing in the wind on the washing-line, they often became marked with sooty smuts emitted with the smoke from passing trains, and she got fiercely annoyed. When I walk along this road towards my mother's house, I realize that such net curtains are a mark that the house is lived in by someone who is growing old.

I stare out into a road peopled with ghosts, but I don't see them. All is quiet now, except perhaps for a car engine being warmed up before a car is driven away from the front of a house. A front door might bang, a garden gate click shut behind someone leaving a house. An Indian woman walks by, the pale silk cloth of her sari fluttering in the wind, a thin hand-knitted cardigan covering her gold-bangled arms. She pushes a child in a push-chair, but he is hidden from view by the privet hedge, but no doubt all that will be seen of him by passers-by will be a glimpse of dark eyes and honey-coloured skin. He will be snuggled down and tucked up in soft padded clothes, protected against cold weather.

The only people I recognize now are old ladies. One hurries by, pushing a tartan-patterned shopping bag on wheels, dry bleached hair worn out with bleaching and gingering over the years. They often remind me of the mothers of children I played with long ago, but I am never sure exactly who they are.

Cars, some new and shiny, but most not so new, are parked along the kerb, but no one I knew in my childhood had a car except the headmaster of my junior school, and he stopped using it when the War broke out, and then he walked to school each day, just as we did. By the time of my father's death and subsequent funeral, many families had cars. It was whispered to us most discreetly when we arrived for the occasion in our car, that it wasn't really smart enough to be one of the cars respectfully following the hearse to the crematorium, and we were told where we could temporarily park it out of sight, where neighbours wouldn't mind and would understand.

I used to think our road was the best place in the whole world to live. The top end was a cul-de-sac, it led nowhere, so all the best street games were played at our end. On a summer evening, I would stand at the top end, near the allotments, look down the road at all the skipping, roller-skating, children on bikes and scooters, playing hop-scotch, see all the running around and the ball games, and feel, with some emotion, that I was privileged to be there. It was the hub of the world.

As I grew older, the evacuees left, and we didn't play so much in the street anymore. Things were never so good when I left the junior school. We became divided: some went on to the senior school in Derby Road and others of us were girded up in unaccustomed school uniform, which we had never worn before, and went off to the girls' grammar school on the other, unfamiliar side of town . . .

Jules Haywood I Was Three Once

I was three once, with hair to my chin,
and wide dinner-plate eyes.
Knees that knocked
and a hold on my mum's apron strings that only the promise of
                    six chocolate sundaes would loosen.
We did everything together, me and her.
When I dropped the jam tarts down the stairs, she cried, too.
Steam from my ears and flames a foot long from my mouth,
                    dare anyone come near her.
Sat on the draining-board, her soft, quick fingers
                    teased my toes in the sink.
On street corners, chatting, would find her and her mates.
I'd press hard on her little finger with my cry of 'Oh, let's go'.
Back home, seducing her into an armchair, I'd curl up on her
                    lap, like a cat in the sun.

We packed a large, dusty suitcase once.
Jonny, my best doll, had her face pressed against the lid,
                              but she didn't moan.
Sea, sand and ice-cream filled my head.
No, we got as far as my aunt's, a bus-ride away.
And were back, unpacked, in time for me dad's tea!

Olive J. Scott
Recollections of a working-class girlhood on Tyneside in the 1930s

After Dad died, when I was nine years old, our mother got the chance to run a newsagent's shop for Colin Veitch, who was a well-known local personality. It was when she helped out at the Socialist Café in the Royal Arcade that Mr Veitch, who was an amateur dramatics producer as well, asked her to work for him. So, not only did she take on the shop, she also kept up her interest in the drama, and I remember being taken to see various productions. Bernard Shaw was a patron and often came to the shows.

My two sisters were encouraged to take part in the plays and one production was *King Midas* starring my oldest sister, Nancy. On the last night she was presented with a most lovely casket of chocolates. It had gold-tasselled drawers. To me, it was a marvellous gift which I could only look at. I was not allowed to touch the box, never mind sample the contents. The box was put in our china cabinet to be gazed at with awe. One afternoon the key of the cabinet was left in by mistake. It was too much, the temptation was more than I could bear. I took out the box and carefully unwrapped the foil, bit off the end of each bottle (they were liqueurs), drank the nectar, re-wrapped each one and put them all back carefully.

Time passed, then Nancy had a small party. The chocs were handed round. I made myself scarce. Needless to say, it all caught up with me and I paid the usual price, which was a belting across the legs with the 'taws', a leather strap with cut-out strips at the wide part. This object of misery always hung at the side of our fireplace next to the cupboard.

We had a stone-floored scullery with a boiler in one corner. It was one of my jobs to chop the sticks to start the fire for the washing, also to turn the wheel of the mangle in the backyard. The steps were done with a donkey stone. It was real hard work.

Mam took washing in for a Mrs Friedman and I used to deliver the washing-basket on an old pram to Sandyford when I would get the money, which was five shillings in an envelope, and a piece of cake.

Sometimes I would have to get two penn'th of jam in a cup out of the corner shop, run by Mrs Crawford who always wore long jet ear-rings and spectacles which only had one glass in. This always fascinated me. I used to think perhaps she couldn't afford two and was waiting till she could, to complete. Anyway, the cup was weighed first, then the jam was spooned out of a big stone jar till the right amount showed by the scale tipping down at one end. The same procedure was used for pickles and beetroot. We kids found that if we kept one finger under the scale (she couldn't see on that side) we always got good measure.

People used to get goods 'on tick' in those days. Mrs Crawford had little black books which she gave to selected customers, usually the ones whose husbands had a job. I remember feeling quite resentful and envious of some of the kids I played with because they were sent to get messages 'on the book'. We didn't have a book. We had no Dad.

The best day of the week was Saturday; that was matinee day, and for one penny we could lose ourselves in another world, always much better than the one we had. I used to be carried away by silent films, which were nearly always serials of the most daring escapades and usually ended with the heroine hanging by delicate white fingers to the edge of a cliff or just about to be run over by a train. This was to get you back the following Saturday to see what happened. Consequently, if I didn't get my penny I was devastated and would do anything to make sure it was forthcoming, hence my appearance as a newspaper delivery kid.

Each afternoon, straight from school, I went to the shop where Mam marked the street and number on each paper and off I went, hail, rain and blizzard. I started off quite keen, but grew very

70

bored, and eventually came to hate it. Just the matinee penny kept me going.

There was a family in our street called Caisley. There were nine of them including the parents. They kept hens and ducks, also a very noisy cockerel in the backyard. They often got out into the back lane and walked in anybody's yard where a door was open. Once, the cockerel came in our yard and our cat, called Peter, went for it. There was such a noise and the feathers flew! Later, one of the Caisley kids came in to collect the loose feathers. They never wasted a thing in that family! Mam would often send me for two-eggs-for-three-ha'pence and Mrs Caisley would ask me into the kitchen. I was amazed to see the hens strutting around – a couple were on the settee and one on the table. The place was very dirty and I just couldn't describe the smell.

One of my greatest pleasures was books and the *School Girl's Own*. If I started a book I just couldn't put it down. Before I could join the library I had to get the signature of a parent. I used to pester Mam to sign the card, and it seemed ages before she did.

In the meantime, I used to borrow books or mags from anybody who'd lend me them. Sometimes, at night, the gaslight would start to go down just when I was at an exciting part of the story and had no pennies for the meter. Often we read by candlelight, and usually my sisters would blow it out when I could have read on and on.

When I was accepted for the big library I was in seventh heaven – two books at a time. I was getting, on average, four books a week when, one day, I returned my books to choose some new ones and the man behind the big counter told me Mam had dropped them a card instructing them to issue me no more books. To this day I remember so well the desolation of it. I was shattered and felt that the bottom had dropped out of my world. I walked away from that library numb with misery. I wanted to run away and never go home again. I cried bitterly, but when you are poor and underprivileged you develop a kind of cunning and I was determined I wasn't going to do without my books, so I got Doris Montague to join the library – her parents were only too delighted to sign her in – and she let me have the loan of hers.

The trouble was, I had to become a sneak reader and the only place I could read in peace was the back yard lavatory. I used to sit there for hours on end, then hide the book in a paper bag in the coalhouse, high up on a shelf. There was never any danger of it being discovered. We never had coal more than two feet high. In fact, Mam used to send me with a bucket to Maxwell's who sold coal in their back yard. It was twopence a bucket, or a stone in weight. I was minded to be careful not to drop any pieces and if I did, to pick them up immediately before anybody else did. How I hated that chore, but we did have our good times, too, if you could call them that.

I remember once being asked to a school chum's birthday party, along with Doris and Elsie. They were discussing what they would take for a present. I began to worry, knowing that Mam would never be able to afford even a simple gift. So, after asking, I was told, 'no party'. I threw myself on our bed weeping, then I had an idea. Somewhere in one of our bedroom drawers I'd seen a brand new card of safety pins. I started searching, and to my delight found them, shiny gold, all in a row in graduated sizes. I had my present! It never entered my head that not only was it an awful gift, but it was also stealing. I wrapped it in tissue paper and managed to convince Mam that a present wasn't necessary after all, and off I went to the party. I'll always remember that girl's face and her mother's, when they unwrapped the card of pins. Everyone there just stood and stared at me.

The kennel lads used to get their evening dinner at our house. Mam got paid by the trainers, so much a meal. She seemed to be always cooking and that meant more errands for me. She used to give me a list with all the groceries, and one thing that was most important was the dividend cheque number. These cheques were saved up for a whole year when the Co-op paid out one shilling and sixpence in the pound. I can still remember the number – 4045.

Mam kept a string behind the cupboard door with a big darning needle on the end, and every cheque was threaded on this string. The delight when it got near divi. time was felt by the whole family, because it usually meant something new for the house or some treat. Once I went cold with dread when I realized I had lost a cheque with seven shillings' worth of purchases on it. I didn't dare go home without it, but neither could I carry the parcel of groceries around with me for long, as they were needed at once.

I got my friend to help me to look for it. She said, 'Why don't we ask Saint Teresa to help?' We were near our church at the time. It was next to the Potts Street Co-op. In we went, straight up to the statue of Saint Teresa. On my knees, I begged to be shown where the lost cheque was, although I didn't really believe it would turn up. I came out in tears. I would just have to go home, so I lumped the parcel under my arm and as my friend said 'Cheerio' to me at our corner, she said, 'Look what's tucked into the string tying the parcel.' It was the cheque! The grocer must have tucked it in when he put up the goods.

From that day to this, I have firmly believed in miracles!

Heather McCracken Photographs

They got married in early summer. A June wedding. Visions of soft sunlight slanting through stained glass church windows. It rained. The whole day it just poured and all the wedding photographs were pock-marked with heavy black umbrellas shielding the couple from the downpour. But they looked so happy. She, shyly beautiful, smiling quietly, her eyes soft and the tiny pearls nestling gently at her throat. She told me much later that they were borrowed from her cousin, but on the day they were hers, frozen, forever.

At her side, he looked smaller, more boyish than I remembered. His ears stuck out rather comically and his hair was slicked over to one side, with a parting so perfect it might have been pencilled in. They were posed on the steps of the ivy-clad Church of Ireland she had attended since childhood. After their marriage she had left the church she loved, with its quiet beauty and familiar rituals, for the cold, hard austerity of Presbyterianism – the faith of his youth. But on that wet June day there was no hint of sadness or regret for lost loves. The future was theirs, a new life, filled with fresh hopes and unsullied dreams.

More photographs followed, of the honeymoon spent in some quiet corner of the West of Ireland. He had a way with the camera and captured the sunlit splendour of the countryside, posing her amid trees, lakes and hills like some imagined spirit whose form was a perfect blend of earth and air. Years later they had gone back to the same spot for a spring holiday, taking with them his sister and her husband. His photographs were more earthy now, perhaps because of the swollen bellies of the two women, both pregnant with their first babies. She wasn't part of the air any longer. Her feet were firmly planted in the burgeoning earth, the tiny form within her rooting her to the land.

How she laughed at those photos when I found them in a dark corner of the attic! I'd been looking for old bits of carpet to fit the stairs of my new flat when I found the box. It was one of those old chocolate boxes with painted clusters of faded flowers at the feet of an elegant, crinolined lady twirling a parasol. A dusty blue rosette clung in a crumpled heap on one corner and a piece of old knicker elastic held the sides together.

I shouted down the stairs for her to come up and have a look. Together we sat amid the clutter and giggled over the small black and white images. But now and then she'd be silent and would seem to be drinking in a scene, gazing at herself with a puzzled look as if she didn't recognize the eyes that held hers. Then a small sigh would brush past my cheek, like the gossamer breath of a passing ghost.

I wondered, looking at them in their youth, what had they hoped for? Was it what they had now? A house, car, central heating, double-glazing? They certainly seemed more contented than in the stormy days I remembered as a child. Then, the house had often been a harsh, frightening place, full of anger, bitterness and pain. The frayed furniture, the cracking lino that she scrubbed every Saturday until the pattern was almost worn away, the sour smell of bleach on the back steps and on her red, chapped hands. The glistening fat of the mutton stew that used to make me sick and earned me a cuff on the ear if I wouldn't eat it. All those things were buried in the past, but were as much a part of the present as the new shower unit and thick bathroom carpet, real luxuries to which I looked forward on my odd visits home. But under the carpet I could still feel the cold lino and see the rusty stains under the bath taps.

Could this cosy present be their only reality? It seemed so. If I ever mentioned the past as anything other than happy, she, in particular, would say my memory was distorted, and would tell me her truth, her reality. So I'd let it drop. Now, when I visit, we look at photographs, drink tea, and try not to argue. My brother, on a holiday, home from Australia, bought him a fancy camera and he took up his old hobby with all the zeal and fervour of a new convert. But she isn't in his pictures anymore. Not as their essence. Instead, she might be a tiny blob at the end of a windswept beach or a speck somewhere on a hillside. He takes close-ups of ducks, icy puddles, marram grass, children at play, but none of her. I make the right noises and he is pleased. But inside, I am choked with sadness for her and the young girl locked inside a faded chocolate box, waiting to be discovered.

Sandra Grayson
Saying Goodbye to Booba★

'Hallo, darlink!'

The voice was like no other that I had known, the accent Eastern European. In her tone warmth, concern and indulgence all played their part.

Booba's shape could not be pin-pointed. She mostly wore loose-fitting clothes and a shawl. Her grey, dishevelled hair was pinned in a chignon. She had one glass eye, but the good one noticed enough for two.

I never saw the house in Boreham St, E1, but once an uncle drove me there to look at the new council flats. It was in that area that Booba and Zaida raised eleven children.

Zaida was a toff. He wore a smart grey Homburg hat with black petersham ribbon. Facially, he was Ben Gurion's double and his ferocious temper depended on whether or not he had won or lost at cards or at horses.

My grandparents had fled from the holocaust and Booba never did learn to read or write, but so vot?

Mother occasionally talks about the East End. Everyone was poor. Every door was open to one's neighbours. The children played 'Knock Down Ginger'. You tied a cord to all the door-

★ Booba is a Yiddish word for grandmother

75

knockers in the street, gave a quick tug and then ran for it. The greatest treat was making custard on Friday nights. You took sweets to the cinema, put them in the hat-brims of the 'swells' and waited for the clatter when the owners stood up.

It was in that locality that some of my aunts mixed with the Communists and met their future husbands, either in the local youth club or, as in Gertie's case, in the street. She worked in a milliner's shop and every day greeted Alf, who worked opposite in a gentlemen's dry cleaners. One day she went into his shop and said 'Ah, a breath of fresh air'.

After the war, the family moved to a larger house in Stamford Hill. Its French windows were of a dull gold and blue and overlooked a tiny courtyard and there were rooms in the basement. The toilet was a porcelain hole in an oblong block of wood. No sooner were you inside the hall than Booba would say, 'You must be hungry,' and she would offer Lockshen soup, roast chicken, pickled gherkin and smoked salmon. She used to feed her children in rotas and never sat down until the last one had been served. We grandchildren were taken into the garden and introduced to the neighbours with a great flourish. It was by the rosebush that Booba told me not to take life so seriously.

After tea I would accompany my father along a road of peeling facades and broken down walls, past the Orthodox Jews in their kuppels, with their long sideburns and beards that almost reached their knees, until we arrived at the tailor's workshop on the corner. There was a tremendous din from the sewing machines and the voices that joked and shouted out orders. Every year, from the age of ten, I designed a coat or jacket to be made exactly to my specifications. The finished gift never ceased to seem miraculous – like the coloured pencils that I bought for sevenpence each with my pocket money.

After Zaida had died, my father returned to live with Booba. 'Your mother wore black at her own wedding!' I was told. 'She cut herself off. She wanted something better. She's very anglicized.' The secure days of fairground treats and afternoons spent in icecream parlours had come to an end. For some time, I refused to see Father, but later we met three or four times a year. He was a generous stranger who spent some of his time reading novels of a lurid or political content and in working out *the* system to win a fortune. Although he was sent to business college, he wouldn't accept a job from a family friend – charity! How he hated the workshop. He paced up and down in the garden as if to take out his frustration on his feet. Zaida made life difficult, through his inefficiency and irresponsible attitude. One day my father did not just wave goodbye to me at the front door, he walked down the path to the gate. Soon afterwards, he died of a coronary thrombosis and Booba failed to climb the stairs and go to him when he cried out. She thought he was making a fuss about nothing. My brother attended the funeral alone and when I came back from abroad, I crossed the threshold and burst into tears.

Booba had faced many tragedies. One daughter suffered from mental illness, Alec was shot down into the sea by the Germans, Zaida asked a daughter to leave the house to bear her illegitimate son elsewhere.

She didn't forget all this when she sat in state at the numerous Barmitzvahs and weddings – 'Please God, by you'. Always 200 to 300 guests, rows of banqueting tables, the children playing beneath white linen cloths, a Master of Ceremonies to announce the guests. There were flowers everywhere. The orchestra played schmaltzy melodies and Booba was attired in her latest black diamanté or silver lurex creation. She beamed happily, her head nodding out of time to the music, even when Zaida had passed on. 'We were kissing and cuddling to the very end,' she admitted.

I see her now, a slim-waisted young woman, her posture erect, sitting in a deckchair at the seaside, expression serene, a stillness about her.

Not only was she coquettish in dress, but she also enjoyed a good chat. Her telephone bill must have been exorbitant. All day long she would gossip to Mick and Ronnie, Debbie and Lou, Jean and Gertie, Polly, Mossy, Esther, friends and grandchildren. She had the knack of boasting about one person to another and about the second to the third, until the family was one seething mass of competition.

'Do you know, she never once walked in the street. Because of loss of balance, she feared falling, so she always travelled by cab or car.' She had eleven children to care for, and she knew all about balanced diets and was well-organized. She attended every school and club event. Their cliques and rivalries are still apparent. At

77

least four are Sunday artists. Her baby, now over fifty, sits aloof—linguist, writer and psychologist. Most of the grandchildren have conformed, but a few of us cannot bring ourselves to.

In widowhood, she insisted on living alone, despite a bad hip and aching joints. Polly rang daily to advise her on which TV programmes to watch. Her party clothes hung in the wardrobe, awaiting the next celebration.

It was to her tiny flat that I took Jean for approval. I sat on the bus, embracing him. Booba was ninety and no longer capable of preparing huge feasts. We were offered a cold buffet. Jean, an analytical French Marxist, missed all the family references. I could all but read her thoughts, 'You're not one of us', in the same way that they say of my sister-in-law, 'And how is the beautiful Sawbee-Li?', a slight edge to the voice. ('Didn't you know, they eat matzohs with their rice?') Nevertheless, without looking at Jean, she scolded me: 'Look after him, pour out his coffee, see that he has enough to eat.' I'm sure that she sensed we would part. An uncle accused me of wanting the bizarre.

On the last visit, I caught two buses and a train to the sea. She sat in an exclusive old people's home, a frail puppet, a wig perched on her head. 'It's getting dark, dolly,' she remarked. 'You must go home.' It was only three in the afternoon. I no longer said 'Goodbye. Behave yourself!' and she no longer chuckled.

At ninety-four she had a nose haemorrhage. I went to the shiva (funeral). I thought, 'I sit and shiver. Everyone will be weeping'. But I was wrong. They said that her life had been happy. Smilingly, they passed round sweets and photographs. 'Look, there's Lou!' I had forgotten that my father's hair had gone white. Debbie said, 'She understood young people. If she could have had her youth back, she wanted to live like you do'. The shiva was interrupted by a telephone call: 'Sawbee's having contractions every few minutes!' Kim would have been her thirtieth great-grandchild, and she had twenty-five grandchildren.

I read in one obituary, 'Her great delight in her family, her love and compassion, always her love!'

It's the end of an era.

Jane Toms Remembrance Sunday 1982

I watched her touch your lips
your mother
to keep you quiet while we stayed
silent.
The sounds you tried to utter
drowned.
I looked at all around and thought
about those dreadful years.
My childhood broken at the age of
eight.
Best not to think too hard.
My thoughts unspoken.
Some stay away, their grief
so painful.
Poppies and carnations carefully
displayed
upon the Communion Table.
Another generation here today,
new blood to put this world aright.
And, on another cold November morn,
they might remember.

I was in the church family service, and when the minister said we would stand silently for a couple of minutes I felt trapped, as usually I do not attend these services. As I stayed silent, I wondered what it was that I should be thinking, and realized that there were many at the service who were not even born at the time of the last war.

I could only think of the effect it had had on my own family, being evacuated from Jersey. One evening all was normal, the next morning we were going on boats to different parts of England. I left behind my favourite teddy bear, who was as big as myself, and I felt safe with him by my bed. Also my dolls. All these my father gave away to other children during the War. The War was a blessing in disguise for my father, as he was able to carry on a relationship with a woman, started previously, now that my mother was out of the way. I left at the age of eight, and did not see my father again until I was twenty-four or twenty-five.

During the service, I thought of all these things. Had I lost someone who was actually fighting, I think it would have been even more painful for me.

I would be interested to hear how others cope when in this two-minute silence. Around me were babies murmuring, and it reminded me of the cities which had been bombed, and after a while nature took over and plants began to grow. Here were children – another generation – and, not wanting to dig into my mind too much here, I stopped. It would have been too hard to imagine the next war – God forbid.

Karen Liljenburg Coming Home

Has almost become a mechanised process;
A matter of fitting myself into timetables.
I sit by myself in a bus, hot with people
Noting coolly the accent I grew up with.
It takes sweat to find some feeling
At the sight of a city dying.

The tedious procession of tatty shops;
Shrivelled figures leaning on lintels;
Grey things draped in the window
Of a store called 'Misfits'.

At one stop, a woman picks at the gutter.
The passengers queue away from her.

In the prestige offices
Every cell hums with barren Workers.

Over the dirt of a disused railway
Someone's daubed 'Get about with the Tories'.

Alleys, chimneys,
Lead works, leather works,
Roads, roads, roads –
To the end of the ride.

I run at last up the narrow street
To the terraced box where my heart beats.

Mary Bird Firecrackers

Has anyone got the embarrassing habit that I have? My problem
is that I giggle at the most inappropriate moment and even
though I'm over sixty, I still do it. If I see the funny side of
something, my body quivers like a jelly doing the rumba. I have
often asked myself if it's due to a warped sense of humour, a form
of hysteria, or some nervous reaction. Whatever it is, it makes me
feel very foolish.

I was born in Tooting, in London, and, judging from early
photographs, it seems that I was a podgy baby, with a head that
looked like a toilet brush and a body like a Michelin tyre. My
mother was an absolute dear, so kind, generous and understanding and I loved her very much. My father was just the opposite; he

had a hard, cruel streak. My sister, Joyce, and I were scared stiff of him. The beer he consumed would sink a battleship. Mind you, he did have his witty moments and often he would say, when drinking a pint, 'If my mother had fed me with this when I was a baby, I'd never have left her'.

The first few years of my life are a little hazy, but I know that home was an unhappy one. We lived in the basement flat of a very large house. It had dark cellars; the lighting was bad, owing to the dim gas mantles. It was a very eerie place altogether. The house was owned by a family of quite substantial means, and we were the caretakers. My mum had once been nanny to them and was much loved by them. My sister and I were really scared of the dark shadows, especially when we went to bed with our candle-sticks. When I come to think of it now, gosh what a danger those lighted flames were! The smallest draught used to blow the blessed things towards us from our bedside table and nearly set light to the bedclothes. Under these circumstances, I was very nervous at night-times and had dreadful nightmares.

My father would come home from the pub and ill-treat Mum and I was terrified that he was going to murder her. Her dressing-gown used to hang on a hook on the bedroom door, but in my dreams it was not the dressing-gown, but my mother hanging there.

During the day I was a different child, very popular with the other kids, and would do anything for a dare and used to laugh most of the day. I loved school, because I found all the lessons, apart from arithmetic, fairly easy, but, oh boy! owing to my giggling and daredevil ways, I was constantly in trouble. In those days it was quite in order for a headmaster to cane us girls. I got so used to it, that it didn't bother me. You only had to lick your hands first, then it didn't hurt so much. Sometimes I would pull my hand away and the headmaster would hit his own legs, which caused much laughter in the classroom and, being a right old show-off, I giggled and got another whipping for that.

Secretly, I wanted my teachers to like me, and I picked flowers for them from other people's front-gardens on my way to school and would say that they were from my garden. One day I was dared to pinch a new piece of chalk from the classroom cupboard so that we could play 'arrows' on the way home, never dreaming that the teacher would follow the chalk marks to my house and have a word or two with my mother, and at the same time thank her for the lovely bunch of tulips she'd sent. Mum naturally answered that we didn't grow tulips in our garden. It was only because I wanted to be loved by everyone that I did these outlandish things. Unfortunately, it had just the opposite effect, and my reports reached my father with the words, 'Kathleen is good at her lessons, but is very, very naughty'.

Further education was out of the question, as my parents couldn't afford the uniform of an upper school. As it was, the clothes I normally wore were in the pawn shop quite regularly.

So off I went to find a job, not even knowing where to head for. I found myself in Wandsworth High Street and went into a few shops, without success. I was about to pack up, because my poor old feet were killing me (I think I had my sister's shoes on), but said to myself, 'Come on, Crackers, don't give up,' and walked into a shoe-shop, asked to see the manager and to my amazement he took me on as a junior. I was so thrilled I nearly kissed him.

The young girls of today would be shocked if they knew how hard we had to work and the number of hours we put in. If someone came into the shop and we didn't sell them anything, we got told off. I developed the gift of the gab pretty quickly, and it wasn't long before I managed to talk a customer into buying a pair of wellies, even though they'd come in originally for a pair of bedroom slippers. Ten shillings a week was my wage, with commission on our sales. The first week, all I did was dust boxes and put them in order, but I was allowed to sell one pair of stockings to a customer and at the end of the week had to sign for one penny commission on top of my wage. I gave my mother most of the money, but kept a shilling for the local Saturday Hop and a sixpence to pay for a bicycle that I was saving for.

One day I arrived home from work to find my father back from one of his jaunts. That night when Joyce and I had gone to bed, we lay listening to another awful row, which only ended when my father went off to the pub. About ten o'clock we thought we heard the back door quietly close. We didn't take too much notice and thought we must have been mistaken, but after a while the house had an eerie silence and we realized that Mum had gone out, a thing she never did. We lay awake and heard our father stagger in and go to bed. We didn't know what to do. At first we thought we would dress and go to the police station for advice, but we were frightened we would be heard. Eventually Mother returned, about midnight. She came into our room, the tears streaming down her face. She said, 'I couldn't leave you, after all'. Apparently, she had walked to Putney Bridge and was going to throw herself over. She had had enough. Luckily, as she was about to do the actual deed, a lady and gentleman happened to be walking over the bridge and, guessing what she was about to do, they managed to talk her out of it. She ended up sobbing on the woman's shoulder. That kind couple brought her home. They must both be in heaven now, but I shall always be grateful to them.

The next two or three years went smoothly for me at work, and I was happy there, but although I became the senior assistant, I knew I had to do something better with my life.

Walking along with a friend one day, I saw two women coming down the road in what I thought was the smartest uniform I'd ever seen. I was very interested and really fancied myself in one of those outfits. My friend said, 'Dare you to ask them what and who they are'. Of course, I didn't have to be dared twice, and found out that they were fire service girls, and that they went to the fire station once a week for some sort of training. We didn't stop to ask what you had to do, but went straight to the fire station to join. I wasn't at all concerned at what was involved, all I knew was that I wanted one of those uniforms. The big disappointment came when the station officer said that only women of eighteen and over could join. My friend, Pat, was already eighteen and the look of woe on my face must have melted the heart of that officer, because he said, 'Of course, I am not to know that you are not the right age', which was good enough for me. So I wrote down the wrong age on the application form and signed it, not even having read the thing. Little did I realize that I had signed on for the duration, if there was to be a war.

There came a day when my whole life changed. It was 1 September 1939. I was serving a particularly awkward customer when a telegram arrived at the shop for me. I hardly dared open it, thinking something awful must have happened at home, but when I read it the words were, 'Report to Wandsworth Fire

Station with a blanket and toilet articles, etc. at once'. This sent me into a real tizwaz and I thought, 'Oh dear, whatever have I let myself in for?' All I wanted was the uniform. Anyhow, I thought I'd better obey the order, and dashed home to get the blanket, etc. My mother said, 'Where are you going to sleep, then?' and I replied that I didn't know and would be in touch as soon as I found out what was happening.

I was loving every moment of the attention I was getting, being as I was the youngest member on the station and was thoroughly spoilt. I remember thinking, 'Gosh, there is a rotten war on, yet I'm happier than I've been for ages'. We had two days on duty and then one day off, but I didn't take my leave day because it was just great to be with so many nice people, all a bit older than me and far more sensible. The girls were included in all the chores that the men had to do. The first two or three days we were filling sandbags, drinking lots of tea and having lots of laughs.

It was with guilt that I felt that I was neglecting the folks at home, so thought I had better start taking my days off. Things hadn't changed, and one night father was so bad-tempered and I was so unhappy that I packed a suitcase and left home, telling my mother that I would go in every day to see her. I had no idea where I was going and had only a shilling in my purse. I went down the High Street and looked at the adverts in some of the shops. They were very difficult to see, but I always carried a torch. There was a room to let in a road near Wimbledon Common, so, making my way in the blackout, and getting one or two stares from passers-by (perhaps I looked as if I was off for a naughty weekend), I knocked at a big eerie house. A frowning, serious looking woman came to the door and asked me why I was knocking at such an unearthly hour. It was about 10.30 pm. The tears were beginning to well up by this time, so I thought I'd better tell her the truth. She eyed me with suspicion, but finally said I could have the room at eleven shillings a week. I sent up a silent prayer that she wouldn't ask me for it in advance. Luckily, she didn't, and I was shown the room on the top floor. My last shilling went into the gas meter to heat it, but even then, I shivered half the night.

Next day, I popped back home to have a long chat with my mum; she didn't blame me one atom for leaving, and I always kept my promise to go and see her every day, even if it was only for a few minutes.

Whether our family has a thing about uniforms, I don't know, but my sister, Joyce, decided to join the women's air force, my cousins joined the navy. It meant that all of our family have been in uniform at some time. Joyce was sent somewhere to help look after a barrage balloon. In April 1941, I was introduced to a friend's brother, Harry. He was in the army and was stationed on a gun site at Clapham Common. I'd heard quite a lot about Harry. He asked me if I would like to go out with him on his next day off. I said that would be nice, so got myself ready, complete with a high-heeled pair of patent shoes on my feet, and wondered where he would be taking me. I was a bit disappointed when he said, 'Let's go for a walk on the Common'. Yes, he was a man for his fresh air and athletics, football, etc. Oh, how I wished I hadn't put those high-heeled shoes on. I returned from that walk with blisters on my heels and was dying to get me feet in some water, therefore declined the offer his mother had sent, for me to go back to his house for tea. I didn't tell him why, but I knew I couldn't walk any further. I promised to go to a film with him in the evening.

Eventually we were married. Most brides say that they don't remember all that happened on their wedding day, and I don't think I was any exception. I remember a sea of smiling faces and the long walk down the aisle. Unfortunately Dad had a limp, due to his wound from the 1914 War, and I tried to keep in time with him. I wanted to go up, down, up, down and the thought of it made me want to giggle. I pleaded with myself not to be weak and to control myself and luckily it worked. When we came out of the church, most of the fire station's personnel had come to wish us luck and we walked through an avenue of raised axes. Thank God, nobody dropped one.

Harry and I had rented a flat in Putney, and there we spent the weekend. During that weekend, we both discovered, or at least admitted, that I wasn't a very good cook, and that Harry wasn't in any way a handyman, but who cared? We had time to learn each other's faults. Unfortunately, that is where we were both wrong, because when Harry got back to his unit on the Monday morning, he was told that they would get their embarkation leave and were off to foreign lands. It was a bit of a shock, because we hadn't had time to really get to know each other properly.

Anyway, a fortnight later I was at Kings Cross Station waving goodbye and not knowing where Harry was going, or for how long. He turned out to be away for four-and-a-half years.

Miriam Carney Paris

In the Impressionists Museum
the tired tourists
study
the tireless ideas
of dead artists

Paris is peopled by
hot–eyed art pilgrims
emerging from hotels

mystics in raincoats
drinking coffee
in pavement cafés
while Paris turns
to autumn

Margot Henderson In the Old Stories

In the old stories
of your service days,
so vivid I can see the sheen
of polish on the brass
you come to light,
the quiet, laughing girl,
in lace–up boots and hand–me–downs,
the costume jacket of a second aunt
that doubled as your Sunday coat.

It seemed I was beside you
on the steps
with faces pressed between the railings
hoping to be missed,
by the keen eyes in the courtyard
where the women danced
still with their peenies on;
and men smoked, squatting by the side,
acknowledging the rhythm
of the dulcimer and fiddle as their own.

In no time
a griddle would be on the go,
and far from being put to bed,
once someone got their eye on you,
you would be sent
to pass round scones and butter and the tea
before the tide and washing went back in.

You saw your share of washing in those years,
your mother helpless in her bed.
The neighbours left you spare
hot water and the dolly barrel tub,
and for your youth,
they came to sit a while
so you and Davie could get out
to shed the darkness
in the picture house
for a pocket full of dreams.

For me, you were the film stars
in the photo box.
I try to place
the perfect manners of the age,
caught in the quickness of your eye,
the swagger of your coat;
a match of style and grace.

Kitty Fitzgerald Lizzie

I only met her once, my paternal grandmother, and that was at my dad's funeral. She was small and solid with the same large, dark eyes, inherited by my dad and me. Her Waterford accent was rhythmic and throaty from decades of tobacco. My dad had done pilgrimages to Liverpool from time to time throughout my childhood, trying to find her. She left a confusing trail, but eventually he found her, living on a variety of park benches with several other Irish natives. They were a rowdy bunch, and she was undoubtedly leader of the pack. That day, she told my dad that he had a sister five years younger than himself and living in Manchester. I remember he came home glowing, having seen her at last and at discovering more family.

She changed her name frequently, but I'd always known her as Lizzie. All those years ago she'd gone, at sixteen years of age, to the little village near Cork, to work as a maid at one of the big houses. Her employers were race-horse owners, I've heard tell, and they worked her as hard as their animals. She is remembered as being a mostly silent girl who took orders grudgingly and used her eyes to display her anger and discontent. Unlike the other girls who worked at the house, she didn't gossip and, consequently, didn't make any friends.

After she'd been there a few months, the cook noticed that Lizzie was getting fat and took to watching her, thinking she was stealing food. When it was discovered that she was, in fact, pregnant, the housekeeper dismissed her at once. The cook was not an unsympathetic person though, and something about the young woman reminded her of one of her own daughters away studying in England. She found Lizzie lodgings with an old farmer, who she knew would appreciate the company.

Lizzie 'did' for the man, Christie, then sixty-eight, who had no family left alive and had never married. She 'did' for him as long as she was able. He, in turn, doted on her and made several trips into Cork each month, to buy items for the coming child. At night they'd sit together by the fire, reading or playing cards in an easy, comfortable way they'd soon developed with one another.

Of course, the tongues wagged round and about, claiming that Lizzie was 'wrapping the old man round her little finger' or that 'he must be getting something for his troubles'. Rarely was a kind word spoken or visit made to their quiet cottage. Even the priest stopped calling, afraid of the reaction from the rest of his flock, which included influential race-horse owners.

Lizzie didn't want to go into hospital to have her baby; she'd heard terrible tales of misery about the place. The cook, mother of five and deliverer of scores of babies, agreed to see her through the delivery. Every morning of her ninth month, Lizzie and Christie would go through the ritual of checking that they had everything they required for the birth. It was debatable who was more nervous as the weeks went on.

Despite much delving and probing, no one had been able to find out who the father of Lizzie's child might be. She had no intention of disclosing his name, and enquiries in Dungarvan, where she'd previously worked, proved futile. A number of interested parties kept digging. Christie admonished them at the entrance to the church one Sunday, declaring that, 'The Devil made work for idle hands,' in a shaky voice. The priest kept a beady eye on him all the way through his sermon about people who live in glass houses.

It was four o'clock one Friday morning when Lizzie's pains began. Christie stoked up the fire and filled up pots of water and set them to boil. Then he hurled his pony and trap through the lanes like a rogue elephant, to fetch the cook. His hair stood on end like a hedgehog, and his eyes burned feverishly by the time they got back to Lizzie.

The cook, Mrs Cahill, was a large, comforting figure of a woman. Her red cheeks, bright green eyes and ample arms were reassuring. Christie darted around or stood to attention, according to her instructions. His sixty odd years dropped away in his fervour to assist. He felt young, strong and purposeful, and yet dreadfully inadequate, as he watched Lizzie's labours.

When, around midday, he heard the first sound of a new life crying out from his back room, his face broke into an uncontrollable grin and tears drenched the front of his waistcoat. Lizzie sat up in bed, her hair hanging in wet ringlets, holding the tiny dark-haired bundle. Her expression was, as usual, unfathomable.

It's amazing how the baby changed things. People who had previously shunned Lizzie and Christie, called with gifts and murmured with pleasure over the cot. Some of this was Mrs Cahill's doing. She'd stomped around the Mothers' Union meeting and the village shops spreading encouragement for compassion and fixing her sharp eyes on the worst gossips. Still, born out of wedlock, the baby was refused baptism by the priest, and Lizzie's proud bearing and new clothes – purchased by Christie – caused the tongues to wag again before long. She didn't look for work because Christie was more than happy to employ her as a housekeeper. The child, Liam, he treated like a Second Coming. In his turn, Liam soon filled the cottage with the burps and gurgles of a growing life.

As the child became more demanding, Lizzie became more silent. Some days, Christie could hardly get a word from her lips. Once or twice she stayed away a whole day and night and Christie coped as best he could with the nappies and bottles. He dredged his memory for songs to sing the child to sleep and surprised himself with the vast catalogue stored in his subconscious. He no longer fretted about getting old; the coming of Liam had taken decades off his age and filled his life with meaning.

The opposite seemed to be true for Lizzie. She grew paler by the week, she ate hardly anything and slept most of the day. In the end, Christie asked Mrs Cahill to call and see if anything could be done. She arrived, laden with home-made bread and preserves and spent a good part of three hours sitting in Lizzie's room. Every so often she came out to refill the teapot, but revealed nothing to Christie except for raising her right eyebrow occasionally. Liam and Christie played and walked and talked and eventually fell asleep on one another.

Mrs Cahill woke Christie as she lifted Liam into his cot. Lizzie was sleeping, she said with a sigh, then placed his newly-woken hands around a mug of amber tea. She sat across from him and the two of them, unspeaking for a moment, looked more like fireplace ornaments than living people.

'What's to be done?' he asked after a while.

'Ah, sure I've seen it before, dear. You'd be surprised how often. Some girls can be persuaded to carry on, but they're never truly happy, Christie love. There's only one cure for Lizzie,' Mrs Cahill said.

'And what would that be?' he asked.

'She must be allowed to go, and leave the child behind, or very soon she will die anyway,' Mrs Cahill said quietly.

Christie was amazed at her words, but he knew her as a woman of strength and conviction who would never make light of so grave a matter. His main surprise came from the newly-acquired knowledge that women were prepared to die rather than be burdened with children. It was an alien idea to grasp, but accept it he did.

Lizzie left the day after Liam's first birthday, the colour back in her cheeks and a smile on her lips. Christie bought her a boat ticket to England. She sailed from Dublin to Liverpool in November 1928. Christie received a letter from her in the New Year. It bore a street name but no number, and was barely literate. It was the last time she wrote.

Liam grew up lean and full of mischief. He was spoiled, of course, by Christie, but Mrs Cahill kept a foot in the door as well. He became tough at an early age through suffering the taunts of 'bastard' from other children, and one or two adults who should have known better. Mrs Cahill got him work in the stables of the big house, 'mucking out'. He worked hard and his sense of humour won him friends easily, but there was a broodiness about him at times which reminded Christie very much of Lizzie.

In the autumn of 1946, Christie died in his sleep, clutching the letter Lizzie had sent him all those years ago. Liam was devastated, he got drunk more than once, and often ended up at Christie's graveside, crying. But life had to go on.

Everything he'd owned, Christie had left to Liam. It wasn't much, but at least he had a roof over his head. The letter from his mother he put in a bamboo frame on the windowsill as a reminder that somewhere he had the makings of a family. Before long the frame became dusty, as his attention was taken up with a young servant at a nearby house. She was called Kate. He followed her to church on Sundays and told his friends with a frightening certainty that he would marry her or marry no one. A year later, the marriage took place and Liam was as happy as he'd ever been.

I was born in Christie's cottage, with Mrs Cahill, now grey and wrinkled, but still in charge, standing by. By the time I was five, we were living in England and Dad's quest for Lizzie had begun. It took him eight years in all. He saw her three times before he died. At the funeral, with the bravery of youth and sadness of my loss, I asked her if she'd ever regretted her decision to leave him behind. She fixed me with her still-dark eyes and told me she never had, as she believed the love of Christie and the cruelty of the world were better child-rearers than she could ever have been.

RELATIONSHIPS
. . . family, friends and lovers

Our relationships with other people dominate a large part of our emotional lives. Sometimes they make us strong, sometimes weak . . . sad, happy, angry, jealous, hurt, bitter, lonely, grateful . . . they touch on a whole range of complex and deep-felt emotions. Our involvement with other people shapes our development, alters our views, changes our lives dramatically.

As working-class women, our relationships are as diverse as anyone else's – as serious, as devastating, as passionate, as complicated. The stereotypes presented in most newspapers, magazines, TV programmes and films suggest that such emotional involvements are the exclusive pastime of the middle and upper classes. Working-class 'relationships' are frequently reduced to family squabbles, nagging wives and hen-pecked husbands, meaningless and cheap sex, unwanted pregnancies, bickering neighbours and bitchy factory girls.

It is true that, very often, economic pressures put a lot of strain and limitations on our relationships; it is much more difficult, for instance, for a working-class woman to walk out of an unhappy marriage when she has children to house and feed. We do not usually have families who can give us financial support in such circumstances. For many of us, finding ways to 'make ends meet' often seems to be a necessary preoccupation, and sometimes we do not have the luxuries of time and energy to devote to our emotional lives; but our relationships are still an integral and important part of our lives. We, also, are mothers, daughters, sisters, friends, wives and lovers.

Our first experience of attachment to others is usually with our immediate family. This is where our roots lie; it often defines our identity, and perhaps more than any other relationship, determines what we are today. For many women, the example and influence of their mother remains particularly powerful throughout their lives – and many of the pieces of work in this section analyse the bond between mothers and daughters – from both the mother's and the daughter's points of view. For other women, their relationships with their fathers have had a profound, and at times shattering, effect on their lives. Family ties are not ones we choose, however, unlike our other close relationships – our friends and our lovers. These are the bonds we need and desire; we need the support and the shared sense of identity; we desire love and affection.

The poems and stories about love (lesbian and heterosexual) deal with all the ecstasy and the agony of longing, pursuing, loving, losing, grieving and longing again. Some pieces deal with our loneliness, our shattered illusions of love, our oppression within certain relationships, but they all seem to show that, through our varied experiences, and despite the heartbreak, we emerge resilient and strong – maybe stronger – having learnt much about ourselves in the process.

Annette Kennerley

Susan Hoult In Remembrance

My mum liked things to look nice. When she left the house she'd always glance back to see if everything looked perfect. If the curtains weren't evenly drawn she'd go back and correct them. She never left the washing-up until later and never left the dishes to drain. She washed, dried and put things away straight after a meal, then wiped over the work surfaces with a cloth. She would leave the stainless-steel sink and draining area dry and shining. When everything was completed she would join us in the front room. I used to say, 'Leave it, Mum,' or, 'Relax, Mum,' and, 'The house isn't really important.'

Now Mum is dead – thirteen distalgesic and a glass of whisky – a tidy death. I don't take flowers to the cemetery, but I do polish the stainless-steel sink and drainer and see that the curtains are neatly drawn.

Krishna Sadhana The Old Photograph

My mum is now reduced to an old photograph. I would like to burn it, but I think I would regret that. The worst thing about her being sick was shaving her legs for her. She had varicose veins and I was always scared that I would cut one. Watching the injections was easy, but now I haven't got the stomach to watch someone die in bits. Another bad thing was seeing the child slowly creep into her eyes and face. I couldn't look at such vulnerability, it made me want to die inside. She turned grey when she died, and I went to kiss her goodbye. 'Goodbye, Mum,' I said. I was the last person that she talked coherently to. I loved her because she was Mum and Dad and everyone in the world to me.

For a long time I felt as if I hadn't done enough for her in that last year. If I had known she was going to die, I think I would have been more patient. I was too young to understand. I was too young.

Although, when I look back, I can't remember very much any more. Especially before that last year. I just remember the frail body, washing it, feeding it; the varicose veins, the injections, the scar where her breast used to be. Her hair had turned completely white. Her crying; I had never seen her cry before.

For Christmas, us kids left a sack of presents at the foot of her bed, just as she used to. It was too late . . . she was too far gone to really enjoy that. I think I disappointed her.

In the last few days, her breathing changed. She would take three or four breaths and stop for a long time and then breathe a little and then stop for a while. I used to wipe her head with Eau de Cologne. When I went into the room I would wait to hear breathing again, and rush out before it stopped. Someone told me later that it's called the 'Death Rattle'.

Annette Kennerley My Mother's Mother

A small, strong woman,
Proud and plain.
Some would call her face hard . . .
But I see only strength and wisdom there.
A dark, plain overcoat,
A small-brimmed hat, no smile.
Annie Matthews.
My grandmother.
My mother's mother.
I never knew her.
At 52, hard work cut short her life –
Seventeen years before I came into this world.
And yet, through my mother's tales,
She lives with me.
My mother was forbidden to read books –
Only the idle could indulge in pastimes such as that.
So she read by candlelight in bed at night, secretly.
Annie Matthews –
Working to feed four children,
With an invalid husband, shell-shocked from the 14/18 War;
She was a fustian-cutter in a local factory.
Long hours, low pay,
Women's work.
Treading the boards in her wooden clogs and starched white apron,
Cutting the loops of a velvet pile with a thin, sharp blade –
Up and down the long benches with a steady hand.
When my mother was small, she would often be taken to the
                                                    mill with her.
Curled up to sleep under the benches,
She would sometimes wake and see,
By flickering candlelight,
Vague female figures, dressed in white,
Gliding silently along the room,
And she'd think she were in heaven in her dreams.
Annie Matthews –

She threw a clog at my mother's brother when he told her, at 26,
                              that he wanted to get married.
She threw my mother's first dance dress on the fire – because it
                              had a low-cut back.
She reared my mother's sister's illegitimate son as if her own.
She believed in the after-life and feared God.
She took my mother with her to the Spiritualist Church.
One day, the minister said he could see a small, grey-haired
                              woman on the other side,
Feeding some white hens in a yard.
'That was my mother . . .' said my mother's mother.
My mother was the youngest of the family.
She was just 20 when her mother died,
The year the Second World War began.
That's all I know of her.
One faded photograph, these handed-down memories.
And yet I know her well,
And feel her with me now,
As I prepare to be a mother, too.

Billie Hunter Mothertongue

She defines herself in mirrors.
She looks.
There are always
mirrors
carrying back
people she doesn't want to be.

When you are older
will you ask
why didn't you write a poem for me, Mum?
and what will I say
to be honest?
That I was tired and porridge-minded

and even forgot what I'd gone to the supermarket for?
And often I was exhausted
because I'd pushed you for miles
just to get out
to be away from the nappy chores
and the grime settling on your toys
like scum on washing–up water
and the cat's hairs sticking to everything
your bibs and your vests and your mittens
while I sterilized,
manic with boiling water and shuddering nose.

Will I tell you I was often confused
about who I was now
a horlickshovishoneyvoiced mum
or a shrillshriekingshrewsiren
hearing the nag in me,
and the I-know-best mother
and all the time
lost and troubled
and wondering who I was?
my spirit is kitchen-bound by your smile
and your skin
and, do you know –
that is probably why I never wrote you a poem?
– they are for the men to write,
the doting father poems of six pm babylife.
For the women, tied as they are
by soaking clothes and salty tears
and smiles that make your heart go tight inside,
the poems are there,
minute by minute,
written by chapped hands in words of Persil foam,
pouring out with the PG Tips
and the bathwater
unobserved
undefined

I wrote you a poem a minute
my gladeyed boy
my raspberry rascal
but they had no words
there are never words for such extremities.

Maxine McCarthy
Extract from 'The Thin Line'

I think it started years ago, really. There was the time when my mum would sit in the chair for hours on end and gorge herself on liquorice allsorts. She used to send me down the road for an *Evening News* and then sit there, absorbed. She would drink her coffee with small, precise sips; I would watch her sometimes as she pursed her lips and then swallowed very carefully. Her mouth seemed tight, then, like it did when she told us off. She would appear round the living-room door and catch us with our feet up on the settee. Me and Lynn used to call it 'her face' as it was quite funny. We'd nudge each other and say; 'Mum's got her face on . . .' then fly out of the room before she started.

I reckon that my mum's drunk coffee for as long as I can remember. It was like a ritual with her when I was a kid; two spoonfuls of dried Marvel milk mixed with a little bit of water in the cup, then a spoonful of coffee. Then the hot water and a Sweetex. The milk used to make sticky blobs in the bottom of her cup, but she didn't seem to mind. She used to drink it really hot, as well. Two or three on the trot, boiling the kettle in between. She always used a white glass cup and saucer, never got a bigger one. Maybe forcing it down was the only thing that kept her going. Now I've got kids, I drink big mugs of tea all the time and smoke myself silly, without giving it a second thought.

It's vague, isn't it, memory? I've got a whole vision of her now, as though I had observed a particular event with a view to memorizing it. I don't think she went out for months, that time. She refused to answer the door, may not have even gone shopping. I remember her, with a chiffon scarf knotted under her chin, slouching by the fire with her nylons rolled down and her legs slowly mottling with the heat from the gas.

Although I don't remember it happening, I know that Mum really went through a change after that. I remember her starting work again, very smartly dressed. She lost a lot of weight and kept herself busy. She never really said a lot about it, but sometimes, in a lowered voice: '. . . after my Breakdown . . .' and then go on to say, '. . . the doctor did insist that I must keep working . . .' whenever I asked her why she stuck at the job that upset her so much. She related chapters of brush-offs and incidents of rudeness to me; I think the Unpaid Bills section at Water Lane had a lot to answer for.

Mum always found it hard, for as long as I can remember. My stepfather was really strict and it was very hard to stand up to him. I think he just kept on and on at her for years, while she crumbled slowly away under the pressure. I remember us going to stay at me nan's once, she convinced Mum to go back because he was earning a few bob. So we all went back again, to more deadly silences and not daring to move.

Mum had four sisters, who she was alternately superior to, and in awe of. No matter what the state of the game, none of them ever came round. Our neighbours were the fussy, curtain-twitching type. There was only one other kid in our block, so we had to be really quiet coming in and out. They used to go mad if the kids from up the end came round, so we used to meet them down the alley or under the tunnel. The old man next door used to come out and shout, then hang about until me mum came in from work, so he could tell her. He used to sprinkle all his speech with references to his Back Passage and his Waterworks. (I used to think his home smelt Brown.) Gawd knows what me mum thought.

It got odder, anyway, over the years. Mum was always too tired to come to open night at the junior school, and I really wanted her to, every time. I drew a picture in the juniors that they put on the cover of the school magazine, but she didn't seem that interested. I was always trying to impress her, one way or another; I never seemed to measure up to what she wanted.

When I got older I ran away twice, then I started bunking off of school all the time, in the last two years. I left school before I took my exams, then got a flat a few weeks later. I kept leaving jobs and then get behind with the rent and she used to do her nut. I often tried to talk to her about things, which always ended up in a great big row.

My sister used to say I was a mug, that I should keep me mouth shut and not tell her what I was up to all the time. I just went on being more and more outrageous in Mum's eyes, which drove us further apart. She used to go on about the neighbours, always worrying what they would think. Once, when I was working in a holiday camp, I cut all my hair off and bleached it white, with Titian Red streaks all round it. The manager said it lowered the tone and asked me to leave. I rung up Mum, crying me eyes out. She said: 'You're not coming here with bloody red streaks in your hair.'

In the end, I became pregnant and got a top floor flat on the main road. It was great after all those bedsitters and shared houses. Mum was working up the road, so she used to come round on Thursday nights, drink two cups of coffee and sniff at my friends.

I was getting on with it by then, although still saying what I thought. Mum used to convert everything into lurid headlines, with countless imagined outcomes which were sparked off by some casual comment. I was always falling short of the mark.

The funny thing was, Mum used to tell everyone about her two lovely daughters, how well we all got on and how much she loved us. I used to find this a nightmare, as I could never feel it.

I used to scrutinize every moment, trying to glean some good feelings from it all. She would jump on any little thing and wade into battle, tight lipped and disapproving. I scrabbled around for ways to explain, frantically trying to justify everything.

When I got pregnant again, I packed up my things and moved. I was like a refugee when I got here, with a small son and a large lump.

Against all odds, I really fell on me feet. I've met some great women and I haven't looked back. Women who are married, single, with or without children; educated or illiterate. They talk to me so clearly, about living. I'm still a bit mouthy, but have managed to sift through the huffs and rejections. I've discovered that some rebuffs are other people's business, that others are because I don't listen or am being downright boring. These strong women have taught me to value my own experience and acknowledge my own worth.

Jan Turnbull Gentle Giant

Gentle giant, kind, grey man.
Home for your tea.
Sausages and mash and six slices of bread,
washed down with a mug of tea.
Two sugars.
Weathered, smiling face
trowel handle peeps over the bib of torn overalls,
unassumingly.
Broken ruler in your back pocket.
Pat your thighs, and send talcum clouds rising.
Sit. Take off your tired, heavy boots,
whitened by caked-on plaster and cement.
With hands greying with plaster and asbestos, cracked and cut
take off the holey socks,
that fail to hide ingrowing toenails.
Strong fingers carrying their nails of sand
take off the flat, checked, press-stud cap, to reveal
proud, black, shining with Brylcreem hair,
thinning now, older now,
not concealing the innocent new-born head.
Or the pencil behind your ear, always ready to work.
Strong man, bulging biceps, hairy arms.
My provider, constant.
Always somewhere nearby
as you were on my wedding day.
Dancing with me and wishing me happiness.
Did you realise that this was probably the first time
that you had held me in your arms since I'd been born?
I realised it, I felt it, and the memory of that dance
makes me cry, even today.

Unseen pillar that my life clung to.
I'm very proud of you, my dad
I love you very much,
and I wish I could tell you
before it's too late.

June Burnett Father 1947–86

My daddy was a black man.
My daddy went to war.
Numbed by cold, in a cold climate
he sits and toys with a plastic fork.
Gone back, inside his head travelling.

See the black man,
watch him stalk the pale corridors,
his past unravelling.

Couldn't be a white man.
Sent to war to kill.
Going back to Africa, still travelling.

My father is a black man.
Others silenced him.
He pushes the medicine trolley
following the nurse.
He travels still.

Alison Guinane To my Father

I sit and read the *Guardian*
opposite an old man who
watches and dreams in
silence.
Ash drops noiselessly from
his desultory cigarette
on to the pale velvet pile;
slowly the light silvers
the smart metallic slats
of the Venetian blind
and long tortured shadows
ebb and flow beneath his
hard-polished
shoes.
Still dressed for Sunday,
he sits on the edge
of the chinoiserie settee,
his head inclined, his eyelids
quietly drooping; he creeps back
unnoticed along his life's tunnel
of thread-like webs, to where

a girl once sat and dreamed
and watched him read, in
slippers;
where strange colourful shapes
chased and twisted across the worn
flat rug, stained with the
etched fantasies of childhood;
where frilled chintz filtered muted
sunlight across deep green chairs
and cracked Toby jugs shone
smugly from the
shelf.
One Sunday soon, we must gently brush
all the powdered frost from the
bent shoulders of our memories,
gather up our great soft ball of
silence and hurl it into the
sun.

Caron Freeborn Tea Party

Debbie had been a plump child, a fat adolescent and was now an extremely obese adult. She had grown as a cactus might: larger, rounder, more prickly, yet somehow more lush, as the years had scorched her with their merciless pressure. She needed fewer soothing words rained on her with each day, which was fortunate as she received less than even she desired.

David, her husband, was tall and thin and straight; he paid each week for his wife to attend whichever slimming club she was currently a member of, although from her wages she could easily have found the money for herself. Debbie never went with her husband to parents' night; she starved herself for weeks before the annual dinner and dance where David worked; she bought her clothes from a special mail-order catalogue and loathed each item.

There was only one escape, one refuge from the children's shame, David's scorn and her hated crimplene: Debbie had a secret world in which she danced dressed in purple taffeta, was loved and admired, and, most importantly, was free.

The incident that first trapped her roots in the soil of an imaginary world happened when Debbie was fourteen. A boy at school had publicly asked her out – it had seemed impossible that such a popular, handsome lad would do so; in shock, she had replied that she would think about it. The boy's best friend turned on her and said viciously: 'Go on, you'll never get anyone else.' Debbie's clear, soft skin flushed a hideous red and she accepted the offer; her 'suitor' had been joking, of which everyone was aware but herself. It was thought tremendous fun and Debbie began buying wonderful records to lose herself in.

Joyce Fowler was nearly fifty. Her once bright red hair had faded to a dull orange in the process of bringing up five difficult children, and her spectacles grown thicker as each year she tried harder to see where she had gone wrong.

'You KNEW, you knew and you closed your stupid eyes to it! You didn't want to see, you thought it was easier to betray me!' Lisa Fowler fired abuse at her mother down the telephone, blaming her mother because her father had raped her. It was something she did almost daily, even nightly, for the calls came at hours as diverse as noon and five am.

'How could I have known? I'd have killed him, or anyone else if I thought they were hurting any of my kids! I've left him, Lee.'

On and on it went, hour after hour of the same scenario, an improvisation without surprises and with no conclusion. Joyce suffered high blood pressure, nervous indigestion and constant reproach, but hers was a generation of silent anguish; she thought seldom of distributing portions of her guilt to others, would certainly never have entertained a public sharing of that cake.

She was generous with what little money passed through her aching hands, lavish with what time was not taken up with her job as a runner in a bingo hall, yet she would not part with her pain.

Evie Fowler sucked miserably on a barley sugar as she sat in the smokey airport lounge waiting for her taxi. The long flight from Australia had confused her. Every few minutes she started to get up, stopping herself each time as she recalled Charlie's strict instructions to stay where she had been put. Presently, her need to go to the toilet would become really desperate, but were she to wet her knickers she would care little: she had already suffered the ultimate mortification.

Charlie was Evie's son, the only boy out of six children. He had moved to Australia four years ago, and when her husband died a year after the emigration, Evie decided to follow the son that so resembled her Bill.

Charlie had moved to another town after two years; Evie was once again alone. When her son wrote to her of his intention to visit England for a while, Evie jumped at the chance she saw to travel home in safety to live with one of her daughters. Parsimony was Charlie's least attractive trait. He brought his mother to Heathrow, ordered a taxi by telephone from Joyce's town in order to avoid paying a ravenous-looking black cab and abandoned Evie, knowing she was without English currency, and running to catch a train that would take him cheaply to his Brighton friends. All this, Evie could have borne: she possessed an animal's capacity for instinctive maternal love without judgement.

'I'm so ashamed!' she murmured softly, causing the people near her to look away, embarrassed. Charlie had added one last, unforgivable, act of uncaring: he had made a placard from a cardboard box, written FOWLER on it and forced Evie to sit holding it for the taxi driver to see. An unwanted piece of luggage, labelled but not retrieved; a mangy cur with 'My name is FOWLER, please give me a home' tied to its scraggy neck. Evie wept.

The initial emotion had subsided by Sunday; Evie Fowler and her daughter, Joyce, were getting used to one another again. Together they had set the table for tea, as they had so many times when Joyce was a girl, but now it was no longer Evie who was in charge; her hands, once so deft, were not reluctant to hold a minor post. As Evie's small frame began to tremble a little, a heavy knock on the door announced Debbie.

'Granny!' Tears flow on such occasions, but Joyce had cried hers on Friday. Checking that the telephone was off the hook, sitting her mother and daughter in hard chairs at the kitchen table whilst they were still babbling incoherently, cutting huge slices of cake, she gradually becalmed. Two cups of strong, sweet tea later Debbie asked for a third iced fancy.

'Sure, pet – don't have to ask!'

'This is smashing, this. When I was in Australia I didn't have family . . . well, there was Charlie.' Joyce had told her daughter of Charlie's crime: 'Wouldn't do it to a dog!' Debbie had cried furiously. All she said now was, 'Have another sandwich, Gran.'

The mild afternoon sun came out from behind a cloud to shine through the spotless kitchen window, adding still richer highlights to Debbie's thick chestnut hair.

'You're a rose, love, you really are!' said Evie quietly and tears filled her old brown eyes. Her granddaughter smiled and stood to turn the radio on low: 'A nice bit of background music.' Joyce poured more tea and fetched a small blanket to warm her mother's knees, which had grown used to blazing Australian sun.

'You'll remember this, Joy,' said Evie. 'I used to mash tea for the bus drivers round our way and let them use our outside lavvy if they provided their own whatsname, disinfectant. During the war it was, so you'd be a little girl, but I bet you can remember, because we was quite glad of the few coppers it brought in.'

The radio played an old, sentimental love song to which the three women listened in silence. Lucy, the cat, miaowed to be let in from the garden; her wish granted, she marched over to the old lady and made a nest on the blanketed knees.

'We always had cats, didn't we, Joy?'

'Yes we did, Mum. Remember what Charlie did to Bess?'

'Fixed an elastic band to her foot so as we wouldn't lose her, so we'd know her if she got out, and it was so tight the poor thing screeched the place down all night!' The three women laughed, but Debbie added, 'My boys hate cats'.

The sun went back to its shelter but the clouds, like the shadow of the day's mood, were full of chinks to let the warmth filter through. Plates were emptied and refilled, crumbs escaped to laze on the scrubbed floor, appetites were sated. David could not find his new shirt; Joyce's phone stayed off the hook and Charlie was cold beside the sea. The three women ate, talked and laughed, a world within a chaos.

'Let there be light!' said Debbie, clicking the switch, her beautiful smile infecting those who saw it. Evie pulled the soft blanket further around her, disturbing the cat but momentarily. Joyce slowly stood to begin piling the empty plates ready for washing-up: a star performer in a gloriously predictable play.

Violet Verlaine Our Children

A hand softly caresses my cheek
whilst a secret to me is whispered
I am kissed on the nose
then the truth is disclosed . . .

. . . 'I love you, Mummy'.

Jane Fell Cold Morning

Inside, life grew strong
Dreamed for freedom
My fear for you so helpless
My need to feel you breathe
Beats the heart
Breaks open

My courage fails
Waters parting, draining me
Drawing me inside out
In cold dawn cracking
The sky bleeding
Me empty

The moment is yours
Shivering at your scream
Born screaming
Here I go again
Blood baptises flesh
Once mine
Arms cradle and comfort

Sun outside rises
High and higher
Out of reach burning
Cold in my flesh and so tired
Struggle not over
I name you innocence

I kiss your virgin eyes
And count your fingers
Complete I sleep
And wake to hold you

You know nothing and
You cry
I try
To feed you

Sally Flood The Master

So small, curled in a tiny ball
face red as the blood in a vein,
yesterday you breathed thru' another
now you lie exhausted, as though
you've journeyed far.
Anxious eyes wait for your command
and watch your changing expressions
'Is he hungry?' the new Mum asks
'Don't spoil him,' says exasperated nurse
'Can I manage?' asks Mum
'You'll manage,' says experience.
Mum lies stitched and in pain
nine months of wonder and fear
lies clean and content
'Isn't he lovely?' says visitor
'Sssh, don't wake him,' says Mum.
Too late, the face wrinkles
like an old man

while the lips quiver
Mum holds him to her
and rocks gently to and fro.
He holds her finger in a vice-like grip
while freedom slips quietly away.

Chaucer Cameron The Merge

Living with central heating
is like living alone with a four-year-old son as a feminist.
Dry.
Living as a feminist is no fun, it's real.
Trying to live in a real way alone, is to encourage despair to
saunter in between the strengths and weaknesses,
the highs and lows, and to hammer the latter into my
    numbskull.
To live with a numbskull is no joke,
the joke's on me.

And then she came,
Support, drifting haltingly through the open doors of choice
with Life doing a foxtrot behind her, in front of her, to her left
and to her right, trying to trip her up, trying to keep her in line
right behind.
Reaching for Support, Life jumps in and drags me passively
    through
the door of Hope, leaving Support out in the cold, away from
    my smile
and screams.
I see what I'm looking for – potential,
in pink, violet, green and white,
in likeness and empathy,
in form and shape,
in hostility and understanding,
in fear and strength,

and in feminism and knowledge.
High, I think (that's the word)
until I wink and Life and Despair have been hiding behind a tree
and laughing at me; jumping up and down and holding their
    bellies
swollen with past conquests.
Am I to be next? There is no cross over.

The pattering of tiny feet has come to find me and I return to
    numbskull
with a pinned grin, to reassure my bundle that I am in control
and together and so pleased to have him again in my arms
my body, my brain; staining me with wind-milk, heinz
    regurgence
chip vomit and semen marks.
Oh, the joy, the joy.
I look to Support, I'd forgotten in my double-edged ecstasy
my axe to see, that she had become frozen in my forgetfulness
and the effort to thaw her is beyond me at the present time,
    being
two o'clock in the morning and he has german measles.
The effort to ask, the fear of rejection.
The boring, boring fear.
Without Support and her warm paraphernalia, brings strength;
painful aloneness but never a feeling of complacency.
So I suppose I'll keep fighting and grabbing at her every now
    and again
and maybe, just mabye, if she yields and we embrace, my
    feminism my woman love
and my son will merge as one.
and i can smile as i did before when i was young.

Annette Kennerley Little Boy Blues

It's a boy
Boy blue
Boy joy
Weapon
Toy
Rough and tumble
Mustn't grumble
Boys will be boys
With guns for toys
A proper little lad
A fine little fellow
A cheeky little chap
So I dress him in pink
And keep him from the guns
And try to teach him
Gentle, caring ways
I'm the mother of a boy
And I'm doing what bit I can
Because I know some day
I'll be the mother of a man

Susan Hoult Single-parenting

I lived alone with my new-born baby, loneliness crept under the door and haunted me with its emptiness. My thoughts became my only companions – deep and disturbing. The baby kept crying, I walked around the rooms, rocking her on my shoulder – my eyes filled with tears. I put her in the pram and took her for a walk, but she kept on crying. The sharp cries cut right through me, I could hear nothing else. I pushed the pram faster and faster until I was running along the street. Tears rolled down my face – I did not know where I was running to.

Susan Hoult Parenting

We have a daughter, her name is Billie – my choice, she's three.
Billie lives with me – it's difficult at the moment. 'Don't worry,
just a phase,' they tell me. 'All children go through stages of being
aggressive, destructive and demanding.' Perhaps it's the additives?
'Don't blame yourself,' they say, but it's very hard. Sometimes I
feel as if I'm going mad. Her dad takes her to the park now and
again with his girlfriend – they have lots of fun. He contacts me
whenever he wants to take Billie out. I never know when he will
ring. I can't contact him – I have no address or 'phone number. He
sends postcards to her – Andy Warhol ones, leaves, flowers,
conkers or perhaps a small abstract painting he has done. She
looks like him. He made her a kite for her birthday. He enjoys
having a daughter.

Margot Henderson
For my daughter in darkness

I watch her closely for the signs,
the twist of fingers in the hair,
a blankness in her look.
I look for outbreaks
of blotching on her skin
and search the darkness
underneath her eyes.

Last night, she slept badly,
I could hear her grind her teeth and turn.
I saw her eyeballs flit
from side to side
and watched her fingers pick at the blanket on her bed.
I did not wake her.
I could not break the dream.

She was pale this morning,
like the sky.
I touched her cheek.
She sat listless
by the crack of window
out of habit.
She is afraid of birds,
things are not what they seem.

She has stopped eating
since yesterday.
She says it tastes of ash.
She has not moved
for two days now.
She does not speak.

She is my daughter.
I wrap her in my arms,
rocking her awake.
I sing her childhood back to her.
I am her mother.

Somewhere, there is still a garden.

I close my eyes
and bring my breath
into my belly.

We begin to rise.
She feels heavy but she comes.

We slip through layers
of ceilings and smoke.
We drift through the broken city,
out of the dark time
light as vapour, bright-eyed.

Wilma Murray Competition Day

'Oh no! Not now!' I wail, as the first red drops hit the table.

'Keep it away from your clean blouse, then.' Mother leaps to the sink at the window and pushes a wet cloth into my hands. As I lean forward, the blood from my nose drips disgustingly into the yolk of my boiled egg.

'Oh, Mum, if this doesn't stop soon, we're going to be late.' I visualize the train puffing out of the station. The cloth becomes a murdered pink wad and the clock is swallowing up time. It is competition day and we have a journey to make.

'Calm down, now. We'll get there somehow.' Mother is helping me into my coat, while I move the cloth from one hand to the other. 'These nose-bleeds can't be normal.'

It clears at last, and I grab my music case off the bed, check quickly that the precious familiar music is in there, and we race to the train. The sweet, round, imagined shape of the day is already rolling away and threatening to disintegrate.

In the train, Mother takes at least ten minutes to recover, her face blotched and wet, her breathing inflating her coat. Errant strands of her hair have strayed onto the velvet plush and she is wearing her harassed look now. I try to fix my mind on the day ahead, but it is still bouncing. At the first station along the line, a woman joins us in our compartment. Mother tucks her hands neatly in her lap and smiles.

'Nice day.' They nod the required greeting.

'Sit up, Meg. You'll get your skirt all creased, slumping like that. She's going to play in a piano competition in town, you know.' I pretend not to hear and wish hard for her to stop talking. The notes are getting clearer in my mind, now. Their shape makes music my fingers can touch. The start, so clean and controlled, then the hard bit that pitches the theme into minor and back, sweet change . . .

'She won't win anything, of course. But the experience does them good, don't you think?'

I shut out the chatter with determination and concentrate on my fingers, feeling their way through the sonata, performing miracles of interpretation in my head. Then my teacher's voice threads through the daydream. I see her rings, and those ugly hands with bitten nails that can, nonetheless, magic a sigh or a shout from the keys with equal ease.

My own fingers feel suddenly clumsy and I fluff a trill, even in my head. 'It'll come. Relax. Just relax your hands. Don't strain after it. That way you'll murder it. See?' She does her magic. I hold my hands tightly together, making the music in my head stop, before I ruin it.

The competition hall is half empty, the audience made up mostly of competitors. There are few other mothers. We are held back at the door with a warning whisper until a competitor finishes. Our progress to our seats rings loudly on the wooden floor. A woman turns to shush us as the next competitor takes the platform. In the peace of the performance, I greedily drink in the atmosphere of the hall. Everyone is straight-faced and serious. The adjudicators at their table look not quite interested and the ushers look bored as they hug their big cardboard numbers.

'When are you on?' Mother whispers.

'I don't know yet,' I hiss back at her, and flash her a warning look, which she misses. She is fumbling in her bag and passes me a barley sugar, just as she does in church. I begin to feel hopeful that she will behave.

Between competitions the cards and numbers on the platform are changed and the noise grows back to normal.

'It's running late,' I tell her, after getting a programme. 'We had plenty of time, after all.'

The hush is back in the hall, and a new class starts. It is the 'Bach Two Part Invention' class. I am drawn willingly into Bach's tidy old world with the opening phrases of a familiar piece.

Mother's head is keeping time. She knows it, too.

'You used to play that, didn't you? What is it, again?'

I point to the piece named in the programme.

'Oh.'

The competitors perform the piece at various speeds and levels of accuracy. Missed notes seem to me to pile up under the piano, and I feel myself blush during one badly stumbled performance. The adjudicators' faces remain blank throughout.

'Well. That was a mess, anyway. I hope you do a bit better than that!' She shifts uncomfortably in her seat and I am touched with sudden panic. What if I go up there and . . . I shut out the thought.

She is still wriggling. 'I wonder where the Ladies is?'

'Ask an usher.'

'I think I'll have to.'

The adjudicator wants to start the class without delay, as time is short. My thumbs start to make sweaty prints on my music as I feel the girl on my left get up to take the stage. On my right, a boy with light grey trousers fiddles with his watch. His music is a different edition from mine, and the terrible strangeness of it confuses me. I check twice that I have the right piece and then relax with the girl's performance. She is good. I feel my fingers working in sympathy. I can do that, too, I tell myself.

The next minutes pull me tight into a knot of excitement. The stool is too high. I adjust it. The keys are very white. The stand is slightly high. I take a moment to let my eyes settle to the new position. I dare not look away into the body of the hall. I set my hands to the keys and they seem very remote from me. But the notes I look at are starting the Mozart sonata in my head, and my fingers know how to follow.

'But that's my daughter, up there!' I hear her clearly, but I am coming to a trill and have to concentrate on relaxing my hand. There. A door rattles noisily in the background, but I have only half a page to build to the climax and then run it sweetly down and back into the theme. The last chord makes a very satisfactory resonance in the half-empty hall.

Mother is clapping very loudly from the doorway, her face flushed. I cannot get to her yet. I have to sit back into my place. I dream easily through the other performances, sitting light and easy on my seat. I agree with everything the adjudicator says about the others, but immediately forget his words to me, knowing only that they sound fine.

'Oh, Meg, I'm sorry. I couldn't find it, you see. And then that woman . . .'

'It's all right. I managed.'

I enjoy her guilt all the way home, with the medal clasped tight in my coat pocket.

121

Eve Featherstone We Sit And Pick

We sit and pick over our faults
Finding all the bad bits
Discarding the good
And you do too
What about when
You don't love me
You don't even like me
Because I say so
I want some space
Odd to think of you
All newborn and so tiny
Red wrinkled face
Sucking at my breast
Flouncing out you fling
One last statement
And you didn't even want me
Ouch how true
It doesn't mean I
Don't love you I
Mutter to my tea
Lighting up a cigarette
It's worse than a lover
Eight-and-a-half years
My longest-ever relationship
Except mine with my mother
And she chased me round the
Kitchen table with a knife once
The problem with bringing up
Your daughters to be assertive
Is that you end up with
Stroppy young wimmin.

Clare Sambrook Two Sisters

1972

Helen's head was clamped between Sally's knees. Sally gritted her teeth. Faces hot and tense with fury, their muffled gasps had not yet given way to cries of pain. The carpet burned her arms as Sally fell back onto the floor, her head jolting hard against the sofa. Hot tears swept through her determination not to cry. Tears fell, and there was only pain to fight over. Sally's grimace collapsed into a pout, her muscles weakened, and Helen sensed victory. For Sally, the will to win next time grew stronger . . .

Sally's face was red-brown. A white nose protruded from the caked mud. Helen laughed but did not copy. Helen laughed and Sally smeared more mud until her arms and legs were covered and Helen was lying back in the long grass, her stomach aching with laughter. Mr Cowdell, the surveyor, looked on from his garden next door, convinced of his wisdom in not allowing his children to play with them. Council house kids were always the same. Helen shrieked with happiness and the joy that this show was only for her . . .

Sally had never noticed before how small the room was, nor how airless. They normally came visiting in threes, but this time everyone was there. The big white cake stood waiting by the wall. Helen's name was on it, too, and she had a present like Sally's, but Helen's birthday wasn't for weeks and weeks. Another thing Sally hadn't noticed before was Mum using the breathing mask. There was a thin red line around her face where the hard plastic pressed. Dad was trying even more than usual to be cheerful, but Helen and the older ones looked miserable, in a way that only grown-ups can, usually . . .

It must be a mistake, thought Sally, but there were seven priests saying the Mass and the coffin looked real enough. The church was full, and everyone said that was a credit to Mum, but Sally felt uncomfortable squashed between Mrs Hodges and Mrs Kelly; she wondered what Helen was thinking, wedged between Mrs Kelly and the edge of the pew. They didn't want to go to Communion – it wasn't a Sunday, so they didn't have to – but Mrs Hodges said Daddy would be upset if they didn't. Sally wondered how he could be more upset than he was already, but they went up to the altar anyway. The host stuck to the roof of Sally's mouth. She had cried herself dry. Sally didn't understand why everyone went to the cemetery except her and Helen and Mrs Kelly. Sally and Helen played Monopoly on Mrs Kelly's living room floor, but for once it didn't matter that Helen went straight to jail and didn't collect two hundred. Even landing on Mayfair with money to buy couldn't dull the realization that grown-ups lie and bury people. That night, Sally couldn't sleep for Helen's crying. Sally wondered how anyone could cry so hard or so long.

1982

Sally's 'hello' got caught in her throat as her eyes found Helen, but not her Helen, perched on the edge of their step-mother's velour settee. Helen's eyes were dull and staring, and her face was swollen by an ugly sore on her lip. Sally's hand reached out tentatively to touch her sister's face. Helen shuddered and drew away. Their step-mother stood up and quickly left the room, but Helen didn't seem to notice. She stared ahead and chewed her lip. Sally realized that the musty smell was coming from Helen, that her clothes were dirty and rumpled. Helen's nose was running and Sally fumbled in her pocket for a handkerchief.

They said that schizophrenics often had a go, but Sally knew that Helen would never do a thing like that. She put her books aside – she needed a break anyway – and walked across the hall towards the bedroom. It was strange not having to climb stairs anymore, but Christine's house was warm, and Dad seemed happy enough. In any case, Sally had only one more year at school and Helen could go back to nursing as soon as she was better. There was no sign of Helen, so Sally went back through the kitchen. She could see from the utility room that the garage light was on, so maybe Helen was in there. Sally felt too old to be playing hide-and-seek. Gently, she pushed the garage door open. Guilty-faced, Helen backed away. 'What's wrong?' said Sally. Before the words had left her mouth, the matchbox clattered on the concrete floor and the thick smell of meths surged up to meet her nostrils. Helen's clothes were wet. Before she grasped the meaning of the signs, Sally moved between Helen and the matchbox. Sally wanted to ask why, but all she could do was stand and stare. 'I have to,' said Helen, 'they'll get us all, if I don't . . .'

Helen's big toe poked through a hole in Sally's favourite socks. 'I'll leave you alone, then,' said the nurse, and her heels clacked down the ward. The barefoot woman wailed that the plate was too big to fit on the table and the door was too small for the man to fit through. 'She's off again,' murmured the boy who rocked back and forth on his chair. The barefoot woman wailed her distress, and the nurse tip-tapped back to quell the noise. She smiled at Helen, who, thank God, was one of the quiet ones. Helen sat quietly and still, not rocking or wailing, but calmly explaining to Sally that she was an angel, like their mother, and had been sent to bring the message . . .

Mr Grady's footsteps echoed through the school gym, and Sally breathed a sigh of relief that the exam was over. For the last hour there'd been no one else in the gym except Sally and Mr Grady. Three hours was a long time to have to think about history and objectivity, and towards the end Sally had thought about Helen, of how she might fetch Helen from the house and take her swimming. Helen would like that, and it was good to keep her occupied. She hadn't had much exercise in the hospital, she'd lost weight and her skin was spotty. Sally thought that, once Helen was fit and her skin was clear, she might not want to cry all the time. Sally handed the papers to Mr Grady. Just before he took them, an ink blot appeared on the page, and Sally looked up, embarrassed, to see him crying. 'There's been a fire,' he said, 'your sister's dead.'

June Burnett Vanishing Point

David, near his 80th birthday and just before his death.

I sit with you
in this quiet place
imagining your single occupation,
and watch the clouded night go by.
Hour by punishing hour
I am separated from sleep
grounded from flight.

You pore over sun-scalded photographs.
Faces turned pale and interesting
by dint of service
in a drawer.

I watch you connecting images
with remembered voices,
hard hands, soft remonstrations.
Lips with kisses and lies.
The past makes them dumb
all seized and impounded in
mid-grief, mid-laughter.

You celebrate your past
in silence with a smile.
Not vulnerable
as I still am
your thoughts speed on
to vanishing point.

Marian McCraith The Pear Tree

The two girls could not have known it was to be their last summer together. The season was long and dry, with every minute until evening spent out of doors, in the Mortimers' garden.

'I wish we were sisters,' Claire Mortimer told Penny, as they sat cross-legged on the lawn, tearing syringa leaves into tiny pieces and letting the fragments fall. And they planned a distant future in which they would marry and have children and live next door to one another.

Penny knew, and had come to love, every inch of the rambling garden. In the moments when she was alone there, when Claire was called in to the house, she took possession of it. There wasn't a part of it where she and Claire hadn't collected caterpillars or smooth stones, made camps or dug for treasure. On her hands and knees, she had crawled among laurel bushes and under rhododendron shrubs to discover long-lost tennis balls, wet and muddy at the end of winter. And there were the giant daisies at the foot of the pear tree, the clumps of frilly fern leaves along the borders of the lawn and, at the far end of the garden, behind the young plum trees, the old, unused toolshed.

'Would you like a drink, darlings?' Claire's mother called through the French doors. Claire looked at Penny. 'Would you?' she asked.

Penny liked the way Claire looked to her to decide these things. Claire didn't take advantage of the fact that it was her house where they played, by being bossy or taking charge. Claire went, on her knees, to the flower border and threw a handful of soil into a metal bucket. She stirred it with a stick.

'Looks like stew!' They laughed.

'I know! It can be a special potion and we have to give it to people to stop them from breaking our spells.'

Handfuls of dandelion leaves and daisy heads floated in the muddy brew. Penny fingered the petals of a yellow rose. Claire glanced towards the house.

'Pick it off,' she said. 'Go on, it's alright.'

The head of scented petals was thrown into the pot and beaten till the petals were frail and translucent. Mrs Mortimer approached, carrying a tray.

'Are you making another of your concoctions, girls? It does look appetising!' She put the tray of pink milkshakes and chocolate bars down on the grass, and stood with her hand cupped against the sun, looking into the branches of the pear tree.

'Did you tell Penny we're going to look at your new school tomorrow, Claire?'

The girls went on eating their chocolate bars.

'When Claire starts there in September, Penny, you must be sure to still come and play.'

Claire wiped chocolatey fingers on the grass: 'I wish Penny could come to that school as well.' She looked at her friend. 'It has got a swimming pool of its own, and a green uniform with a hat.'

Penny busied herself with the milkshake, embarrassed by Claire's remark. Claire's innocence was one of her endearing qualities, but this time it was irritating. She seemed to think that just by wishing for something, you could have it. Penny and Mrs Mortimer knew better.

'Well, darling, that's for her mummy and daddy to decide. It might be that they prefer the junior school up the road. And that's a very good school, too, of course.'

Penny observed the woman's tanned arms and throat, as she stood with her head tilted back.

'I think I'll get Daddy to cut that pear tree down . . . I don't think we've had a pear off it in years.'

From then on, the girls didn't talk of September, when they would be going to separate schools. It seemed to Penny that Claire had simply forgotten, whereas it was always in her own mind. And there were the practicalities of it, like the day when Claire and her parents went off in the car to meet the headmistress, the trip into town to buy Claire's pleated skirt and blazer and striped tie and hat. And then there was the day when Adrian came to play. He, too, would be going to Vale Preparatory in the autumn. He arrived in the afternoon, just when Penny and Claire had their witches' den almost built.

'Duck down!' Claire whispered as a car pulled up the drive. 'It's him!'

128

'Claire, darling! Come and meet Adrian,' called Mrs Mortimer.

'Come with me, Penny?' said Claire.

Adrian was standing by his mother, twisting the hem of his T-shirt, as the girls approached. His mother ran a hand through Adrian's fringe.

'If we can get them to play together, it won't be half so daunting for them when they start at Vale,' she said.

Penny turned away and picked the leaves off a honeysuckle trailer that hung from the fence.

'Adrian, perhaps you'd like to give Claire the sweeties we got for her. I bought Claire and Adrian a packet each. I didn't realize there'd be anyone else here.'

'Darling, why don't you show Adrian the den you've been making?' said Mrs Mortimer. Penny studied her friend, who was characteristically chewing the ends of her hair. After a moment, Claire pulled the wet strand from her mouth and said: 'Shall I show him some of my toys upstairs, instead?'

In Claire's bedroom, Adrian picked his way through the toy box, studiously turning each small item over in his hands. Claire and Penny stood watching him.

'What's this?' he said, holding up a flat-ended arrow.

'I've got a dartboard to go with that. I'll go down and ask Mummy where it is.'

When she was gone, Penny went on watching the boy as he rummaged in the box.

'Are you staying here for tea?' she asked. He didn't look up, but twirled the wheels of a small metal car.

'Yes, of course I am,' he said.

It was at that moment, studying his wide brow and full, serious lips, that something became clear to Penny: she was going to lose Claire. Claire was branching off in a new direction; it was more than just a change of schools – it was a different world. This boy was part of it, Penny was not. He had more right to be here in the Mortimers' house than she did.

Claire entered the room, breathless after running up the stairs. 'There you are, Adrian. There should be two more darts in that box somewhere. Come on, Penny.' She led her friend out of the room.

It wasn't until the girls had, a little nervously, resumed their game in the den that Mrs Mortimer walked across the lawn, followed by the boy.

'Darling, what *are* you doing? I found poor Adrian upstairs on his own. He's come to play *with* you, so just you be kind and let him join in. After all, you're going to be together a lot when you start your school.'

She guided Adrian inside the den and returned to the house.

'What are you playing?' Adrian asked.

'Oh, nothing,' Claire said, chewing her hair and prodding the soil with a stick.

'I know! Penny and I can be witches, and we'll try to capture you and bring you to our den!'

'Alright, but you've got to give me a head start and not watch while I hide.' He stepped out of the den and hurried across the grass. Penny and Claire covered their eyes with their fingers and counted to a hundred in fives.

'You start looking for him, Penny. I'm going to go upstairs and see if I can find our cloaks to wear.'

There was only the sound of unseen birds as Penny turned slowly round, expecting to catch sight of the white of Adrian's T-shirt behind the toolshed, or hear movement along the border shrubs. But all was still. She was, she felt, alone in the large, enclosed garden. It was, for the moment, as though Adrian was not here, had never come in the first place to change everything.

There was a scuffling sound, and she turned to the pear tree. She saw a flash of white in the upper branches. She had often climbed the tree, and knew off by heart where the footholds were. Left, right, left, then a gap where she had to stretch her arms to take hold of the next branch and haul herself up.

Adrian was a long way up. He was sitting on a branch, looking down at her between his legs, saying nothing. She continued to climb until she was almost close enough to touch his foot. His face was pale and serious. Quietly he said: 'I'll come down.'

'Okay, come on.'

Penny started to make her way down and, slowly and carefully, Adrian followed.

'Come on.' She waited.

'I'm . . . stuck.'

'Turn round a bit, this way, and reach your leg down to here.' She indicated the only available foothold, a bulbous notch on the trunk. His foot reached down, but the flat sole of his sandal would not flex to grip the notch. 'Hold my foot!' he demanded.

Penny stood secure, at the join between two thick branches. She put her left arm round the trunk, holding her body close to it, her face up against the rough, flaking bark. She raised her right arm and bent back her fingers to form a flat platform for the boy's foot.

'Right,' she said. 'Come down now.'

Adrian's toes jabbed at her fingers, trying to find a hold. Gradually, the full weight of his body came down onto that one foot, resting on Penny's hand as he let go of his branch and clung only to the rounded trunk.

'Have you got me?' he murmured, his lips hardly moving.

'Yes.'

She looked up at his scared white face, and saw in it the fear he had of trusting himself to her. One jerk of her hand and he'd be falling through the branches, landing with a thud among the daisies below. To let him would be to rid herself of him, to be alone in the garden again and to have Claire back for herself.

Her arm was aching from the weight of the boy. Her palm reddened and her fingers stung. She couldn't let him fall, of course. Another few moments and she'd carefully bring him down. For a little longer, though, they remained poised there on the tree, while Penny counted silently to a hundred, in fives.

Lauren Smith Yesterday

We walked in single file across the beach
Over the white wet sand
Marching as the sea birds do
And all around other lovers held hands tight
In their own silent spaces
Stepping in other people's footprints
For the incoming tide to catch

And I wanted to say I love you
But the words would not come easy to my lips
So we walked in silence
Still in single file
And I wanted to get closer to you
As we walked
Marching as the sea birds do
But I gazed instead at the marbled clouds
And there was blue reflected all around
From the sea to the sky
Deepest blue colouring my thoughts
Then you turned
Reaching out to hold me in your arms
And the silence faded
As my darkest thoughts changed to light
We held each other in our own silent space
Stepping in other people's footprints
For the incoming tide to catch
As the sea birds marched around in single file
Over the white wet sand.

Theresa Verlaine Dear Juliet . . .

I remember when I first began to think of you in that way. Finding the claustrophobia of Sunday cooking smells and 'his' moods over-bearing, I set off on a lengthy trek of the district, supposedly in search of cigarettes. I walked for quite a time and, as usual in moments to myself, I began to think of you.

I knew he had been seeing you for some time. You would send him letters. Occasionally, I would intercept them in the post . . . scented secrets surreptitiously slipped into the pocket of my dressing-gown. Of course I read them, who wouldn't? You always wrote on pale-blue paper, the long, elongated waves of your handwriting sliding across it. Sometimes I hugged those letters to my aching breast, the only clue I had to the anguish we shared, and one which you could now not share with him.

Over and over again, I read your hurting pleas to him; 'I love

you . . . Please ring me . . . I love you . . . Why are you ignoring me? . . . I love you . . . Please leave her!' Your words were all I needed to slip back into domestic bliss. I laughed at my temporary paranoia. Of course my husband loved me. What husband doesn't lose interest in a pregnant wife? You were just a passing fancy . . . I was the one that he married, after all.

The months passed, and your letters reached a crescendo of desperation. Then stopped. I snuggled close to my husband, so glad he had decided to remain with his wife and child. So glad he had made the right decision. But, of course, I was so ignorant of him . . . and of you. The letters had stopped because he had started to see you again. How did I know? I began to smell you on him. A woman smell that could not be denied. You were in his hair and on his chest, and with it I mixed the bitter tears of naïvety.

So what did I do? I ran to my child, the only sanctuary left to me. However, deep inside, you became an obsession. What did you look like? Were you pretty? Clever? Posh? Of course, I never asked him. Not because of his temper, oh no. But because I was afraid of the answers. All I knew was your name . . . Juliet. Juliet . . . I whispered that name to myself time and time again, through sentient breath. Whilst I cooked for him, and cleaned for him, and, yes, even when making love to him, I still couldn't get you off my mind. You were the woman who foolishly loved him as I did, and, consequently, the one I feared more than any other.

And so it was, on that Sunday afternoon, that I felt an overwhelming urge to meet you, to touch you, to hold you in my arms, and to share your pain. I was shocked by the candidness of my thoughts, until it struck me that it was the only option left. I had compromised my pride for so long in this sordid episode of deceit, that all I could do now was forgive . . . and try to love again.

That wistful spring walk was glorious. I imagined your body next to mine, combining our love for one who was not worthy. Of course, I was deluded. I shook my head in alarm at the hidden contingency of thoughts I had discovered. I was totally unprepared, and attempted to satisfy my fears with the belief that, should my secret fantasy ever materialize, I would probably run a mile. And besides, I wasn't about to give up my husband for anything.

I continued the walk home, pushing those troubling, questioning, and challenging thoughts to the back of my mind. When I arrived back, I prepared the dinner with the usual diligence, for once succumbing to the hateful feeling of indifference, as I humoured the ancient Sunday habit. How could I begin to explain the feelings I now had for you? You were the woman I had wanted to hurt, to maim, to kill even. As he had me. You were the woman I had wanted to drag through the streets crying, 'Homebreaker'. These feelings were no more. They became replaced by a secret empathy, a sort of love I couldn't describe, for one I'd never known.

And so, three months later, as I prepare to leave him, I'm leaving you a letter and not him. That brief but previous moment that you unknowingly shared with me, was the moment that I found a part of me that I had lost . . . the moment that I learnt to love again, and to respect myself. Dear Juliet, for being my partner in that illicit voyage, I can only thank you . . . Yours.

Annette Kennerley Unawares

You caught me unawares
The day you arrived in my life
I was daydreaming in the bath tub
Mentally writing a thousand lists
Of Very Important Things To Do.
You were not on it.
You were my flatmate's girlfriend
Dave was my flatmate.
There was no lock on our bathroom door;
We had this system
You were not part of it.
You crashed through the door with the subtlety of a thunderbolt
And hung in the doorway like my un-worn winter jacket –
New and interesting, so I hardly dared put it on . . . yet.
I longed for *Badedas* bubbles to pull up over my head
I felt vulnerable
You were not aware of it.
You came round more and more
As the months went by.
I was often in the bath and you were often barging in on me.
We spent a lot of time there, talking
Then we fell in love – or was it the bath-tub?
I only remember the warm water flowing over us and the soap
Smooth on our skin.
Dave was often out somewhere and anyway he didn't mind.
It was a winter for staying in, really.
And we did.
But spring came round and one day the pipes froze
And we had no hot water.
I thought we could do without
But you were beginning to feel the cold.

136

You opened the window one morning and flew away
To some warmer climate, I believe.
You never wrote.
Winter is coming round again.
The water's hot now and I bought some *Badedas*.
And I've put a lock on the bathroom door,
In case you should come back one day and catch me
Unawares.

Suzanne Doran The Parting

I was late. Both of us were always late for everyone else except each other. But today I was late and she was there already, as I had known she would be.

'Sorry I'm late.' I was at a loss, I had no idea why I was late – why I was deliberately late.

'That's alright. I knew you'd come.' Her casual response belied the look of relief that momentarily crossed her face.

The Lounge Bar was cold. It was still only just past ten am and the cold February weather seemed to have crept through the door and up the stairs behind us.

'What would you like to drink?'

'Coffee.'

'Two coffees, please.' What I needed was a real drink. She handed me the white carrier bag.

'They're all there. If there are any missing it isn't deliberate.'

I took them and shoved them on the floor between my feet. Our history in my handwriting. Her potential weapon.

'You know it's not because I don't trust you, don't you . . .

I just think it's better if I have them back that's all.'

'Of course.'

For a fraction of a second our eyes met, and then shifted. I didn't trust her, and she knew it, just as certainly as I knew that there would be some missing, and I could almost guarantee which ones.

Something looked different about her.

'Your clothes,' I said surprised. 'Are you going somewhere?'

'I have to meet Ma. We've got to sign papers at the estate agents.'

'You're going, then?'

'Yes.'

'Soon?'

'Yes . . . I still feel the same. I don't know how I can, after everything that's happened, but I still feel the same.'

She sounded bewildered – I wasn't.

'We'll always feel the same, it's inevitable, but there's nothing we can do about it. It's too late for us.'

She didn't reply. I felt slightly dizzy, as if I were an onlooker, or dreaming. I knew this conversation was happening, but it lacked reality. We would never see each other again. I could tell she had made up her mind; this was finally the end.

'Here,' she said, taking off her rings and laying them on the table in front of me. 'You know how I never take these off. I wouldn't part with these, but I want you to have one. Any one you like.'

I studied the three rings whilst she went to the bar and ordered two more coffees. I studied them, but thought about her clothes. The navy suit, tights, high-heels. Her long dark hair tied neatly in a French roll, painted nails, long earrings. Attractive, but not the way I liked her to look. Unreal, false, only vaguely similar to the person I knew. Yes, she looked nice, but not the way I wanted to remember her.

I kept my face expressionless, but inwardly I was seething.

'Why are we here? Why the hell are we in here?' I asked myself, all the while studying the rings intently. Battleground of our last furious argument, and the scene of our feeble attempt to patch things up.

When she returned, I tried on all three rings once more, already aware of the one she wanted me to choose.

I decided to try the test, the test I always tried, to prove to myself what I already knew.

'This one.'

'That one? But I – I was sure you'd pick this one,' she pointed to my true choice.

'Really? Oh well, I'll have that one then.' I feigned indifference as I put it on, with the sudden conviction that soon this scrap of silver would be our only connection, my only proof of her existence in my world.

My world is flat, it ends with my last acquaintance and she, the brightest of my planets, was about to step off the edge.

She stood up, 'I'll have to go.'

'No, not yet. Look, just tell me one thing . . . tell me, promise me, you'll come and say goodbye, swear you won't leave without seeing me.'

She sat down again.

'I promise. I'll come up before I go. I promise.'

'You won't. I know you won't.'

'I will. I will. I promise you.'

We were whispering frantically, both aware she was lying.

'Just tell me the truth. Tell me if you're going to go off without saying goodbye. Just tell me.'

'I will come up. I will. I will.'

'What if I'm out?'

'Then I'll come back. I'll keep coming back until I find you in.'

'Alright. I believe you . . . I have to believe you. What else can I do but believe you?'

She stood up again.

'I'm going now, but I'll see you before I go.'

'Goodbye, then.'

'Goodbye.'

Instead of watching her leave, I turned my attention to the white carrier bag. It took me about three minutes to work out which two were missing.

Two weeks later, someone told me she'd moved to Galway. I wasn't surprised. Our relationship had always survived everything except the truth.

Viv Acious A Day in the Life

of one lesbian

W
E
Dnesday

clean windows   oven shine
sweeping brooms   and
    Still,   AUTUMN LEAVES.

Biscuits,
        biscuits,
                biscuits

reading poems newspaper music
tapes with liz
pool lager trish and crisps.

Viv Acious To Alice

I just wanted to laugh
and roll into bed with you.
Jump off the pillow
and leap from high cliffs
            with you.
and smother each other,
but not quite smother
each other with kisses
        and touches and
laughter licks along our spines.

But it just didn't quite happen like that!

Maud Sulter
Like Blood in the Rain

CLAE: I'll still love you

September nineteen seventy six. Two years to the day since they first met. The words hung between them like baggy white drawers on a line. Pristine, deodorized. With an air of prissiness that suggested them not quite fit for the human eye to confront in a one-on-one relationship. Bloo looked into Clae's eyes. The yellow-amber tigereye which saw the future, past and present, blinked, while the right one welled with a saline diamond. The terror that Clae felt somewhere to the left of her ribcage was reflected in her tear. Swallowing hard, she touched Bloo's shoulder and was gone.

'I want you to be a conveyor-belt. Each a component part of a system producing, oh, whatever you want, working together, yet still an autonomous part of this vast mechanical unit.'

The charged energy of the group advanced towards the tutor and he realized that he might be being too ambitious – after all, it was only their first day at drama school.

'Okay. Let's just talk this one through.' In the end, the class improvised working at a conveyor-belt and were content.

'God. I remember ah nearly died when he said, Be a machine.' Clae beamed at Bloo. Sensing impending friendship at enrolment last summer, she caught the divine profile in the corner of her eye and waited patiently. Now, they sat together for the first time. The dirty fair hair silhouetted a strong jaw. Framing blue eyes which, in turn, were framed by the longest lashes Clae had ever seen. Bambi lashes she called them – later.

'Yeah. I suddenly thought that fuckin' drama school was going to be as middle-class and posey as I'd feared. It's taken me a year to take up the place. My body was willing but the psyche weak!' chatted Bloo, whose birth certificate read, Margaret Mary Campbell. The eyes had it.

The hot chocolate with its toupé of whipped cream that Bloo drank had left a creamy brown foam on her top lip. Clae reached

141

out her little finger and ran it along the break, collecting the bubbles as it went. Without hesitation, she flicked her tongue to it and the foam was gone. Suddenly embarrassed, she lowered her large and expressive brown eyes to the deck.

The lino on the café floor was cracked, and the pattern of interlocked Lego bricks worn away down the passage from the counter to the four little tables at the back. It was, however, spotless. Obviously a down-on-your-hands-and-knees job. A task carried out by a woman, probably in her late forties, for a pittance. Perversely, it made Clae proud that the one traditional occupation in her family other than joining the forces was still available to a few. The only shitty thing about shit work was the pay and status. A view she had seen confirmed in a dogeared copy of *Race Today*. As her eyes probed every inch of the place in an endeavour to avoid Bloo's gaze, a discomfort manifested itself physically in a cold and clammy sensation between thighs encased in ridiculously tight Levi's. Period time. She noted that it was only women with pain-free periods who indulged in mysticism and the cult of menstruation.

'Back in a minute,' she mumbled, and took a wad of paper hankies from her bag.

The jeans clung for dear life. As she fought to extricate her thighs from their corset of blue denim, a clot of dark, gunky blood slid down her left leg. Catching it with a hankie, she observed its viscosity, then tossed the soiled paper in the loo. Blood flowed between her legs and was caught in the jeans, which were tightly woven and impervious to this first flush.

Her head swam as her hands pushed towards the walls of the cubicle. The tiles, cold and slippery, offered no hold. Her nails slid vainly to the floor, followed by her limp and semi-conscious body.

Christ of St John on the Cross soars above her. An inky, ecclesiastic blue incense engulfs her sensibilities. Lips part. Her parched mouth opens and tastes its richness. A note. Pinned to the apex. Her long black and boney fingers reach out. Crocheting the air alerts her to the bloodbrown stigmata on her palm. The note is wordless. No language, great or small, has sullied the paper's woven plane. She is now ready. Ready to write, in her woman's tongue, a message. In blood. To her sisterhood. A society closed to the taint of men. Ready to leave her mark of the past. For the future.

Salvador twitches his paint-brush.

In surreality, her body floats. Cloudward. Her sphere being the moon, she is neither constricted by forces gravitational nor the chains of enslavement that are inhumanity. Her blood drains from head to feet. There, old nails. Nails with fist-sized heads. Hammered home by gladiatorial men. Nails which flake rusty, coppertoned fragments onto her flexing feet.

Dali's moustache tickles her nose.

Consciousness returns, like a lamb to the fold.

As the Glasgow Art Gallery sped past the cab window, Clae sensed that a hand, proverbially lily-white, and smooth as Mary's herself, was cradling her head in the lap of its owner.

'You sure she hisny hid too much tae drink, cause ah don't want her spewin' up in ma cab. It's always the bloody same. Dae they say, "Hey wait a minute, Jimmy, gonny stoap the cab?" Naw. Up it comes. The eight pints or the gin 'n' bitter lemun if it's a wummin. That, wi' the fish supper some idiot goat them tae eat. Yer supposed tae hiv it before ye go fur a bevvy, no efter.'

The taxi bloke nattered on and on, unlike an auld fishwife. The glass panel between him and the women symbolizing the divide of sex. There was, however, no such clear divide between the women. Yet. As they drew up to a redbrick tenement near the Botanic Gardens, the cabbie was paid, the body of Clae eased out of the cab and womanned up the stairs to Bloo's studio.

Daylight stalked tigerlight through the bamboo blind. A diffused stream of light percolated into this oasis of calm, nestled within the harsh reality of the inner city.

Clae felt well-grounded. Except for her left arm. It had wheedled its way under Bloo in the night and then decided to go to sleep on her. Lifting the milky shoulder she extricated her dead limb.

Kissing it, like the frog prince in the fairytale, to bring it to life. Like real life, it didn't work, so, to divert her attention, she cautiously drew her index finger the length of the spine next to her. Vertebrae one, two, three . . . suddenly, with no warning, Bloo pounced.

Laying in her own sweat, her sexual passions sated, Clae felt some poetry come. I am now powerless, having abdicated, having abdicated the power to you of my own destruction.

The words would overtake her, seeming to have come through her, not from her brain, but her soul. She felt cold, yet it was July.

'Bloo?'

'Yeah?'

'Have you slept with a black woman before?'

There was no correct answer. 'Yeah, sure,' meant that the odds were this woman had a taste for black skin. If 'No', had she even seen, let alone comprehended, her Blackness? She might even say, 'Does it matter? How is it relevant?'

Lay your bets.

'I haven't slept with anyone before, Clae . . .'

In Clae's head, thousands of little bells went aclang–clang. Woman, the water sure is deep, but runs so cool.

'. . . and it sure gives you an appetite.' The eyelashes lifted provocatively. In one bound, Bloo was out of bed.

Breakfast in bed is an adventure at the best of times. And here, in the best of times; orange–juice tasting a little salty, and the bedclothes a little stained, was no exception.

'Do you fancy seeing a picture? There's a road movie called *Janice* at the Film Theatre. Directed by Strick. 'N' guess who the music's by? The mighty Joan Armatrading.'

'Yeah, OK. But I've got to drop some catalogue stuff off at ma aunty's in Parkhead first.'

So it was, on this fine 12 July, that two women in an inter–racial relationship could walk the streets in peace. Today was the Orange Walk. Not just another Saturday night. No. A day when bigotry, religious spite and bloody violence would spill onto the streets. Top-hatted, becaned Lodgers trooping the streets to Queen's Park. Whistle-flute bands stirring hatred on a level untempered by *democracy*.

Seeing the march stirred it, even in her. A chant came into her head. Repeating itself over and over in an insistent rhythm. Almost numbing her individual consciousness.

'*Catholic cats eat the rats. Two for tuppence ha'penny*'.

With the image of the school gates, the response came back in chorus.

'*Proddy dogs eat the frogs . . .*'

And so, children from five up would learn to despise the Other. And the Sash played on and on and on and on.

THE PARTING IN ONE ACT
SCENE: FOURTEEN MONTHS LATER
      LUIGI'S RESTAURANT

TABLE SET FOR DINNER. RED CHECKED TABLE-CLOTH. TWO PLACES.
CLAE AND BLOO

CLAE: Caz has cast me in her new play, '*The Love of a Good Man is Hard to Find*'. Rehearsals start ten o'clock tomorrow. I'm leaving for London tonight.

GLASWEGIAN ITALIAN WAITER APPROACHES. CONVERSATION HALTS. TWO STEAMING PLATES OF PASTA JOIN THE CARAFE OF RED WINE ON THE TABLE.

BLOO: You're packin' in college? Just like that. Off to the bright life. Wonder Woman hits Metropolis. Wine, women and song. Leaving me. Here. Ma last three weeks in Scotland. Ah mean that much tae ye, dae ah? Over a year of lovin' ye. Puttin' up wi' yer ranting as Lady Macbeth, '*Out, damn spot*'. Puttin' up wi' yer hysterics when the mark on your palm wouldny go awae. Even wi' creosote. Free central heating in bed. Menstrual cramp relief on demand, on command . . .

WAITER RETURNS, OSTENSIBLY TO POUR MORE WINE. CLAE FLASHES HER LEFT AT HIM. NO, WE

WILL NOT BEHAVE LIKE LADIES. WE SET OUR OWN
VOLUME. OK, PAL? HE BACKS OFF, WITHERED.

CLAE: So yer daddy canny find work in this godforsaken place.
Yer ma's goin' tae. You can get into college there. That's
cool. Have you heard me murmur?

BLOO TOYS WITH THE FOOD IN FRONT OF HER.

BLOO: Ma fuckin' spagetti's cauld.
Let's get pissed 'n' go tae bed, eh?

CLAE SHAKES HER HEAD. THE RECRIMINATIONS
DON'T STOP THERE. BLOO GRABS FOR CLAE'S
WALLET. SNATCHES THE PASSPORT-TYPE PHOTO
FROM A UNIONCARD. CLAE LOOKS INCREDULOUS.

CLAE: Where will you keep it? Do they only search your luggage?
BLOO: I'll write to you. Maybe . . . maybe you can visit.
Christmas in the sun.
CLAE: I can't cope wi' this crap. Bloo, I don't want to be left on
my own when you've gone. Nothing will be the same
again. Can't you try to understand that?

CLAE RISES TO GO.

CLAE: I'll still love you.

PAUSE
CLAE TOUCHES BLOO'S SHOULDER, THEN EXITS,
DOWNSTAGE LEFT. LIGHTS DIM. BLOO SLUMPS
FORWARD ONTO TABLE. FADE TO GREY.

The heights on the outskirts of the city's urban sprawl slid into
view. Green, white and gold buses, Irn Bru adverts, separatist
graffiti. Clae was home again. Hogmanay. The last day of
nineteen seventy six. Glasgow's frosty morning mist was lifting
in ice bursts as the 22.10 from London–Euston drew into the
central station.

Lugging her bag up and onto her shoulder, she swung down platform one and into a taxi for the ride home. Sleepy eyes. A page of poetry.

The driver, denied the pleasure of talking incessantly at the attractive wee lassie in his cab, retaliated with booming Radio Clyde. News flashed, weather reported. Victorian architecture jarred by modern chaos. Devastated white holes. Derelict buildings. Bulldozed pasts. No Oxbridge spires. Within minutes of arriving, the council estate. Taxi paid. Her mother's home. Breakfast on the table. Ham, no eggs, potato scones, black pudding, square sausage, fruit pudding, grilled tomato and fried bread. After that lot, up to bed. The overnight journey takes its toll. What with the drunks 'n' all. The joy of the New Year spirit.

'You've got some mail there, Clae. In the top drawer of your dressing table.'

'It's alright, Mammy. Ah see them!'

Four or five envelopes slipped, unread, under the bedcovers. The nappy head on the downy pillow drifts off to sleep.

Laying in her now cold sweat, body odours permeate the bedding. Clae feels the realization come. That the Kaapstad, Sud Afrik postmark on the Christmas card beneath her pillow has taken its emotional toll.

The words read, 'Looking forward to my first Christmas dinner on the beach. People here keep asking me to describe snow! Dad is working in Windhoek. College is dull as dishwater. I do love you – miss you so much. Take Care. Bloo.'

Where is she? Where is she? Woman with the seeing eye. We need her. Like blood in the rain. My sister dead. Load aim trigger release. Bullet leaves. Air. Target meets object. Entry. No force meets resistance. Explode. Flesh burst. Fragments bruised. Blood pumps steadily, rhythmically. Covers distance forcefully. Its colour. The blazing sun. Remember Soweto, remember. The eye that could see all: the future, past and present. Stilled by reality. Kassinga approaches.

Black Madonna on the Cross soars above Soweto. A smokey, folkloric green incense engulfs her sensibilities. Eyes focus. Her lipcracked mouth opens and tastes death's stench. The note. Pinned to the apex. Her long black and boney fingers grasp it. Crocheting the air, a quicksilver bullet passes through her palm.

147

The note is legible. To the left, the embedded bullet, stilled by the wood, explodes. She is now prepared. Prepared to speak in her mother's tongue a message. Of blood. To her people. A society opened to the taint of Kassinga. Ready to leave her words of the past. For the future.

Bloo adjusts her sun shade.

Labouring, her body plunges. Groundward. Her aim being redemption, she is neither constricted by forces military nor the chains of enslavement that are apartheid. Blood splatters her from head to feet. There, children's bodies. Bodies with fist-sized wounds. Shot through by fascist men. Bodies which ooze slimy, soldertoned mucus onto her flexed feet.

Bloo's tongue arouses her labia.

Consciousness returns like a squatter to the Crossroads.

Eve Featherstone
An Elbow in the Consciousness

Such a happy family group
Sitting round the telly watching *Gone With The Wind*
You ask how I bruised my eye
After last week's incident of the guy with the knife
You presume I was fighting men
No I laugh and explain how we were in bed my lover and I
How she put her elbow in my eye
Accidentally while reaching over to turn out the light
Oh Mum comments
What a good job you weren't wearing your glasses
Glasses in bed quips Dad
I sit back and think how easy it is with my parents
No need for trauma or pretence
Should I wash my hair calls my daughter from her bath

When did you wash it last
Oh Wednesday when it was lesbian support group
Mum's sharp intake of breath
Echoes as my father coughs and shuffles his feet
Odd how the word lesbian
Used by an eight-year-old can elicit such shock
After all I've been out for years
They know I'm a dyke met my lovers and friends
They chat about holidays in Crete
No we didn't go to Plakkias we hear that it was nice
My mother who changed her trousers
In my sitting-room full of astonished lesbian writers
Can't be easy with her granddaughter
Who uses the word lesbian in a normal everyday way
Lesbian – only three syllables but such a big word.

OUR BODIES

Most women, if asked whether they would like to change something about their body, would answer 'yes'. We are bombarded every day with images of 'perfect' women – an ideal constructed by fashion magazines and advertising, by television, films, art and literature. Our bodies are taken and abused by the media to sell, to entertain, to decorate and to make us feel that our main object in life should be to aspire to their 'ideal'.

Few women, and especially working-class women, can afford the time and money to devote to pampering and preening their bodies with expensive cosmetics and fashion-model clothes. And such conditioning denies the wide variety of women's shapes and sizes – it does little to encourage us to celebrate our differences or feel good about our bodies.

The pieces in this section deal with some of these differences and cover experiences many of us share, such as menstruation, childbirth, abortion, growing old. They deal with some of the sufferings we face as women – physical abuse, rape, incest, and how, for working-class women, disability often means much more hardship and suffering when it is accompanied by financial hardship, too. We cannot always buy the privileges of private health care, therapy and the gadgets and surroundings which might bring greater comfort and less pain.

But what the work in this section also emphasizes is the strength and determination women have in coping with and overcoming even the most devastating physical hardship. This strength is the woman walking out of the door, leaving a violent husband. It is the girl feeling anger at the world's judgment on her decision to have an abortion. It is the woman laughing at the small revenge on an uncle who abused her. It is the woman with arthritis feeling anger at the shop assistant who treats her as though she were invisible, seeing only the wheelchair and not the person in it. It is the mother fighting drug dependency. It is the strength of the woman, no matter how weak the body.

And finally, there is the tender plea, 'Apology at 41' – which makes the point that we, ourselves, sometimes fail to give our bodies the respect and love they deserve.

Annette Kennerley

Kate Hall Menarche

You called to me
and in your voice
I heard
your trembling womanhood
that long-awaited moment
red between your thighs.

A strange shyness
gripped me
and
just for a second
I could not come to you,
a new woman
unknown to me,
the last traces
of the child I held
slipping
laughing and excited
from my arms.

Miriam Carney Genesis

She shivered all night
In the morning the blood stained the sheets
Like red wine on an altar cloth.
She was frightened
Her mother gave her bandages
sent her to school.

Lauren Smith 12 pm

12 pm
Tired again
But wanted to keep awake
Wanting to do so many things
Evening slipped away
Listened to records
Smoked
Drew in felt-tips not painted
Thought of writing poems
Wanted to write verses and lyrics
Maybe for songs

But didn't
Nowhere to go except bed
Done mundane washing
Clothed the kids
And fed each mouth
Cups of coffee and bread
Watched television
'Ploughman's Lunch'
Had another cigarette
Monthly blues stay with me
Wanted to read
But bled.

Pat Moy
To my daughter, Jen, about your forceps birth

I went to classes with other women.
In we sailed, tummies taut,
proud as blown sails.
Great with expectation
we lay our humps
at our teacher's feet,
puffed and panted,
on dry land
practised all our strokes.
I read all the books.
It was going to be so right for you and me.

But like a small craft
on a boating lake,
when they said it was time
you wouldn't come in.
So they reached
with a ten-inch surgical boating-hook,

broke my waters
drained your pond
left you high and dry.

They put rows of tablets
under my top lip – pushing it out
like a boxer's with a gumshield in.
This was going to be a bout
that would go the full distance.

Still you wouldn't come.
My stomach was tearing slowly
like a telephone directory
being ripped in half,
or a sail slowly splitting.
I had injections; gasped for gas and air,
not because I couldn't bear the pain
but because I couldn't bear it if it got any worse.

'Go home and get some sleep,'
they said to Dad that night.
'Nothing's happening.'
Only me hurting the whole night through.

At 12 the next morning,
they summoned my GP
'Taken me away from a round of golf,' he said benignly.
I had laboured round the course all night.

He put my legs up in canvas slings,
like they use to swing cattle into ships.
Couldn't trust me
to position my legs willingly
as I had for your conception.
He couldn't wait to be off
to tee off.
Unlucky for him that his 13th hole was mine.
He took out his irons,

determined to dislodge
that little white ball of you
from my bunker.

And out you came
bruised, with bloodshot eyes,
but beautiful, despite him.
It wasn't the way I wanted it.
But doctors and golf wait for no woman.

Ann Lofthouse Our Bodies, Our Choice

There's an empty space
inside my body
where once life
claimed existence,
feeding from my blood,
breathing my air,
asking nothing of me
but protection.

A life conceived in haste,
sweaty bodies
simply screwing
never making love,
time governing all –
time running out,
'my mum'll be home soon,'
he said, ripping off his undies,
time of the month,
'but I haven't any johnnys',
time calculated orgasm,
'yes, I'll be careful'.

Sixteen-year-old smiles
and sixteen-year-old hopes
collapse quicker than at
any other age,

seem more devastating,
more final.
Dreams of marriage and
a happy ever after
cut dead by the cold silence
she met when she told him
her news –
happy expectation died within her –
ice cold –
as he walked away.

At sixteen it's hard
when you're on your own,
and, yes, I believe in abortion,
I believe every woman
should have a choice,
because he did –
and he left.
And no one ran after him
and painted 'baby killer'
on his back,
no one expected him
to weep and repent.
There'll always be
an empty space in my
body where once
my baby lived –
but there'll never be
an empty place in my
heart for the men
who are as much a part of it
and as much to blame.

Jill Aldred
No Earth Moved, Just The Rear Suspension

I met Neil when I was sixteen. I had just left school after an unhappy and fruitless education. I lived in a working-class area, where the only major aspiration of women was to get married. At this time, I was very shy and very naïve. I was also sexually ignorant. My parents had not bothered to explain what sex was. My knowledge of the subject came from magazines and romantic fiction.

I was desperate to obtain a boyfriend. Neil collected the pools coupons that my dad filled in every week. He seemed to take an interest in me, something that no one else had done at that time. Everyone kept telling me that I was stupid, and I was beginning to believe it. I started going out with Neil to pubs and discos in the town nearby. I was drunk for the first time, on my very first date with Neil, drinking Cherry B's all night. My mum shouted at me when I got home.

On Sundays we would go for drives in the rural areas nearby, in Neil's old car, which he called Bessie. I sat beside him while he was driving, wondering what it would be like when we were married. I did not realize that I was not the only girl that he had his eyes on. Everyone could see marriage in my eyes, so they did not mind Neil too much. My parents had never had high hopes for me.

He had come on strong a number of times, but I had somehow managed to deflect his lust, without really knowing what he was trying to do. We had been going out for several months when it finally happened. We had been to a pub and I had been fed Babychams all evening. Consequently, I was pretty drunk. My efforts to protect my virginity finally faltered. As we were driving away from the pub, my head began to swim around. I began to feel sick, which surely I would have been, if the car hadn't stopped. It would have been better to have been sick, as Neil might then have been unable to take advantage of my condition. I could feel him moving my buttons, then leaning over me, breathing heavily as he did so. I pleaded with him not to. He took no notice, and his dominance suddenly overwhelmed me. I felt dirty. I began to cry.

The next day we did not see each other. He said he was busy. I began to count the days to my next period. Nothing happened. My mother began to notice that something was wrong. She then insisted that I should go to see the doctor. He did the test and told me to come back and see him in a couple of days' time, when he would have the results. For those two days I sat in my room, wondering and waiting for the outcome, hoping and praying that I was not pregnant.

I sat waiting in the doctor's shabby surgery, looking at the four grimy walls. Half of me felt happy about the prospect of becoming a mother – having something to cuddle and look after, to push around in the pram. The other half of me felt confused and unsure about what my mother would think. My thoughts were suddenly jolted by the ringing of the doctor's bell. I walked into the room where the doctor was sitting. He opened a large envelope and took out the results. It read positive. I was well and truly pregnant.

My mother was outraged at the thought of having an early grandchild. She told the doctor that she wanted me to have an abortion. He said that he did not agree and that I should have the baby. He then sent a letter to a hospital in Manchester, where I would be seen by another doctor.

The following day, my mother asked Neil to come around and talk to us. We told him what had happened and what the doctor had suggested. He did not want the responsibilities. He wanted to be free. So he walked through the door to his freedom. I can remember his mother calling me every filthy name she could lay her hands on. For the next couple of days I tried not to look pregnant, because Mother did not want the secret out. I was sick every morning and tried to sneak past the neighbours, as I was sure that they must know.

A week or so after I had visited the clinic, the hospital rang to say that I was to be admitted. The next day, I packed a suitcase and moved into the hospital ward. I unpacked the suitcase with the nurse who would be looking after me. As I got under the sheets, she came back with my details to place at the end of my bed . . . my age, my name and condition. The crime awaiting the sentence. I lay there, staring up at the ceiling, wishing that there was some way out, but all was lost.

The next morning, the doctor came along to explain exactly what they were going to do. I felt sicker than ever. Before long, the sentence was carried out. I was first given an injection to make me drowsy and then wheeled into the theatre, so that they could kill the life inside me. I was lying on the operating table. Three surgeons looked down at me through their masks. The large door opened and the consultant entered the theatre. I felt a needle in my hand and I began to drift away into sleep.

The surgeons were busy inside me, I knew that this would be the end of the baby talk, the knitting, the end of the fun and enjoyment that I had thought I would have. No more. My parents would make quite sure of that. For the rest of my life, I would have to be a good girl and conform to my dad's rules. I hated my dad. I began to come round. The operation was over. The cork in the bottle had popped, but the shattered pieces of that bottle were scattered on the floor. My mind was screaming, but only tears flowed. I cried for three solid days. I was desperate for somebody to understand my loss. When I needed it most, no one understood.

When I read in the papers of people who have experienced abortion, and note the seemingly callous disregard for life that some people display, I feel myself becoming angry. Those people who set themselves up in the rôle of judges of the nation's morality, and pontificate about the evils of pregnancy termination, to me, display an ignorance that numbs my mind. There is no such thing as an easy abortion. Those people who think that a woman can terminate a pregnancy in the same nonchalant manner as she might renew a prescription for the pill, should think again. I know what an abortion can do to a person. I have experienced those feelings of utter loss and emptiness. I am still paying for a sexual encounter that I did not want and, moreover, one where I did not realize what was happening until it was too late. I lost my innocence to a slob, and lost a part of me because of a slob. No earth moved for me, just the rear suspension.

Janet Hawkins The Abortion

Inside I blossom
against my will;
my blood
nourishes
the intruder
who harbours,
seeking shelter.

Conversations:
how it happened . . .
does the father know?

Anaesthetic
to deaden nerves;
I tense every muscle
awaiting freedom
from inner devils
who argue.

Eyes open;
room blurs;
voices echo,
full of hollowness.
A trickle of blood
but no tears;
the relief
overwhelming
even pain.

Taxi waiting:
I emerge –
unscathed?
Feeling crumpled
but strong . . .

Favourite

A young woman hurries along a narrow, high-walled passage. Shadows are closing in around her, and a man is waiting at the far end of the hall, his arms outstretched. He is seated, a giant, and her eyes are now level with his knees. He reaches down, his enormous hands pulling her on to his lap. She struggles, as he forces her head into his groin.

The woman is outside now, running. Her hair is sticky with drying semen, and still running, she drags her fingers through her hair, desperation turning tangles to knots, until eventually she begins to tear it out at the roots. All the time, her mind chants: they won't believe me, they'll say it was my fault . . .

The dreams were becoming less frequent now, sparked only by specific reminders: a letter on a problem page, a TV documentary, a drunken conversation. The last time was when a lover had tried to revitalize a failing erection by asking how old she was when she'd had her first sexual experience. Four, actually, she said.

'Go and sit with your Uncle Gregory. You know you're his favourite.' Uncle Gregory, two years after his initial assault on her, and well practised by now, was becoming brave, complacent almost. It was a weekly ritual, getting more brazen with repetition: he would pull Jennifer onto his lap, one arm around her waist, his other hand free to tear at the soft flesh between her legs, whenever the family's gaze was directed elsewhere. Sometimes she would be forced to sit like that for an hour or more, panicking each time her parents looked the other way, dreading the moment when they might leave the room altogether.

He liked it best when they were alone. Alone in the house was ideal, but alone in a room was enough. She would immediately occupy herself with a book, a drawing, or searching for a record to put on. Always, he was just one step behind her. Gregory, her daddy's favourite brother. Jennifer, her daddy's favourite daughter. She feared hurting her father by telling him the truth, but could bear still less to risk being called a liar by him. Little girls frequently have such fantasies, said Dr Freud. Case dismissed.

Jennifer once called to her father during an assault, Gregory's dry fingers burning into her, his clammy face pressed against her ear, a voice feigning normality, urging her to tell him how much she was enjoying it. Dadeee, she shouted, and Gregory fell to his knees, pleading no, darling, no, it will never happen again. As a six-year-old, Jennifer had an amazing capacity for compassion.

Happy families. Mum, Dad and four lovely kids. Everyone said so: Anne, she's the beauty; Jennifer, a little difficult, a bookworm and bed-wetter; Jim, a proper lad, a chip off the old block and handsome with it. And young Suzie, who started life a sickly, squalling baby, but look at her now – a livewire, a real bundle of fireworks.

Suzie and Jennifer were thrown together, really. Anne, at thirteen, was beginning to establish her independence, preparing to leave school, following fashion, picking out a steady. And Jim, progressing into an archetypal working-class tearaway, had started to engage in acts of harmless vandalism, stealing useless items from building sites, smoking down the back alley. The exclusive world that Jennifer and Suzie began to build around them laid the foundations for the most powerful, intense and consistent relationship in Jennifer's life. Love seems such a small word, sometimes.

The two would huddle together in the bedroom they shared with Anne, playing elaborate and complex games, speaking a secret language, defying anybody to interrupt them. Gregory did once, striding across the room, his smile sweaty and anxious, his arms already open, his eyes on Jennifer. The girls turned their backs on him, willing him to leave them alone. Gregory stooped behind them, faking interest in their game while slipping his hand into Jennifer's knickers. She winced and said nothing. Just as long as he left Suzie alone. Shortly after this, Jennifer warned Suzie never to be on her own with Uncle Gregory. It was years before she would tell her why.

Jennifer looks back now, and can remember nothing and everything. Week after week, for ten years; fear and pain, repulsion and panic suppressed into a fact of life she discussed with no one. The secrets he stole: his fingers testing each stage of her maturing body, thieving the private pride of her first period.

And Jennifer, like most women, learned how to please men. Be smart, but not too smart. Turn on the tears. Widen your eyes, shave your legs hairless like a child, sit on his lap, little girl lost,

lost, lost, another little girl lost to some sex fiend, you know, the guy next door, the one she calls 'uncle'. Turn on the television and get the saucy schoolgirls, toddlers in high-heels, grown women in a helpless, lisping parody of childish innocence. Nothing wrong with making a man feel protective.

As a teenager, Jennifer became expert at dropping smart-ass, cynical remarks, designed to keep would-be suitors at a distance. While her friends developed crushes, junior romances, and swapped stories about How Far They Were Prepared To Go, Jennifer affected a disdainful aloofness. She opted out of discussions on the right age to lose your virginity, a question that held a desperate fascination for hormonally haywire Catholic adolescents. She was cool, superior and vitriolic around young men. For one thing, she found them boring. Above all else, she was frightened.

She decided to conquer her fears – cure herself – at the age of eighteen. She picked up an incredulous thirty-five-year-old psychiatrist, went back to his place one Sunday afternoon, and silently laughed her head off at the sight of him naked. She had expected something a little more imposing. But this and other sexual encounters were difficult. She viewed them all as assault, and responded accordingly, shrinking from any touch, no matter how gentle, trusting no one.

Healing began with the gradual realization that trust is nobody's right. Strength is beginning to replace the protective shield she wears, as she learns how not to be a child.

Like a series of snapshots occasionally unearthed, the memories are still with her. Uncle Gregory, his proud and so-nearly middle-class wife – they stopped sleeping together after young Gregory was born: What happened? What awful fantasies did he try to exercise upon her? Here's one: Jennifer's regular trip round to Trevellyan Road, off to take a message to Uncle Gregory. The picture shows a small girl, hesitant in a doorway, praying, please don't let it be him, please let it be Aunty Dot. Come into my parlour, said the spider to the fly . . .

And a postcard. At fourteen, Jennifer went on a family holiday, somewhere on the South Coast. Gregory, Dorothy and young Greg also went along. Jennifer's terror of the opportunities that lay ahead for her uncle forced her at last to spell out the danger to

Suzie. An historical moment followed when Suzie fell completely quiet. She then stood up and declared her intention to kill him. Jennifer pleaded with, bullied and cajoled Suzie into silence.

About a week into the holiday, Gregory had managed to catch Jennifer alone. They were standing near the edge of a pier. Gregory had slipped his hand into Jennifer's bra and was trying to force his tongue down her throat. Jennifer was kicking and struggling. Suzie emerged from the shadows and pulled at his jacket, screaming, shrieking, piercing the night. He turned around, stricken. 'I was only playing, darling.' Suzie continued to scream: 'I saw you, you filthy bastard, you were hurting my sister.'

'Please, darling, I didn't mean any harm, please, darling, don't spoil everybody's holiday.'

The girls left Gregory at the end of the pier, shaking from his final assault. The snapshots blur, going into and out of focus. Jennifer is left with an almost phobic hatred of deceit, and an extraordinary power to detect lies, even the smallest. She has an open and manic detestation of power games.

And a vivid, sunny memory of a day in June when her telephone rang, her mother's voice fretting the bad news: Uncle Gregory, she said, had been savaged by a dog and was in hospital. Did she want to send him a card? Sixteen stitches to the face . . . a card would cheer him up no end, Jenny, you always were his favourite . . .

Jennifer smirked into the receiver, unable to fake concern. Gregory's poor little terrier had got into a fight with an Alsatian, and he'd felt compelled to separate the two. That was when he got his face bitten. Are you still there, Jen? 'It must have been a real trauma,' said Jennifer, by now clutching her sides in soundless laughter. 'I mean, for the Alsatian.'

Unable to contain herself, she choked out her goodbyes and, still giggling joyously for small mercies, walked outside, blinking against the sunshine.

Dedicated with love to my sisters and brother and their children, and to PBH.

Julie Rainey
About my friend who was raped

The room has that tense 'exam' silence about it, as everyone dredges up all remaining shreds of concentration. Half-tried sheets of paper lie over desks, chairs, and from walls. Art is no longer the easy option. Although it's not quite time to go, one by one students stream towards the refectory to drown their sorrows in lukewarm cups of gritty coffee. One last person remains, trying to spin out the threads of time to avoid the dark.

Even as she reaches the refectory, people drift out, homeward or flatward in twos and threes, or hauling their bundles alone. Deeply engrossed in the blurred pages of her book, the darkness grows denser, more silent and, aided by imagination, a fertile breeding ground for those creatures, formless, faceless and brutally strong.

But as the lights begin to go off, there is no further refuge in the building and, going through the hall, she steps into the concrete jungle. Even though she's 'better now', like a moth she flits and clings to the pools of orange false security. Even lights, worn like primitive amulets by the city, aren't enough to ward off the monsters.

It's time to move off again, after a moment's hesitation, knowing that when the need arises, you can't move quickly enough. Distant sounds fall into patterns, rhythmically, like footsteps echoing, resounding, faster and nearer and . . . Don't think about it. Just keep walking. Up past the restaurants, full of distinguished clientele, insulated from the outside world by fur and bloody rubies. And now the restaurants thin out into houses, tall, dark and terraced. And then trees. Not wanting to see what might be there, wanting to shut your eyes, but not being able to for fear of what could be there. Every so often cars sweep past with waxing and waning trails of light, giving a second's illumination, a second's reassurance. Just one more street to go, flying past, and trembling so much, the key cannot penetrate the lock.

Into the room, bolt the door, turn the music on, and back to the wall. Relative security.

Once more checking the locks and the curtains, it's time to sink back to the foetus, holding teddy not too tight. The physical scars heal, a lifetime before the fears. Once again, man believes he has dominated what he sees as his superior, using the only weapon he has left.

Ann Lofthouse
'Thank God She's Dead'

Alone she lay,
her child's body transformed
to womanhood by
death – I stagger away to retch.
Images of her naked
flesh, screwed-up skirt,
gagged mouth,
monopolize my nightmares.
Men who get kicks on
children's screams,
show yourselves,
show us all what kind
of human being
could do what you did.

I close my eyes
and still see her torn crotch
running red with blood
and sperm.
Pumping life force into
a child,
they use their dicks
like daggers,
draw blood to feel power
then kill
when the horror
seeps into their consciousness,

they run away and
blame their mothers,
their wives, their sisters –
anyone but themselves.

We pick up the pieces,
the mutilated body
and give her back to
those who loved her.
Her eyes never close
but keep staring,
not angry, not sad
just aware of
what can be done,
of what hatred burns
in men's hearts.
I say, 'Thank God she's dead,'
and curse myself.

Joan Batchelor

1. The Bitter Ore (the first marriage)

'You hit me, Dan Evans, and I'll wake the whole street with my screams,' she said breathlessly, throat tight. He halted, scowling. She had too much pride to yell . . . didn't she? He lifted the belt and she dodged his arm, and fled out into the clear night. It was beginning to freeze over the melted snow. Roads glistened. Walls twinkled diamonds in the light of the ringed moon. To her horror, the door slammed closed behind her. She had a fleeting glimpse of his grin. She wore a nursing bra and one of Dan's old sweaters. On her feet were slippers that were fast soaking up water. She knocked at the door. From a distance, within, she heard her baby cry out. Gareth screamed . . . a curtain next-door twitched, but they wouldn't help. A cloud blew over the moon and the lamp at the side of the road was out. It was dark. She crept around to the back of the house. The kitchen blazed with light. He chuckled as she tried the back door. It was locked. The baby cried lustily in his pram. The only guess she could make was that he had kicked out at the pram to frighten the child and make him scream. She was cold. She tried to prise open the bathroom window. Stuck. With horror in her eyes, she watched him lift the kicking baby from the pram.

'You want this?' he yelled, through the window. She nodded, choking on the tears. The bolts screeched and the child was thrust into her cold arms, shawl and all. Then the door slammed shut again and the bolts rang. She stared through the window as he settled down, feet up before a roaring fire. She tapped on the glass, teeth clenched. He grinned.

The baby was silent, looking up at the moon with wide eyes. She wrapped the shawl about the little figure. Her hands were stiff, and her teeth chattered. This was silly. Childish. So she had dared to strike him? A fat lot of harm her small hand could do. How dare he treat them like this? She was his wife . . . a good wife and mother.

'I shall go to my mam's house!' she yelled. He shrugged and closed his eyes. To her horror, small flakes of snow began to fall. She knew it was the tail end of winter and would most likely turn to rain by morning, if the temperature rose. But they were out in it. She was freezing. She looked through the window. His mouth had fallen open, slackly. He was asleep, and nothing would wake him now.

An hour later, her mother looked up, startled, as her daughter walked into her bright kitchen. Her pleased expression turned to one of concern.

'Hello . . . What are you doing here, love? Nearly ten o'clock, it is . . . you shouldn't have the baby out at this time. The night air will kill him. What's wrong? Where's your coat, girl?' She bustled the girl and her baby to a battered but comfortable, and so familiar, chair by the fire. Her eyes widened as she saw her daughter's soaked feet, encased in sodden fur slippers. The girl rocked the baby in arms that shook so much that her mother took him from her, tutting and clucking. The front door opened. The girl's father walked in. He was rubbing his hands. He reeked of drink, but wasn't drunk.

'It's a cold one again,' he said to his wife. Then his eyes fell on the baby.

'What the hell . . ?' He stopped as he saw the girl. His mouth tightened. Eyes hard.

'I don't know . . .' his wife began nervously. 'Just walked in, they have . . .'

'What's wrong, girl?' Her father's voice was deceptively quiet. Eyes steely.

'I've left him,' the girl said, flatly. She stared into the fire. Her father sucked his teeth.

'Left him? Left him? What do you mean, you've left him? Just like that?'

'You said to marry and give the child a name. I did. You said I could then get a divorce. You said I didn't have to stay with him. So I left.' She trembled.

'Get a divorce? On what grounds? Are you mad, girl? I thought once you had married, you would see a bit of sense. Grow up . . . too hot-headed, you are. Big ideas. Feminist stuff.' His daughter turned her deep brown eyes towards him, and he faltered, staring at the bruises on her face and neck. Her mother cried out in horror.

'I can divorce him for cruelty,' the girl said, slowly and sadly. Her father gasped.

'I won't let you bring shame upon yourself in this way. You're no daughter of mine if you can't put up with a belt now and then. It's a way of life here, you know.'

'Do you beat Mum?' she asked.

'I don't need to. She knows her place better than you.' Her mother looked away, unable to meet her daughter's eyes, rocking the sleeping infant. 'You can stay the night,' her father said, 'but back to your husband in the morning.'

With her father in bed, and the baby asleep in a padded-out kitchen-draw by the fire, the mother and daughter talked in whispers.

'Mum, it's not right. Why should I just take it?' The girl was in tears, not sobbing, but emotionless, as tears dripped down her face.

'They keep us, love. They earn . . . What can we do alone? You know what a bad name a woman has who leaves her husband, around here.' Her mother wept.

'I won't go back, Mam . . . I'll work, get a job in the factory.'

170

'But who will look after the baby, love? You know your dad won't let me.'

The clock ticked in the silent room. The fire spat. The baby sighed.

'Mam, the suffragettes fought for more than the right to vote. We should have other rights. There must be a way.'

'Love, it's the sixties. It'll never change. Whatever you earn he can claim as his. If you took him to court, your name, and ours, would be dragged through the mud. Go back. Just don't answer back. Think of something else. He is a good worker. As he gets older, he will grow out of it . . .'

She did not know it at the time, but she was already two months' pregnant again. Within months of her daughter's birth, she discovered she was expecting her third child. Dan was furious. He swore she had done it deliberately. Miserable with sickness and worry, she began to cope less. The house began to look cluttered. The children grew fretful and Dan was of uncertain moods that kept her on a knife-edge, until her nerves felt frayed. She cried easily, which aroused his fury. Her sickness infuriated him, too, although it was mainly a dry, painful retching. She had to stagger to the chemical closet at the bottom of the garden, where the smell made her retch even more. She had new bruises each morning; his fists were ever-active. Something had to snap. The strain she carried was immense. The children, sensitive to her despair, became difficult.

The morning had gone badly. The children kicked, yelled and spat out food until she was exhausted by the never-ending round of sickness, bottles, napkins, rain, shopping, cooking, cleaning, ironing, sleepless nights . . . only to be greeted by his fists at the end of the day. If only she at least understood why he acted this way. She had tried to talk to him – to no avail. Why did he refuse? Did he enjoy sadism? She was so depressed that she could not think straight. Post-natal depression, the doctor said, and pre-scribed sedatives that depressed her more. She badly needed breathing space, a rest.

She undressed the children and put them to bed, singing in a broken voice until they slept. She watched the clock. He would be home from work on the ten o'clock bus. At five to ten, she slipped outside to where she could watch the house and listen for the children while she waited for him to return. Her head was light and ringing, her body floated. The bus passed and he alighted, bawdy in his shouted remarks to other workmen. She watched the slight, rolling limp of him, as he walked to the front door of the cottage in the still night, and let himself in, after a slight fumble to insert the key. She waited no longer, but sped swiftly for the hills. Many would have avoided the dark coal dunes as if they were the desert wastes themselves, but to her, it was the home of her childhood . . . freedom. She zig-zagged over the uneven tracks made by the fleet-footed mountain sheep.

Boulders loomed out of the darkness. The moon had abdicated. Darkness ruled. Not a sound. No owl, no scrabbling night creatures, no vixen bark or pony cough. No bat or cat or belly-slithering, cold-blooded creature stirred. Her breath rasped in the silence. She climbed higher, and her feet found the bogland . . . Then the giggling laughter of a brook. Tears ached on her wet face, she was unaware of tears or sweat or pain or life. Gasping, she knelt and drank from the brook, tasting the bitter iron ore of the water in her hand. She stumbled on, missing the narrow tracks now, in her tiredness.

And there it lay, in the sudden silver of a moon that rose full with a new brilliant life. A man-made lake in the hills, cool and mysterious, flooding a sweet valley that cleft the hills in two. A sheep started up and fled, resentful of her intrusion. She fell to her grazed knees at the water's rim. Her work-roughened hands were made silver beneath the soft water. Cool, so it cleansed her. Soothed her. She had lost her shoes. She waded deep, until it brushed her thighs. She felt the silt beneath her bare toes. It was cold. Clear. Her whole self felt at peace. She was radiant. Her mother would look after the two children. She moved deeper and felt the water lap at her pubic region, then stroke at her lower stomach. Deeper . . .

It stopped her suddenly in her tracks. She frowned . . . and as if deliberately, the child within her body moved. A fluttery wittering. She stood still. No . . . don't think. It is for the best. It gave a lurch and a definite knock. She fell forward into the water, on her knees. It reached her shoulders and swirled her long hair about her body. The feeling of final peace vanished. What right had she to murder? To judge? Laws were already being changed. Women fighting, not dying. A new generation of strong women being born. She opened her mouth and tasted again the bitter ore. She rose, water dripping off her strong, young body . . .

2. Confliction (the second marriage)

I honestly hadn't known about his drink problem. When I had found out, I tried to take it with the practical, Virgo attitude that I had taken on my move from the 'sticks' to the 'smoke', and away from my family and friends into the unknown. I had rolled up my sleeves and got on with trying to sort it all out.

It had been his idea to swop roles, but it had soured on him and left him bitter and resentful. At first, it had seemed a new and challenging excitement to me. But then, I had found myself limp from my work and entering the front door to a tirade of drunken bitterness. The child suffered the worst, with the only father he had ever known uttering the words: 'Go back to your own bloody father,' as if the child needed a meal or comfort . . . I watched the eyes of this sensitive boy harden as he approached adolescence. I was horrified. One of the things that disgusted me most about myself was that I had not re-married for love, or even a fondness, but with a kind of pity at his loneliness, and because I thought that my children needed a father. I was paying dearly for it.

I walked slowly down the stairs, feeling my face tighten to greet the complaints. I wondered if my daughter had written, with something like burning longing inside me. My eldest two children had left home at sixteen, the other a year later. My youngest boy was just twelve. Would his young life be spent in this bitterness? Would I lose him, too? The boy did love his stepfather; he didn't despise the man so much as the drink. My hands were shaking and my head felt light . . . the bloody menopause . . . as if there were not enough problems as it was. Still, I knew my dizziness would pass. It always did.

For just a moment, I felt my mouth soften at the sight of the roses in the vase. Yet my eyes remained hard and hurt. He stole the roses, but the thought was there. Like the bars of chocolate he brought me now and then. How I pitied him his struggle. But bills had to be paid, or they would cut off the electricity yet again.

My mug of hot tea steamed sulkily by my cigarettes and lighter on the table. I reached out a shaking hand. I felt him there, by the door, looking at me with those hang-dog eyes, and lifted my own to meet his, questioningly. He shuffled his feet.

'Oh, it doesn't matter,' he mumbled and rubbed his hands together. Did anything honestly matter any more? Tears dammed my eyes. When had I last had a good cry? I couldn't remember. Just this heavy burning. I felt alone. He forgot, you see, the very next day, whatever we had talked about the evening before. Some brain cell damage, they had said. Halfway through a deep conversation, he desperately tried to pull together the words he wished to say and had forgotten. I felt agonized. He had been so keen-minded. His own aggression was the frustration, but try telling that to a twelve-year-old boy.

Hastily, I lit another cigarette as I smelled burned toast. I couldn't help him. Perhaps that was the hardest to accept. It was time to move on and allow him peace to work things out alone. He would sink or he would swim. I was world-weary. I had told the psychiatrist that I could not manage alone. He had wryly answered that I had been doing so for over nine years, and carrying my husband's added weight on my back. It had surprised me. And it was true. I had kept on hoping for a miracle. Expecting my enthusiasm to fire his. But that only happened in story books. My blood chilled when I recalled the times I had, with cold, calm reason, planned to kill him. To put him out of his misery and our lives. Me, who had never deliberately hurt an insect.

He thought I hadn't heard the clink of bottle on glass in the kitchen. How sharp my senses were towards senseless drinking. The subdued clatter and the furtive, foaming fizz . . . My mouth tightened even more . . . it was becoming a thin, sore wound in my face. I lit another cigarette from the stub of the first. I was torn by my protective love, both for him and the boy. My remaining child. The boy needed security. Discipline. Could I, alone, provide it? I must be the strong one, but I felt such a tiny, scrabbling creature . . . young, defenceless and weak. He used many ploys to make me and the boy feel guilty. I now saw through all that. But the hurt, green eyes of my son made my heart constrict.

The house seemed suddenly extra silent. I arose and entered the kitchen. A glass was carefully washed and left to drain on the scummy old drainer. He had crept off to the pub. To pass the window where I had been sitting he would have needed to bend his body almost double, in order not to be seen by me. My mouth twisted.

A year later, we were divorced.

3. A Kind of Calm

There *had* been life after divorce, though it had been a three-year climb that had been far from painless. Without fun, yet not without excitement. I began by giving up cigarettes, getting a flat and building up a close and loving relationship that had been hard work for us both. I was about to train at a city crisis centre, had poetry readings to attend, workshops, childminding. This was my first home after two failed marriages; with three grown-up children, comparatively settled in lives of their own, a nervous breakdown that was a thing of the distant, hazy past, a spinal complaint I was learning to live with, and my youngest son, Jonah, at sixteen, topping my five foot nine by at least four inches. Our moods tended to fluctuate more or less together, so that we either laughed together or had a good yell and cleared the air. He thought of me as a passable parent that he could tolerate a while longer, and I loved him as one does a last child. My boyfriend, Jim, and Jonah seemed to get on well together, after the initial trauma and the rivalry of 'Mum's younger boyfriend', and Jim not being used to children.

Easter was approaching, and here I was cleaning the flat, watering and feeding my many houseplants, washing and ironing, packing to spend part of the holiday with Jim, and getting Easter eggs in for the grandchildren. At some point in this organized chaos, I remembered the renewal of my prescription. Jonah set out for the health centre and my Limbitrol. I had been taking the drug, a cross between an anti-depressant and a tranquillizer, for some years. Not too keen on pill-taking, I had, under my own steam, dropped the dosage from three a day to one a night. It suited me well, and there I stayed, complacent in my new-found well-being. Jonah returned, empty handed. It seemed my drug was a victim of health cuts – it was no longer available. I grinned – this was as good a time as any to come off the dratted things.

Easter went quite well. Jim and I met friends, visited family, ate like pigs . . . We relaxed, and for three whole days I forgot the tranquillizers. I did feel extra cold, and noticed that my skin felt hot and itched, while being goose-bumpy. I shivered and developed a thumping headache. I put spit on my itching patches, wore many sweaters, my jaw ached from trying to control the shivering. Suddenly, I began to throw up everything I ate. I stopped eating . . . I continued to throw up. One morning, the fourth day, the panic hit me like a sledgehammer.

Before I was aware of awakening, I was aware of absolute terror on a massive scale. My nose streaming, I was suddenly trembling, retching, sobbing in sheer, utter cowardice. Then the 'runs' started, so that I was pouring from both ends, itching, hurting, shaking and hysterical. I was high up in a tower block of flats, terrified of moving, terrified of being alone, a strong mental image of myself smashed to red goo at the foot of my flats. Jonah was up to his eyes in revision and Jim was back at work, and I didn't want to be alone. I couldn't bear the physical agony of my terror. Afraid to wash my hair because I feared the dizziness, afraid to bath because I feared drowning. It wasn't worth eating because it seemed a waste of the paltry money I got from 'they-who-keep-us-down', when I couldn't even keep the food down. I drank a great deal, but that came up, too. Jim began to look haunted, phoning neighbours during his lunch break and dashing over after work. Jonah looked desperate, and I had fallen apart at the seams.

Quite by chance, I saw a letter, published in the *Manchester Evening News*, which spoke of the fears of a Limbitrol user about the dependency withdrawal symptoms. Until then, I had not really thought I was, or had been, dependent – that was addicted, wasn't it? I decided to go and see my doctor and ask for an alternative drug until I could cope. I left his surgery clutching a prescription for Temazepam in my hand. I slept like the dead, waking exhausted, sticky, smelly, tearing at Jonah or Jim in my terror. Praying, wanting to die, yet fearing to do so. I clung to everything . . . my son's neck, the bed, the door-frame, the loo, my poor, dribble-soaked rag doll. The vomiting was leaving me drained of energy and in pain. My jaw hurt, my limbs hurt, my eyes looked swollen. Jim took me to the doctor, who changed my pill to Diazepam, to be taken twice a day until I was over the Limbitrol withdrawal. I was sceptical. I could hardly concentrate. I wanted everyone I met to hold me very tightly and rock me to sleep.

One of my hobbies, and greatest pleasures, was to receive and answer mail from many friends all over the world. Now my letters were being hurled to one side as they fell through the door. My doctor asked me if I read . . . I had over 700 books that I was working my way through, but at this moment in time I couldn't read, knit or talk. I sat holding onto myself very tightly, rocking . . . rocking . . .

Jonah went through hell. From dawn, I screamed for him to come and sit on my bed and talk to me. I clawed at him, shivering, sweating and sobbing, telling him over and over again that I loved him, for fear that over the harsher months he had doubted it. My nails dug deeply into his skin, and my nose dripped down his arms. Something had to be done, to allow him to study.

By 8.30 the next morning, I was washed and dressed, after a fashion, and walking towards my daughter's house, six miles away. I was far too anxious to wait for the bus. A hundred yards on my feet, and my nerve failed. My daughter arrived with her own small daughter, in answer to my phone call. It felt good to be taken in hand, to give myself up to someone who lovingly combed my wild hair and cooked a meal, then held my head while I threw up. Who held my hand while we walked along the river, my feet stumbling as I tried not to retch. My granddaughter made me laugh – wild, out-of-control laughter verging on hysteria.

The next day, Jonah took me over to my youngest daughter's. It was a nightmare journey to the city outskirts, with me slumped, limp from Diazepam, having to get off before our stop so that I wouldn't vomit on the bus. I slept most of the day on the couch beneath a duvet, drinking copiously and heaving it back up again. In limbo, I listened to the children shriek in play. I felt cool, featherlight little fingers touch my burning cheek. My head was splitting. When I woke, I wept and laughed in turn, rocking soft, comforting little bodies. It was the fourth week. I stayed the next few days, sleeping in Daniel's bed and hugging his teddy bear. I was afraid to wake up. I couldn't stay asleep. Little chattering voices woke me, and I just drifted awake, weak and giddy, sick and weepy.

We tried various self-help methods . . . transcendental meditation, wholefood diets, herbal tea, peaceful music . . . I went to a faith-healer, with the most surprising results for a non-believer. But this withdrawal was going to take its toll, it had set the pace and there was no stopping it. On the sixth week, I collapsed. Jim was sent for. I felt I was losing my mind. I clung on to the bathroom door, raging at the terrors, screaming and yelling. Jim took me to my daughter's, and there I fell into a state of mind that was terrifying in its finality. I had achieved a kind of calm, but at such cost . . . I wanted to die . . . I had come to the end of my endurance. I had hit the peak. It suddenly seemed clear. I could take no more. I was at peace with this realization. Smiling. Jim called an emergency doctor. I had ceased to talk or react to any of them by now.

It seemed that Diazepam was Valium, and this had not been a suitable alternative to Limbitrol. The doctor was brisk, he asked if I wished to obtain Limbitrol privately, and by now Jim was prepared to do this at any cost . . . but somewhere inside me, a flame flickered and was fanned. Deep from the dregs of my despair, I shook my head . . . I couldn't talk . . . I was finally prescribed Bolvidon, a non-addictive alternative to Limbitrol.

I have been taking Bolvidon for three months, now. It took a while before it got into my blood stream and regulated itself, and there has been this nagging fear that I am dependent on yet another drug, and that someday I will again have to go through the horrendous symptoms I have already suffered. I dare not try yet to stop taking them. I decided that, to become well in mind and body, I needed to get out and work. I have been working in a big store for six weeks. I even went away, alone, to train. I am looking for a business course to study for full-time employment. Life is becoming pretty good. The panic attacks are getting less frequent and less severe with each day that passes. It seems there is life after tranquillizers . . . and this is the very best kind of calm yet.

Bridget O'Connor Reader's Wife

They said it was a disguise, so I must have known he'd send it in –
'cept I never. They kept on at me to admit it, like I hadn't sworn
on the Bible. The wig? That bloody wig! It was yellow blonde,
hat-shaped. I wore it when my hair was dirty. When Mum died, I
inherited it; that and the wall clock.

I never saw it, you know, the photo. Rolf was at the end of the
bed, we were pretty tanked up and I was undressing, giggling coz
I couldn't get nothing undone, and having to shush up just in case
we wake the kids. And Rolf said, 'Smile', whipping out his
Polaroid, so I just struck this pose with my leg out and one arm
dangling over the edge. The flash, it almost blinded me. It was
Exhibit Three, the bedhead, in court, you know it was sometimes
very funny.

Nobody would recognize me now. The stuff they give you
here is shit, it blows you out, potatoes and porridgy things, and all
the custard you can keep down. It's something to do, though, so I
eat it up, all of it. Five years ago, you had to hunt about the room
to find me, skin and bone and nothing jiggling; smoked two packs
a day and sort of picked at food, no appetite, what with the kids
an' all. They grab things, you see, off your plate and that puts you
off and there's always one or other dribbling somethin' or spitting
out his food – and then there was Rolf. Rolf used to joke, Mr
Funny Man, 'cept I didn't think it funny – that I had two backs,
and that got me, that used to really get me. Nothing's fair. Now
they say that's fashionable, clothes hang better, 'cept I never had
nothing worth hanging up. In here, it doesn't matter what you
wear, what you eat, it's like a relief.

You know, he was sort of pathetic, like one of the kids. I'd be
going round the house with my vaccy, up and down all day, and
I'd find piles of this mucky stuff, great big suntanned bums and a
silly grinning face peeping up between. I always thought the girls
looked embarrassed. At first, I'd flick through one when I was
knackered. I'd have my feet up and a cig, but by the middle I'd feel
sort of sick, like I was their mum or somethin'. And then he'd
come home – Rolf, and I'd get up and shout, 'What the hell are

these?' and – you won't believe this – he'd *deny* it, shifting about on his feet. And once, he said the kids must've brought them in and I yelled, 'C'mon, Robbie's five and Jammy's six and a bit. Now is that likely, well is it?'

Men! Sometimes we laugh our heads off. We tell our stories, see, these girls, some of them so young like they just got a Saturday job or something. I look after them, well some of them. Some of them are terrible, hard as glass, they'd stab you in the eye for a cig.

Rolf? He was, well, like a big dog. The hairiest man you ever saw. Not that you'd know that, with his clothes on. He had this big, bald head the colour of a boil; you'd only know it by his hands, great hairy things and from the neck down, like an animal. First, see, I pretended I liked it – all that hair, but I've always had thin blood and in winter, you know, his body was so – like sleeping with central heating, with a very hot dog. His pet name? The Beasty? I don't know when I first started calling him that.

You know, I can't remember much of him. It's like a blank. I can't remember his eyes or mouth or anything about his features – just this incredible hair. Can't even remember what he was like when we were courting. He was just a man and he had a job and wore a tie to work and he asked me and I said yes and that was that. Kids come and I get wore out like every other woman I knew, like me mum and like me sister and like the woman next door. 'Cept I never took nothing, no tablets and no secret drinking, and definitely no going to the doctor. I was busy, I just got on with it.

They said in court, 'Diminished Responsibility', you know. This lady lawyer explained it, she kept hammering at me and what it meant really was, I'm a nutter and I'd get five years 'stead of life. Well, I got twenty. This lady, you know, she come to see me after and gave me twenty fags, 'one a year,' I said, and then she started bawling and I had to comfort her. Wrote me once or twice, and then she must've forgot.

Got that job, see, in the baccy's, just a few hours a day while the kids were at school. Pin money, Rolf called it – more like food money and leccy money and school-dinner money. And it weren't enough, so I got one of those pool collectors' jobs in the evenings, and that weren't enough, and I was ratty with the kids and had to keep dumping them with Myra next door. He kept me short. Had to search his pockets at night, trail of his clothes all over the house. Once, I found a tenner in his jacket lining. God, what a day that was – took the kids to the zoo and got a taxi home. Worth it, to see those kids' faces 'cept they thought I'd take them every week, so in the end it weren't worth it. They expect things, kids, don't they – 'specially when they see their mates with new toys, new clothes, and I'd feel like screaming, 'Well, them kids ain't got Beasty for a dad, have they?' Never did, though.

This baccy's. Had fluorescent lighting, quite a big shop with mags all down one side . . . The light so bright it'd tear your eyes. And all these men come in and flicking through the ones on the top rack, sometimes for thirty minutes! They'd sort of hover and get their courage up, and over to the counter and order fags and matches and a can of something and put this dirty mag down on top, like it was an afterthought. And I'd say, three pounds please, and take the money and ring it up and they'd still be waiting there for a bag, with their eyes going all over, and I'd serve someone else and taking my time, and sometimes they'd whisper, 'Bag please,' and I'd give 'em one of those little ones for sweets. Me and this girl, Claire, used to crack up after. The dirty –

And then I'd get home and clean up 'fore I collect the kids, and it began to seem like the house was covered in 'em, under the settee and under the cushions, two under Robbie's bed and, I dunno, I started to think, 'Robbie's watching me,' he's ten now, and I stopped getting dressed in front of them and you know what, when I was bathing him, I'd look at his soapy little body and I'd catch myself searching for hair, like he was going to turn into Beasty or break out like a little werewolf.

I couldn't leave the kids no more with Myra coz of him, her husband. I didn't tell her nothing, couldn't. He started coming in the shop every other day, see, and he were one of the ones, 'cept he were worse. Didn't know he was Myra's man, they were new neighbours and he's hardly home. Me and Claire used to do the Paper Bag routine 'cept it hit me, 'He enjoys it', and stand there staring me out. The mags he got, the filth, the worst, the kids and dog kind, ordered direct from the manager, and he'd flick through them at the counter and count his change out real slow with his eyes on me, dirty dead eyes with no centres. And I couldn't sleep no more, coz I got to thinking, 'He's on the other side of that wall,' and I couldn't stand Rolf near me, pawing at me. I thought, 'He's just like him, he's just the same as 'im.' Maybe I should have gone to the doctor. I'd clean the house at night, tiptoeing about with rubber gloves on, standing over the flip-bin tearing them up one after the other, and every night the same, like he bought them wholesale, and I'd think, 'If he touched my kids, if he touched my kids'.

That lady lawyer said I should have gone to the doctor, I'd have more of a case, and I were so sick, I yelled at her, 'When did I have time, eh, when?'

Claire kept saying, 'You alright?' I was jumpy as a cat and he kept coming in. I'd hear the bell tingle and my face would go white, I could feel all the blood tightening in my skull – though I tried not to show it. He knew, though. I'd drop his change, my fingers like ice, and I'd have to scurry on the floor with him watching, and Claire would push me out the way and say, 'Here you are – sir,' and give it him from the till.

It don't seem so long ago, now.

Rolf was acting peculiar. All of a sudden he was saying, 'Give that job up,' and I'd catch him looking at me and his face were – frightened, and I'd yell, 'And what'd we eat then, eh? – dirty mags?'

And then, that day. That day, I come into the shop as usual. It was Claire's day off, so I was all on my own. You know, and all the regulars come in, one after the other, and there was no let up, no coffee break and I had this head on me like it would split open. And then the van arrived with the mags and I had to hump ten parcels of them over to the counter and, like I said in court, you can't untie those knots with your fingers. So I cut the first lot open without looking at the covers and up the steps to the top rack and then down again and then up, and the bell kept tingling and I was muttering somethin like, 'alright, alright, I'll be with you in a sec,' and I was cutting and stacking and cutting and stacking, and I heard this laugh and then another and, you know, when you feel eyes on you. I looked up and down the line of them and he was there, and he was passing this mag to some bloke, and this bloke were looking at me and then at this mag, and I just knew what he'd done, what Rolf had done.

They said I'd meant to do it, but I never. It was like a dream. He came up to me very slowly with this thin, stretched smile on his lips, holding the mag out. I'll never forget it, what he said. He said, 'Would you like a paper bag – Miss,' and some man laughed and my arm flew out into his chest. Inside, I was screaming, 'I'VE TOUCHED HIM I'VE TOUCHED-HIM' – and that's all I regret, that and I don't see my kids.

Janet Hawkins The Last Day

The curtains hang drawn in the bedroom. She lays dreaming in a night world.

Colours swirl. Mazes of paths lead nowhere, faces mock and menace.

An hour later, she wakes and rises, stays beneath the shower, trying to rinse away the person she has become . . . Her blue eyes have lost their sparkle, droplets of water cling to their heavy lids like pearls.

She dresses, draws open the curtains, makes the crumpled bed and glides down the stairs.

The telephone rings in the kitchen: her mother.

'Are you okay?' We all know you can never be really safe, not while . . .'

'Yes.' She is okay.

In fact, she has lost all her other fears – of insanity, muggers, rapists and psychopaths. They can't frighten her. She laughs at the thought; walks the streets bravely, cushioned by numbness.

'I'll call in this afternoon. Er . . . will you be . . . I mean, will he be . . . ?'

'I'll be alone. He won't be here.'

She rings off. Eats breakfast. Dusts the lounge. Hoovers the hall. This is normality.

Her left knee is bruised and purple, it throbs beneath her jeans. But at least it is invisible – the public front remains intact.

The milkman knocks. Friday is payment day.

'Hello, luv. How are you?' he chirps, without stopping for her reply.

'Not so bad,' she says, as she closes the door.

And things aren't so bad as they have been . . . She remembers the blow which made her nose pour with blood. More blood than she had ever seen before. She'd held a cold flannel beneath it until it stopped.

Her mother arrives in the afternoon, with a bag of jam tarts to eat with their cups of tea. Company cheers her. She is a sociable sort, really. But some days she feels desperate for conversation . . .

They drink tea and eat the jam tarts, the worried look never leaving her mother's face. Or is it guilt? A choking sensation comes into the older woman's throat and she takes a sip of tea to swallow it down.

'Your father's well.'

Such trivial conversation. But you had to talk about something.

'I miss the dog, too . . .' she replies, looking thoughtful. Yet when she saw him now, he hardly knew her – greeted her as though she were a stranger.

'I see the garden is blooming beautifully,' her mother remarks, even though it is now late September.

Alone again, she switches on the radio. They are playing the song which marked their engagement. It is romantic, sexy, the sort that sticks in your head.

She washes up the cups, dreams of her escape . . . But will she ever? She is too conforming, shy.

She often dreamed of the moment when she could lay her cards on the table – the only cards she had left – and feel triumphant, brave, and somehow invulnerable; that he couldn't hurt her anymore, that no one could ever again. She would pack, leave, walk towards the sun, without glancing back.

Her mother arrives home, closes the front door, shutting out the grey street, and wipes a stray tear from her cheek. She feels helpless. By the fireside, her husband sits silently.

'There, there, don't cry. You've done all you can,' he says, wishing he could believe his own words.

'Our own daughter! I can't bear to look at her! The BRUISES!' she sobs. 'That terrible man!'

'There, there.' He puts the kettle on for more tea, and sits smoking his pipe, deep in thoughts of the past, when his daughter was just a little girl.

That evening, her husband turns his key in the lock. The smell of frying steak reaches his nostrils. She doesn't glance up, but just sits at the table, reading a Barbara Cartland novel. He throws his jacket over the back of the chair and lights a cigarette.

They eat.

Later, they watch TV, sitting in separate armchairs.

In bed that evening, he wants to make love; nothing dampens his desire . . . But she turns her back. He puts his hands to her throat. He could strangle her. Instead, he curses and turns out the light. She sobs, and finally falls asleep.

The next morning, she rises earlier than usual. There is a lightness in her step, a new feeling of being alive. She packs two bags and makes a phone call, then hurriedly drinks a sugary cup of coffee for courage.

She leaves the house, knowing she will never return.

Her new bed is lumpy and old. It stands in the corner of the dingy room. She wept on her first day here, but the other women gave her comfort. They know what she has been through . . . which made her cry even more – for all of them.

That evening, she phones her mother.

'You're not in one of those awful places! Wouldn't you rather come –'

'No.' She was fine. They could meet for a drink in the Battersea Wine Bar, at six on Monday. Her mother replaces the receiver and rushes to tell her father the news.

Marie Roe 'Crippled'

Up the ramp you climb, pushing, turning
the wheels of your chair.
Like a spider, spinning, never tiring,

only half of you functions, like me.
Dare I compare!
'Normal' people having the audacity to turn
in pity, looking the other way.
These 'normal' mortals, who can walk and run,
moaning whilst combing their hair, they say:
'Nose too big, mouth too small,' so vain,
only half-functioning, these 'normal' mortals.

Kay Chell Arthritis

It was late on in the morning, and I had just managed to get myself
out of bed. I had to rock myself to and fro many more times than
usual because my severely damaged leg had set at the knee and
was proving its most unco-operative. It was always painful, but
this particular morning, the sensation of being totally consumed
by pain made me shed tears. Briefly I stood, my weight on the leg
which could take my unsteady body momentarily, before I
swivelled myself into a position where I could dump myself in the
wheelchair.

I sat quite still, looking at myself in the big mirror opposite. My
hair was uncombed and would have to wait until my daughter
came back from the job centre to deal with it. It stood in a kind of
peak on the top of my head like Tufty the Squirrel. I felt a smile
turn up the corners of my mouth, so that in the end I wanted to
laugh. The smile fled quickly enough when I looked down at my
hands which were in my lap, resting in a fold of skirt I'd yet to
have someone help me fasten. They were no longer the hands of
my memory. I still remembered them as skilled and able. Hands
that could knit up a storm, especially if a new baby was expected
in the family. Fingers that in the past had wiped away tears from
my children's faces, and held them joyously while they had taken
their first, faltering steps. Now they lay in my lap like appendages
that belonged to someone else, anyone else but me. The fingers
curled in toward the palm like the twining flesh-coloured roots of
a tree. I faced yet another morning of reality, and the reality was
that my hands were, for all practical purposes, useless, except that

I could still just about hold a spoon, in the way a toddler does when it learns to feed itself.

I looked again at my reflection in the mirror and decided to try my trick of thinking positively. It usually worked, even when nature dealt me a nasty card, like when I hurry to the lavatory only to wet myself moments before lowering myself onto the seat. I thought about my daughters and the unstinting efforts they made to make my life comfortable – my youngest daughter, who turns my humiliation at not being able to care for myself into a joke we can both laugh at – the way she combs my hair, organizes my magazines and books to be all within easy reach before going out, and notices without being asked, those times when I need someone to scratch the leg I can't reach or remove the irritating hair down the collar of my blouse. The friends who come to visit, I always claim jokily, drawn by my wit, and eloquence. Even joking like that makes the wheelchair somehow less significant.

Just before Christmas, one of my married daughters took me to town on a late-night shopping trip. I hadn't seen the big Hanley stores for a few months. To see them all lit up, bright with coloured lights and undulating with thronging shoppers, was a real treat. I had forgotten about being in the chair until we reached one of the counters of a big clothing store. I asked for a slip in my size, as none were displayed on the counter. Ignoring me completely, the assistant turned to my daughter and said, 'Tell her she can always bring it back, as long as it still has our tag on it and it's within a week of purchase'. I sat looking up at her, feeling angry at the way the woman had addressed my daughter and not myself, as though, on seeing my wheelchair, she had immediately labelled me as not having human responses at all, as though I was invisible, an embarrassment, to be somehow bypassed. My eyes flicked to my daughter's face, and I saw that her cheeks were flushed, as though she might at any moment decide to remind the assistant of my presence. Secretly, I was glad that she didn't.

Once we had bought our presents and had got into the car, the chair safely stowed in the boot, my daughter turned to me and said: 'Honestly, Mother, I nearly gave her one. I was just on the brink of giving her a right telling off.' She pushed the key into the ignition.

'I'm glad you didn't, even though I thought she deserved it. It's just ignorance that makes people behave like that, and maybe a bit of fear as well. Anyway, love, you know me. I've never thought differences could be settled by rowing about them. She'll learn.'

I saw my daughter's expression change to a bright smile as I glanced at her in the rear-view mirror. It was clear that she had stopped feeling she had to defend me, and that was the way I liked things.

Carole M. Smith Story of Growth

For as long as I can remember, I have always wanted to write books. This may sound strange in my position, because I suffer from Hydrocephalus and have never been to school. I grew up in a small village, miles from anywhere, on the outskirts of Swansea, and would never in a million years have thought of going out to work. But my mother was in the middle of the Change of Life and suddenly decided she wanted to up everything and buy a general store in the seaside village of Mumbles. My father was absolutely horrified – he was a rather Victorian figure, who believed that a mother's place was firmly in the home. Not so me – this was the opportunity I had been waiting for. I could not serve, having difficulty with adding up, but I could fill stands with bottles of lemonade, sweets etc. What I hated most was when the Cadburys van used to grind to a halt outside the shop, disgorge its load of goodies all over the floor, and leave me in a sea of chocolate. It was my job to scoop everything up as quickly as possible, label, date it and haul it all up a flight of stairs to the stockroom. All this was done to the accompaniment of the family pet wedging itself between my legs.

I made hundreds of friends in the village, most of them I know to this day. Students, teachers, housewives and one queer old stick who used to call me his favourite. He could not have been more than thirty-five or forty, but to me, David looked more like a hundred. He had grey hair, wore a long coat and carried a tatty old shopping bag containing a list prepared for him by his aunt, or guardian. For some reason, he had taken a shine to me and insisted that I serve him. I did not mind getting the things down from the shelf, but come totting-up time, I used to beat a hasty retreat, making an excuse either to tidy the shelves in the stockroom or to have a quick cup of coffee or a choc biscuit.

We sailed along for many a year, doing a brisk trade, and then the supermarkets appeared on the scene. We found that they could sell things more cheaply than we could buy them. About this time, my mother's health began to give out and we sold up. The first few months were like paradise. We bought a brand new house on an estate, with an all embracing view of Swansea Bay. My sister, who had been running the business with my mother and I, took six months off work before resuming her profession as a radiographer, and we lived the lives of ladies. However, all good things come to an end. Once everyone had resumed work, I found myself feeling restless and depressed. Gradually, I began to make myself feel ill – I don't know how, but I am sure I just did. I was missing all the company of the shop and the lovely feeling of being a useful member of society.

I began developing mysterious pains in the chest and armpits, and suffered terribly from insomnia. I kept going back and forth to the doctor, so often that, in the end, he handed me over to the neurological department at our local hospital. I saw the consultant, who told me the bitter truth – there was nothing physically wrong with me, I just did not have enough to think about; I was bored. He was the first person to suggest that I should look for a job. This was quite radical thinking to me, my parents, out of love for me, had always tried to protect me from the outside world and were made very anxious by this suggestion. However, I knew that this was what I really wanted to do, although I was very frightened of taking the plunge. The medical social worker suggested that I should start by trying something like washing dishes in a local restaurant. While she was trying to arrange this, I did part-time voluntary work in a local children's home. I would have loved to work there on a full-time, paid basis but they could only offer me voluntary work.

Finally, I got the call from Woolworth's and started in the catering department, doing pots and pans when required, and various other kitchen work. I felt this was really plunging in at the deep end, as the work was very tiring – on my feet all day and naturally, no one made any allowances for my handicap.

However, people did stare at me a lot, as mine is a very visible handicap, but hard though it was, I just had to learn to accept this, and all my work mates got used to me in the end. I was there about three years when a kind uncle of mine found me a vacancy in an hotel right in the village where we lived. This was ideal as I could now walk to work, and did not have to rely on other people to give me lifts.

The following five years were the happiest I have ever spent. These were the dazzling years before the oil crisis and the recession; business was booming and there was plenty of work for everyone. When the recession finally hit, the hotel got into serious financial difficulties and I began being laid off, and had to rely on social security for half of every year. This was a great blow to my pride, and I had got so used to working by this time that I again began to feel depressed. Fortunately, thanks to the Disablement Resettlement Officer, I was offered a place on a rehabilitation course. Once again, I was frightened of starting afresh in a new environment, but I had been very lucky to be offered the place and transport to get there and back, so I could not, in all honesty, refuse to go. The first day, I was very apprehensive and was started on dismantling cartridges. When I had become adept at this, I was shown how to make toy trucks and then was put on to soldering. I regret to say that I was my tutor's despair at this and was pronounced no good at all at soldering. Finally, they put me in the cookhouse and declared me a born caterer.

When I had finished my course, they sent me on a job rehearsal scheme. I was sent to a popular pub in our locality, and was offered a permanent job at the end. I have been there now for over a year, and am enjoying the variety of work that I am offered. A far cry from the days of just washing-up.

Twenty years ago, I would never have believed that I could hold down a job in the 'ordinary' world. I thought it was my fate to either have to stay at home or, at the very best, to be offered work in a sheltered environment. In my opinion, it is of benefit to both 'sides' to have workers with disabilities and able-bodied people working side by side. It is useful for the general public to get to know disabled people better, to know that we are just the same as everyone else, even if we do look or sound a little different. So, to everyone: Have a go – if I can do it, anyone can.

Joan Howard The Cancer Connection

I was stopped in my tracks in March 1978 with a diagnosis of breast cancer. I joined in the general panic – allowed myself to be rushed into hospital – operation and twelve months follow-up. I was given the usual prognosis – five years' survival. At fourteen months, May 1979, I had developed secondaries. At this stage, I began to research cancer and ask questions. The unsatisfactory answers I got made me decide to approach my cancer from different terms of reference. I reasoned that, if I had no guarantees with the orthodox cut, burn, and poison approach, how much had I to lose taking an alternative route? In September 1979, with the financial help of family and friends, I went to a Danish health resort which treated holistically, cancer in general and breast cancer in particular.

The establishment had been started around 1945 by a Danish woman doctor – Kristine Nolfi – who had successfully treated her own breast cancer with a raw food diet and modifications to her life style. I spent a month in treatment, being de-conditioned by immersion – not in water – but in books, different life-style and interaction with a group of international fellow pioneers. An experience in depth, in which I learned that I could take responsibility for my own health care. That I could die (in one whole piece) and, on the journey, exercise control over choices for a more personalized and less destructive treatment. I learned that cancer is a disease of the system – that tumours are the symptoms. I learned that, with cancer, I could devise an environment to support the body's immune system. I learned that preventative nutrition frames a philosophy which is capable of practical implementation. Commitment to good nutrition breeds commitment to health, which is tied to prevention and control. What I also had to recognize and acknowledge was that my degenerative problems were not only medical, but cultural – economic and political. That my overall response to my situational stressors – sex, socio/economic position, marital status, age – made a significant contribution to my development of breast cancer. Fighting cancer means making all these connections.

I soon realized that, to implement the alternative cancer regime successfully, four vital pre-requisites were necessary: the need to assimilate and process information; the need to recognize the importance of being mono-minded and selfish, the need to conserve energy, in order to sustain the delicate balance in favour of optimism instead of pessimism; the need for a support network who could maintain objectivity through pain and despair.

Returning home seven years ago, I was confused, and felt as if I was to be rendered powerless by engulfment in a tidal wave. The components of the old life had to be broken down, without personal breakdown. I had to get myself together. There was an aloneness in the therapy. I had to learn how to handle fear and discover my own courage. I had to understand and handle fear projected by others.

In objective retrospection, my cancer experience is unique to me, but is connected to all other women's experience. I am now persuaded that there are many paths to ill health – we may all end at a similar destination, but our routes are different. The road to recovery is equally individual and unique. The blanket approach to disease as practised by the NHS is therefore totally inappropriate.

Medicine should be a mixture of science and art, with a bias towards the art. If this bias were to prevail, the tenets of the Hypocratic Oath, 'First – do no harm', could be implemented.

Cancer research has made no significant progress in the last fifty years. The disease has increased dramatically and now includes a much wider and younger age group. More personal treatment choices should be made available within the NHS. Money should be diverted from orthodox research, to research into alternative systems. It is said that more people make a living out of cancer than ever die of it.

If the total picture of treatment was made more widely known, understood and available on the NHS, then patients could exercise choices at no economic cost to themselves, and be a cheaper budget for the NHS.

I must reiterate: – The accumulation of environmental stressors which lead to degenerative diseases are cultural, economic and political, and this fact must be taken into account at the initiation of any recovery programme. 'Know thine enemy.'

Marian Finan Hewitt Breakdown

She moved out of my reach.
The sun shone on
the long grass
turned into meadow
and the wind
blew it silver.

Her mind grasped
and ungrasped
my face at the door.
It was opened and shut.

I walked away frightened
mind meeting broken perception
provoking misconception.
I don't know had she lost anything
only touched what I run away from anyway.

All that evening I thought of her
open-wounded
available now
for drug and needle
ready to be stitched
into manageable conformity
made well, smiling again
welcomed back to normality.

June Burnett Observation

Protected by the talisman of touch
from her patients' piercingly indifferent stares,
she herds them from the green day-room
suddenly turned night

towards the dining-room
where naked windows,
punctured by truthful bleaching light,
bleed scant comfort on to individual fright.
Silent, she nods her head and walks among them
like a sacred Indian cow.
They move in deference before her path
on quiet rubber shoes.
Hands outstretched they beg a dispensation;
clutch at another rainbow fantasy
to drown despair.
She is Circe.
The water that she gives them
tastes of wine
and sedative.

Phoebe Nathan Fattie

I was waiting in the queue for a bus. When it came, the pushing started, and a voice called out, 'Take your time – what do you think we've been waiting for all this time?'

I was given an unasked-for lift up the step from behind. I pulled my coat tighter, trying to hide my fat. Eventually, I got a seat by the window, my legs close together, my arms squeezed up to make more room.

A woman sat next to me, glared at me, and grumbled: 'Do you want all the seat, then?' I told her that I was touching the window as it was. 'Excuse me, please,' I said later, wanting to get off. She just turned her legs to the side and I had to squeeze past! Somehow, after what seemed an age, I managed to get by all the people who were standing up in the bus, and reached the platform.

As the bus reached the stop, the conductor called out loudly, 'Hi, Ma . . . Have you got your ticket?' I hadn't, in the rush. He came over to me, asked me where I got on, told me not to do it again and finally gave me a ticket. I tried to explain that he'd been up at the front when I'd wanted to get off. 'That's right, Ma, and make room for three, eh?' Everyone laughed.

I was near to tears again. After all, I was tired of being called Ma, Mrs, Mother etc, in shops and on buses. I was fourteen years old at the time.

Helena Hinn Food

The food girl was always in the kitchen at parties, but not to eat, rather to just be around food and its presence. Food was like that to her: it lulled and comforted her, it was a safety valve. How can you lose, when food is the most important thing to you? Parties are no bore when you fantasize about fish and chips all the way through them, and you can spend your time planning strategies for late-night takeaways, routes to take, like maps in your head, covering the din.

Men were boring compared to this more private activity. Food was always there the next day, accessible forever, full of mystery. But men were unpredictable and had wills of their own: full of whims. Food had the ability to be controlled – I want to be in control . . .

Phoebe Nathan Letter from Muriel

Dear Muriel,

We'd like to talk to you about the Older Lesbian Network. We heard from a woman in the group that you have been in Gemma (a group for lesbians, especially for lesbians with disabilities) . . .

Dear Susan and Alice,

Yes, I've been with Gemma. Don't get there a lot, but if I can get a lift there, I go. I was with Gemma years ago, before I moved to Brighton and when I came back to London I called them up. They told me about the Older Lesbian Network, who are all feminists. The feminist movement is all new to me. I don't know what to think of them. I'm not a staunch man-hater, even though I don't like men physically. But I get riled up with what men do get away with, what with mugging and rape, and then the judge lets them off – it is hard to believe!

I heard about feminists, but I never came in contact. Back then, there were just clubs like Gateways, and lesbianism was all under cover. I never heard the word mentioned. Even 'homosexual' was a word used in secret. But women being lesbians – they weren't even born! Now people mention the word, but they still get hot under the collar – they think it is a terrible disease. I don't know if it will ever be acceptable. We have only the thin end of the wedge to push up the rock, and it is hard work.

I am a Londoner, I've always been a Londoner, but I went to Brighton with a friend, who I had been with for thirty years. We thought we'd retire to Brighton. But after two years there, she walked out. We'd been together so long. I was in a terrible state, even though she didn't move so far away, and it wasn't for another lover. I'd see her on the street frequently, and sometimes we would talk, but it just chewed me up. I did have a mental and physical breakdown. I was like a zombie. I had to leave Brighton. I never thought I'd be back in London. But I remember my friend saying years ago, how she didn't like old people, or little children. And all along, my friend did not like the gay scene. In Brighton, she had women friends who were married. They thought we were just friends. And we were walking along, and they said, 'I can understand men and men, but women, that's disgusting'. My friend would agree – with me standing there.

I've been disabled for thirty years, although I could get along until three years ago. I have osteo-arthritis of the spine – it's one of those diseases where you look well, but you're in pain twenty-four hours a day. Even a doctor looked at me and must have thought, 'Doesn't look like she's in trouble to me'. There is nothing to do, I just take pain killers – even stopped them a while back, but the pain did get worse, so they do work some. And I need a good bed, and the one I have is old and sags.

I am upset, to put it mildly. I applied to the DHSS for a bed, and I had this reply: I should first approach my local authority, which *may* lead to me getting some help under the Chronically Sick and Disabled Act of 1970.

I do have a disabled cab pass, which is a great idea, but unless I get a lift to a meeting or social, I do not go, as these places aren't local, and the fare is about £5 return. Some groups do help, but I'm too embarrassed to dream of asking.

I think a £50 voucher or something, for one year's free travel for the over sixty-five disabled cab, would be a great help when on supplementary benefit.

And as for closing women's hospitals, I am at a loss for words. Surely it would not put such a heavy burden on the country, for something that is vital and needed by women of all ages? There are words I could use, but you would not like to read them! I am a Londoner, and only know basic English! So many millions are wasted for so many wrong things (my idea anyway), but closing women's hospitals – it doesn't make sense.

I had a phone, down in Brighton, and after I was alone, asked Social Services if they could pay the standard charges. After interviewing me, they agreed as, like now, it is a lifeline to me. I am alone in this place all day. I was told a phone would take maybe a year to install. Lo and behold, it came in two weeks when I explained my situation (top marks given). But a man came to interview me, and later I was refused the allowance, although I had written to Brighton and asked them to verify the fact that they had made the grant.

A few things I've missed, and can't put into words without tears. No one can know the terrible isolation of loneliness; it cannot be put into words.

If only some organization could, and would, find home jobs for those capable of doing them, who could receive a small wage for extras. It would mean so much to a lonely person, to pass some hours away, to help charities maybe, or anyone connected with the lonely, I'd give an arm or leg gladly – that's how bad being alone is. And I mean alone and housebound.

Sometimes there seems no point in tomorrow. But the thought of no tomorrows cannot be dwelt on.

Home work must be found for the elderly lonely. I cannot stress this issue too much. It's so vital.

love, Muriel

June Burnett Acquaintance

There she is again,
the intruder in the smoky glass
of a dress-shop window.
The woman dogs my steps,
her head swathed in a scarf,
her brown paper face
creased with melancholy.

I toss my head and walk on by,
striding proudly within
my cloak's dark dimensions.
I am not old like her.
No cruelty has touched me.
No loss or sickness graved
its mark on me.

Home is the place
I sit in secrecy and pridefully mourn.
Plaiting coarse, unremarkable hair
into submission for another day.

Sue Vodden
A Day in the Life of Betty's Child

I've just started a Women's Psychic Development Course,
it's ever so good, you know.
'What do you do?'
Well, we sit, eyes closed, in a circle and breathe.
There's six of us and the leader.
We relax, open-up, power and protect
find our psychic centre
and go off on Journies.

I'm not very good at it, though
– well my breathing freaks me out, because I smoke too many
    fags
and my flower opens and closes.
I tell it to stop, but it don't seem to work.
I worry I'm not in touch with myself or centred enuf to do it
    properly.

Then we find our power symbol and protect.
The first time, wc went round the circle describing our symbols.
I passed – I couldn't find anything.

Then Diana Hannachild, the leader, child of Hanna, had a blue
    crystal.
Another woman, a shining silver light
But then I got this trunk of a tree,
seemed more like a pole at first.
It was rooted in the ground and it came up between my legs and
    out through my head.
It was pine and it didn't have any branches.
It's changed since then – I'm much happier with it now.

I couldn't find my protection, either, but I wasn't scared.
Diana tried to help – she offered me a circle of shining light.
She's a nice woman!
Oh, and me energy spiral – that's good!
It's lovely!

I got really pissed off on the Journey, though.
Diana said, find a meadow,
and I couldn't think what the fuck a meadow was
– that's because I'm working-class,
and before I knew where I was – we had got to the water and had
    to take our clothes off.

I really got off last week –
I went into a trance,
crawled up my vagina
nosed around the womb for a bit
then had a rest in my left fallopian tube.
And then Diana took us off to Women's City
Mmmmmmmm!
'Oh yeah, and what's that, then?'
Well, it was like a Sioux Indian Camp,
but with women instead of Sioux Indians.

Our guests showed us a psychic film.
I didn't fancy the film, so I sat by the window.
Diana said she saw me.
I still couldn't handle the film so I had a bath,
and there was this woman,

I thought she was going to bath and massage me,
but when I ended up washing myself
I wasn't sure whether I didn't get around to asking her, or she
    changed her mind.
Anyway, she lay close to the water's edge and it felt very
    intimate.

The tea business, that makes me laugh.
Every week we have these different herb teas that do different
    things to you.
They're nice, though!
One woman will go – 'Mmm, I like this, what is it?'
And Diana will say, 'It's rosemary and thyme – good for
    tension relief,'
or 'aniseed and mugwort – helps to intensify psychic states'.
One week it tasted like a bar of soap – LEMON BALM.

Kate Hall Apology at 41

        I have overfed you
        starved you
        danced you
        even wanted you
        I have hated you
        punished you
        even made love to you
        I have ignored you
        reviled you
        and occasionally liked you
        body mine
        please forgive me
        and
        don't let me down
        just yet.

GATHERING STRENGTH:

Oppression, exploitation, fear and grief

Working-class women are not oppressed: they're downtrodden, poor, wretched victims who, because of some basic flaw in their character, have made the wrong choices all of their lives. This is the media/literary stereotype that working-class women have to live with, and one that the writings in this section seek to destroy.

Working-class women's knowledge of our own oppression is a dangerous thing: we have the power to turn the system upside down. It is safer to portray us all as heterosexual victims of our weakness for the 'wrong sort of man' than to name the oppression of women by men, or to acknowledge the existence of working-class lesbians; it is safer to call badly paid, low-status jobs a 'choice' than to admit to the educational and social forces that lead working-class women to take them.

Working-class women, according to the one-dimensional media creation, have no real feelings. In the interests of 'gritty realism', film-makers and writers deal the working-class woman blow after blow, but rarely equip her with the emotional resources to cope, survive and fight back. Finer feelings are the prerogative of the middle-class. Middle-class angst is one of the most prevalent clichés of the mass media age – yet the people responsible can't seem to accept that fear, grief and sadness are part of the human condition, and not necessarily connected with class background. Perhaps we deal with these emotions differently according to class – working-class women's method of coping have not been taken seriously enough for any effective comparisons to be made.

There are no victims here: there are women responding to the world around them. There is a child's fear of abuse by her father; grief at the loss of a baby, the death of a friend, the end of a long-term lesbian relationship; there is anger at our oppression as working-class women; sadness at the destruction of our

environment. Women who have coped. Women who have
survived. Women who are getting ready to fight back.

Julie Cotterill

Sylvan Agass Ground

It's the kitten's first spring. Windy, sunny day. She dances at
every movement, skittering sideways at a leaf, a shadow. I watch.
A dirty powder-puff of a kitten, patting itself round the garden.

Then I move,

crossing its line of vision and instantly, the kitten flattens itself to
the ground, playing the game of being invisible, the game that
young things play.

I stop and look.
    Its body is in contact with the ground, from the tip of its tail to
its chin. Its paws, its belly are pressed tight to the concrete, its
nose quivers just above the dried winter's mud. I wonder what it
smells down there, what it feels, what it is thinking. I know it isn't
fear of me for, when I move, it will pounce, attacking my
slippers.
    And I wonder how long it's been since I felt the ground like
that, all along *my* body, close. How long since I treated the
ground as my friend, the only certain friend in an uncertain
world . . . ?

I lay with my nose in the dust.

I am very still.

I am very small.

My eyes are as big as a kitten's and my ears are stretched tight
round my head. I have found a good place to hide, wriggling in on

my stomach, leaving a trail behind me in the dust. I am not very big and the place seems not much bigger, the iron ribs of the bed pressing down on my back.

It is dark, too, but that is an advantage. The dust tickles my nose but I dare not sneeze. I bite hard with my little milk teeth on one of my hands which are tucked up before my face like the paws of the kitten.

Under the bed, there are long rolls of fluff. I am holding my breath to listen, but when I let it go, the rolls of fluff lift and move. I am afraid to draw in my breath in case they roll towards me, in case I suck them in. I feel them already, at the back of my throat. I want to cough. I am afraid to cough. My chest hurts from the fear of breathing and my neck hurts from being held rigid too long. The dust looks so soft, yet when I turn my cheek sideways to the floor to rest, it is gritty under my skin. I am not old enough yet to have heard the fairytale of the Princess and the Pea but I am aware already of how sensitive skin is, how it feels through layers of grit and fluff the divisions in the floorboards, even the fine-ridged surface of each plank. I can get my fingernails down into the compacted dirt between each board and hold on, pressing the floor to me, a place of safety and a place of dirt, a place where gritty tears dry on my face, leaving tight little lanes on the skin.

Perhaps I doze there.

Perhaps not.

Perhaps I shudder at the movement of a darker patch of fluff stirring, independent of my breath. Please don't let it be spiders. I am afraid of spiders. The spider raises itself on its legs and looks at me. My eye is on a level with its belly. I can look under the body, through the stilted legs, but there is nothing to see, only the patches of darker patches of fluff on fluff. Perhaps I scream, or perhaps I hear the scream in the whirl of words that is my parents' marriage, in the pitch of the row I've been listening to. Even when my ears forget, my body, fingers, cheeks, knees and toes all record the vibrations. They reverberate forever, along with my mother's screams as she drags on the arm of an angry, over-powerful animal. Then the tread of my father's feet, and the heavy breathing and the great boots protruding into the fluff. I wriggle further in, or, flipping over onto my back, grip the great curved ribs of the bed with arms and legs, squeezing myself up off the floor, away from my friend, my only friend.

The bed ribs smell of iron. They are cold, but dusty too. I make myself melt into the darkness. But I am found. I am dragged out. I am beaten. Again, the floor, the good solid floor, that meets me time and again until his rage is spent. Till I crawl at last under the blankets – dusty, too, a grainy, musty smell – and wet my knickers and drift off to sleep thinking on death and the sensation of the body rotting, feeling myself fall apart at the seams and am glad, glad that the ground wins every time, will win in the end. For it is safe in the dust. I am not a kitten. I will never attack. Nor did I know, then, how to play.

Nickie Roberts Frozen Smiles

It's in your oh-so-supercilious faces
and frozen smiles,
the pair of you,
whenever I speak to your child.
You sweat disapproval
at my Northern accent.
You're restrained and arch
with that little boy.
Bringing him up in the middle-class way.

Now I'm scared to pick him up,
swing him round,
give him cuddles,
talk to him.
Most of all, I'm scared
he'll end up repressed
like you.

Ann Lofthouse
One Parent Employment

She decided to lie
this time,
deny his existence
to the cold, dry-lipped man
opposite.
A brief swallow of guilt
was the only outward expression
but, inside,
her body twisted
and turned,
racked with emotions.

I shouldn't have to do this
she screamed from behind passive eyes
I shouldn't have to sit here
whilst you twist the knife,
yes sir,
no sir,
please give me your job sir.

She bites her lip quickly,
swallowing the hatred –
no, she shakes her head at his question,
no children
and a cold pain clutches
her insides
and races up and down her body.
Jimmy's face, freckled and happy
dances before her eyes,
a seven-year-old with
all the ability to love
and believe in human trust.
She'd tried inventing a father once,
and a grandmother who lived just down the road,

and a full-time nursery
but none had worked,
always well-typed excuses
as to why she hadn't got the job.

Crossing fingers on both hands
she stared open-eyed into his
suddenly interested face.
She could read his mind:
no late mornings,
no demands for school holidays,
no time off for silly illnesses,
no slacking for worried parent.

A sticky handshake secures employment
but the cold feeling hasn't gone,
denying his existence today
meant denying it ever after.

Sue Buddin Near the Knuckle

Brenda always had an 'ouch' in the pit of her stomach after being with her mother, who had suffered a wasting condition for the past five years. Washing the old, frail body, Brenda felt a melancholy at the loss of the ample form and quick, robust movements. Brenda also felt a gloomy rage at her mother for letting her down in this way.

In this frame of mind, Brenda put the key in the lock of her agreeable semi that Sunday morning. She had in her mind an idea (a dream?) of pleasing, happy-family Sundays. Reality was two very bored children and a moody husband, the front room awash with Sunday papers, dirty cups, socks, the odd pair of pants and various bits of rubbish. A chorus of 'When's dinner?' hit her before she took her coat off. So Brenda found herself in the kitchen, shifting paints, shoe polish, hammer and nails off the work top.

On the floor, eight inches from the automatic washing

machine, Brenda noticed a rasher of bacon, a back-rasher about
five inches long, hardly any fat on it, which Brenda herself had
bought, together with eight other rashers of bacon, on Friday
after work. She stared at the offending piece of meat, which took
on a magic quality as the kitchen seemed to centre around it.
Brenda was going to bend down and pick up the bacon, but in her
mind the image of her mother, in a bent-forward, hunched-up
position, seemed to scream at her, and then an army – a legion – of
old, bent-forward, hunched women in streets, pubs, supermarkets, after nine o'clock buses, screamed even louder in her
mind; women who had spent their lives picking up after other
people.

She didn't pick up the bacon but, instead, thought about asking
who had had the bacon out. But this would mean that she had, in
fact, noticed it, and today, she decided, she would be like other
members of the family and not notice things on the floor.

Brenda called herself a feminist, only in a whisper, but not at
work where she needed the companionship of women that she
worked with. Her cronies at work thought feminists were very

weird. Quite by accident, Brenda had once read a book that voiced all she had ever felt, and from then on she had a need, a very real need, for this new knowledge. It almost became a religion for her. With great excitement she would read out passages from these books to her mother, who to Brenda's surprise, totally understood.

At one point, Brenda became peeved at her mother for not passing on these 'new truths' to her when she was a lot younger. Instead, her mother had taught Brenda how to be a good wife and mother and to respect and care for other people, or so it seemed to Brenda. Her mother talked of the sadness and the wrath of women in the Thirties, and instead of Brenda teaching her mother the 'new truths', her mother taught Brenda the 'old truths' that generations of women have felt. Brenda began to see a pattern. Her mother gave no end of support and encouragement, and this helped Brenda to feel strong and capable.

Brenda had also attended 'women's days' at various colleges, where her daughter refused to go into the crèche. The helpers were all men. Instead, her daughter, Jade, would sigh, yawn, declare she was bored and wanted to go home, right in the middle of an interesting quarrel. These quarrels were called workshops. Jade would also drag herself over her mother's shoulder, around her neck, lay across her lap and generally pull Brenda about. All the while, the child's sighs would get louder, as if she knew Brenda wouldn't have the nerve to beat her into a bloody pulp, screaming, 'This is my day, this day is for me!'

Brenda bought her daughter books about little girls that went out and did brave things, like rescue little boys, and later books for the young feminist. Jade would thank her mother and then go back to the abundance of make-up pots in front of the mirror and try to achieve the latest look.

Brenda also had a son, Tony (named after Brenda's first love), and a husband, John (who now says he loves being enclosed by Brenda's vagina when making love, instead of penetrating her. He also thinks this is strange for sweet talk). But all this is another story. Let's get back in the kitchen with Brenda.

During the course of the afternoon, Brenda peeled, chopped and prepared Sunday lunch, but her mind was on five inches of bacon, that at different times had been kicked from one end of the kitchen to the other. At one point, her son had done a weird form of break-dancing as he skidded across the room on it. Brenda's feelings lifted; Tony looked down at the substance that had nearly had him on his backside, and for one tiny moment, Brenda thought he would bend down and pick it up; but, no, he didn't notice it. Or maybe the floor is where rashers of bacon should be, or maybe it wasn't there at all. Brenda felt familiar feelings of unreality creep up.

While she was doing things to the chicken, Jade skated past her and landed with a thud against the fridge. She smiled sweetly at her mother, whilst rummaging around in the defrosting fish fingers at various stages of rotting, and found a huge custard tart that Brenda was going to eat after everyone had gone to bed. As Jade disappeared upstairs, Brenda tried to summon up the energy to insist that Jade could not eat ten minutes before dinner, and that the tart was for herself, but Brenda had her mind on five inches of rather dirty-looking meat, which had taken on a fluffy look, and had gathered a few bits of tin foil, the odd match stick and quite a lot of cat's hair, as the cat had tried to kill it a few times and then lost interest.

From the doorway, John questioned Brenda's need to smoke while cooking. He also mentioned the fact that he was quite sure there had been fag ash in his curry the night before, to which Brenda retorted, it was a good job he hadn't noticed the dog end in the apple pie they had had for afters. John didn't see the funny side of this. Instead, he picked up a carving knife and set about the chicken (John liked to do his bit around the house). When approaching the cooker to pour the juices from the chicken into the gravy, John trod on the bacon, and he later said he saw both his feet in the air before his back hit the floor.

'For fuck's sake, Brenda, doesn't anybody ever pick up fucking anything in this fucking house?' His face contorted with rage as he reproached his wife.

What followed that Sunday was an accumulation of rage on Brenda's part that had been massing for the past three hours, or was it fifteen years? Who knows? There was much shouting, raving and tears, dinners went up the wall and the cat got so much chicken that he thought it must be the time of year when all humans sit glued to the television and the front room is a confusion of tinsel, bright paper and balloons, with a tree by the window covered in bright things that are great for a cat to knock off. Only, where were the 'Goodgirl' choc drops and the green rubber mouse that normally went with these trappings?

John asked Brenda if she had a period coming. John said maybe Brenda should get out more. John even said that Brenda might benefit from a chat with Dr Wright (who in the past had told Brenda not to think too deeply about life).

Then John said he was sorry and, yes, he would pick up bits of bacon from the kitchen floor.

Later that week, Brenda and her best friend, Maureen, were trying to recall how many men Maureen had slept with; did she or didn't she sleep with Ben the butcher or Bob the barber, or was it Kevin the car salesman? Who knows? Who cares? Certainly not Brenda or Maureen, halfway through their third bottle of cider. Brenda informed Maureen that she had pinpointed the exact moment that the female of the race starts to bend forward and pick up bacon, or whatever, from the floor.

On the Monday at breakfast, the toast was leaping from the toaster in all directions, and a piece of toast hit the floor with a very loud bang. Brenda felt this toast was meant for John. John didn't see, or hear it hit the floor.

Brenda watched as John took another slice of wholemeal, bran-enriched bread and popped it in the toaster. Maybe he thought the toaster stored the odd piece of toast for reasons best known to itself, or maybe he thought the toaster could make bread just disappear. Anyway, John ate his toast with a layer of sugar-free jam, drank his colour-free orange juice and, together with Tony, who had trodden on the toast, smashing it into tiny pieces, walked out the front door. Brenda was still standing by the fridge staring at the toast, when Jade, in her school uniform, went to the cupboard under the sink and got the dustpan and brush.

Brenda felt cold and unreal (she thought of patterns) as she watched Jade bend forward and scoop up the mess and place it in the bin. She felt sick as she heard her own voice, as if from a long way away, say, 'Thanks for doing that, darling; you're a good girl.'

Brenda thought of leaving.

Marian Finan Hewitt Broken Window

My neighbour in the flat next-door
moved out, a squatter moved in.
Children wanting excitement
broke the kitchen window
and pulled down the net curtain.

I walked over the broken glass,
peered in through the gaping hole
a place abandoned and empty now.

I smothered the scream inside me
at the utter desolation
I staked a piercing yell
in isolation
for the young kids
whose fun was destruction.

I wished that they might hear
a singing bird or catch a glimpse of
a wild rabbit scuttling to the nearest hedge.
Or lay down on a river-bank
and be filled with the sound
and consumed by the images
reflected there.
Or find beauty in a butterfly.

Anything to stop the hurting
somewhere to go to feel peace.
A child needs to know
that more than concrete exists.

He cannot be locked in for long.
It's too much to expect
that a kid might be content
boxed in between the blocks

peering out through a gap
on the balcony
from a high-rise flat.
What view can he have
unless he stands on a chair
and looks over?
That's too dangerous.
By the time he can manage the stairs
or operate the lift
he'll have no need for windows.

Josephine Zara The Yellow Dress

Once again, my father had 'forgotten' to send any money and
I, 'the eldest and the worst', as my mother often said, was
dispatched to beg credit from both butcher and grocer.

If you ever asked me (no one does, why should they?) what I
remember most about my childhood, it is that street. Long, steep,
cobbled. I remember seeing a horse fall down it once. I remember
two women fighting over a man. One rolled all the way down the
hill.

Why did the sun never shine? A feature of old age is that the
remembered summers were hot and sunny.

Not mine. Grey streets, grey houses, grey skies, when you
could see them through the factory smoke. I, at nine years, toiling
up, day-dreaming as usual, trying to find another way of saying,
'Please, could we have half a pound of liver, until my father's
money comes?'

My socks were falling down. My mother had taken the elastic
from my garters to put into the waist of the hated yellow dress she
was making for me.

Anger flushed over me. That dress! Not only yellow, the exact
colour of my skin, but frilled and sleeveless. I, who could never
wear enough clothes, layer upon second-hand layer, must, that
day, *wear no sleeves*. I saw, in my head, my long, thin, yellow
arms, I felt, in my body, the thin stuff, the stiff frills, the hated,
prying women lifting my dress, admiring the frilly matching

knickers. I remembered my mother's patient sewing. I remembered my sisters' blue and pink dresses, their curls and pink cheeks, their plump arms, and their smirking delight at the soon-to-happen, inquisitive pulling and pushing.

I was so angry, my rage spilled over onto the butcher's sawdust floor.

'Ee, luv, don't tak' on. Hasn't thee dad sent any brass? Nay, we s'all 'ave to find summat good for thee dinner. Let's see,' he said, the white gleaming scales dipping under their burden of meat without the brass weights and the holding finger. My tears dried. I was submerged by the waves of a new anxiety. Did he know we couldn't pay? Would there be an enormous sum in 'The Book' for us? What would my mother say?

He licked a careful, flattened thumb, wrapped up the meat in layers of paper and wrote something in The Book, something like 2d. 'Nay, lass,' he said, 'don't 'ee cry. 'Appen your dad'll come 'ome soon. Think on them pretty dresses your mam's mekking for Whitsuntide.'

Ali Raven Outsider

Is it just a class thing
that makes me feel like your servant,
a bystander in your life?

I cook (well sometimes),
and clean (when I have to),
and do childcare (despairing and joyful),
and work hard at not being
super-efficient, domesticated,
in order not to do it all.

And I organize our lives for us,
but always, always I'm around –
my taken-for-granted presence
a support system for you.

And it's so hard
not to give you every little thing,
as you unthinkingly assume I will,
till death do us part.

And when I assert my difference
I'm a bore (to me, if not you).
And when I don't, and float
in my depression, alienation,
I know I'm just mad,
(tho' no one hears me whisper it).

Pat Jourdan The Betrayal

Opening the door into the playgroup always broke any connection with the weather. Whatever the day had been so far, the concrete floor of the corridor always kept its own temperature. Weather, either hot or cold, never affected this corner of the building. Quite often that summer, it was blazing sunlight as Moira approached the door. Once inside, it would be quiet and grey.

Before the children appeared at half past nine, there was a frenetic furniture-moving race. The helpers rushed in and out of the storage room, with parts of the slide, sand-tray, water trough, the portable bookcase and assorted toys.

While the girls loved the dressing-up clothes, and paraded around being princesses and brides and mothers, the boys would become a teenage gang. On the rampage, wearing plastic sheriffs' jackets, they manufactured guns from the sticklebricks and went off to shoot each other.

The women felt uneasy at this, not knowing how to cope; but gradually, with a scorched earth policy, anything longer than a cigarette would be left behind in the storage room.

After a couple of moments, the gunplay would have to be diverted into something as downbeat as jigsaw puzzles. It was inevitable that, in their game of cowboys chased by a sheriff and three policemen in donated helmets, someone would fall over and be hit. Usually they cannonaded into a table corner, or upset some little girl pushing a toy pram, peaceably collecting her empty fish fingers' box from the make-believe shop.

Moira chose her moment, and swooped quickly, sending some boys to the jigsaw puzzle table and promising the others an immediate story of the *Hungry Caterpillar*. It did not always work, but this morning they acquiesced, and she thanked their immedate good natures and tolerance of adult ways.

At this point, one of those who Moira secretly called the 'top brass' called in. There was a strict hierarchy, which most of the mothers were unaware of – it stretched from the chair-woman, Mrs Crowther, down to the mother who bought the biscuits in bulk from the cash-and-carry. While most people who were around regularly soon became 'Liz' and 'Sue' and 'Linda' and 'Mary', Mrs Crowther kept her formal title, even after several years.

'Good morning, Moira,' she said loudly. By now, Mrs Crowther was so much involved in administration, that she did not concern herself with the children at all, and addressed herself only to adults. Committee bred committee in her diary. 'I have some interesting news for you. We have been asked, as an experiment, to take a little girl who is handicapped, a deaf child. She is nearly four, so you won't have any trouble with toilets and all that sort of thing. Her mother is obviously under some strain, and we have been asked to take the child for the maximum number of mornings.'

'How deaf is she?' Moira asked.

'They're trying various hearing aids, but she is too young for the specialists to know which will be the best treatment, yet. Mixing with other children will spur her confidence and perhaps her communication as well.'

'Well, I'm not quite sure,' Moira answered. 'I don't really know how the other children will react, or how we helpers will cope. What good can we really do?' The room was often so rowdy, with a mixture of sounds – hammering, tambourines, shouting, singing – that even a perfectly attuned ear would often have difficulties.

'It's as much for the mother's sake as anything else,' said Mrs Crowther. 'It's a straw she can clutch at. They are waiting for a place in a special school, but of course, it can't be arranged yet. There is a teacher of the deaf who will be calling in, so you will all be helped to be fully aware of how to approach the problem.'

The problem.

'What is this little girl's name?'

'Jenny.' And having settled the business of the morning, Mrs Crowther went across to Sue and Joan, who were cutting out sunflowers from a wallpaper pattern book. After a little chat, she was gone, with, 'Don't forget, AGM next week!' as her goodbye.

Jenny arrived the following Monday morning, with her mother. The girl was not exceptional in any way – merely an average four-year-old girl shape. But her eyes were the colour of wet autumn leaves, a deep brown. Mother, as a 'new mum', was supposed to stay the morning, but chose, instead, to leave. 'She'll be all right. Just shout at her. Keep her away from the water, it'll ruin her batteries.' With this minimum of advice, she left them.

At first, Jenny stood and watched the roomful of children. She did not look back at the green door which her mother had just closed. Moira mentioned to Sue, Joan and the others to give extra attention to Jenny. In no time, Moira was busy, taking children to the toilets, and later washing glue off Tony's hands, then unzipping Janet out of the princess dress. She forgot Jenny.

A hand clutched her skirt. She turned round and saw Jenny, who seemed to be trying to pull her over to the middle of the room. 'Urgh! Urgh!' she was saying.

'What is it? All right!' They both went across the room to the slide. Jenny pointed, agitatedly. Ben was stuck at the top of the slide, his trouser belt caught between the wood of the slide and the edge of the frame. Quickly, Moira unhooked his clothing, and he glided perfectly down to the little carpet at the bottom. He was not upset, in fact, and quite liked the bit of panic around him.

Moira turned back to Jenny and smiled. 'Good girl.' Then, thinking that might not be enough, she took both the child's hands, and held them, smiling at her. 'Thank you, you've been a great help.' It must have taken courage for Jenny to go across the large room to fetch her and try and make her understand. Beyond that, Moira was aware of the girl's concern for another child. After all, there had been several other children nearby, where Ben had been left stranded, and they had done nothing to help at all.

Not every morning that Jenny was with them was a success. Often, she disrupted rhyme-time, when they all sat and joined in singing nursery rhymes together. Unable to hear what was going on, and yet meant to sit still for ten minutes, Jenny would get up, wander around, turn her chair sideways, and tap other children on the arm. Occasionally, she hugged one in sheer delight; they always protested, and claimed she was fighting. Her sounds frightened them.

Storytime, later, intended as a calming-down time just before the parents collected their children, was a similar disaster. Jenny distracted the other children and generally made it even more difficult for whoever was trying to hold the children's attention.

Over the weeks, however, Moira grew to appreciate the warmth that the little girl gave. She would have been different from the other children anyway, even if she had had perfect hearing. She had something of the perkiness and vulnerability of a sparrow, or any half-wild, small animal. This, combined with an amazing awareness and concern for other children. The incident of Ben on the slide was not the only time Jenny drew Moira's attention to fights and other difficulties. In the morning, she ran towards Moira or Sue, hugging their legs, which was as high as she could reach, giving strange, guttural sounds. 'Hello-o, Hello-o, Jenny,' they would say loudly, as instructed.

Her teacher also arrived, now and then, pointing out how they could talk to her more, how to hold her still while they spoke, how to exaggerate each sound. Language broke down under such crude treatment; nothing subtle could be communicated. Frequently, Jenny backed away from such invasions of herself, frightened. They were hurting her with their talking.

Teaching her to say wat-er, sa-and, bo-ok, seemed like attacking her with sledgehammers. 'You've got to get her to talk to you,' the teacher said. 'Don't let a morning pass with her remaining isolated.' At times, Jenny did seem lonely, she was apart, but Moira felt that it was only because Jenny was already complete, with her deafness. The problem, as they called it, was their uphill task of breaking her up and re-making her as a speaking person.

The mother checked her progress. Every morning she would

ask, what had Jenny done? 'Has she behaved? Has she done a picture? Did she say anything today?' Moira decided that she would have to make an effort to keep Jenny under close observation for a morning, so there would be something to report to her mother.

Moira watched Jenny closely the next day. There were so many instances that the mother did not see. Jenny was at the sand-tray, trickling sand through her fingers. Babbling to herself. It was the sound of water, the actual voice of water. It was the sound of streams, of fishes, of open air, light, spray and movement. Moira could not have made that sound herself. Later, standing at home, looking out of the window at the rain, she would think that it was beyond the subtleties of even the most sophisticated scat-singer. Only deaf Jenny could make an all-encompassing language, which reached out so far from the shut-in playroom.

Jenny's mother stood by the door, taut, hurried, almost accusing. She seemed to need something, or maybe she made Moira feel guilty for her own happiness that morning. It had been exceptional, after all.

Jenny was brought to her mother. Slightly loath to go, yet too loyal to show she wanted to stay. Sometimes, children cried at the end of a session; by midday, they had grown into each other and the room, and resented being ripped away from the pattern they had created themselves. Home could mean an empty house and a miserable mother. Perhaps Jenny was not aware that such options were open to her, that she could make a scene.

The mother was still standing by the door. Moira felt sorry for her. Without meaning it to happen, pity grew in her. What could she give to this unhappy, forever-to-be-obsessed woman? She searched for some happy item of news to give her about the morning. Definitely not the babbling that Jenny had done. No painting, no glueing. There was nothing tangible to give.

The mother pointed to a row of labelled pegs where the children's work was always hung. 'She's done nothing this morning, then.'

'No. Oh, wait a minute, she said something today. Put on the dressing-up clothes and said "Hat". She said "Hat". And she's getting on so much better with the other children.' A lie. Moira was halfway across the room, carrying an easel, so this news came out rather incoherently.

The mother smiled briefly. Like a camera shutter, the smile passed over and went. Jenny meekly put her hand in her mother's, and they walked down the corridor.

If Moira had said, Jenny made the most beautiful sounds, that brought back to me all the width of a day in the country, all those sounds made into one flowing, coursing song; if she had been able to say that, the mother would have dismissed it.

That evening, at home, Moira sat and listened to music from James's record collection. It had somehow become the usual thing after dinner. Moira had drifted into a pattern of marriage which seemed to be totally on his terms. One of those terms was evenings spent listening to classical music. James preferred drawn curtains and stereo to the outside world. A perverse corner of her mind longed for a real beery man, who would lurch back from the pub bringing news, fresh gossip from that outside, men's world.

'It's all too safe. I'm shut in at playgroup, and I'm shut in at home,' she thought. Suddenly, it occurred to her that Jenny had 'said' this part of Beethoven's Pastoral that they were now listening to.

'We've a deaf girl at playschool lately. Almost completely deaf. And she said this today,' Moira pointed at the stereo, just like the mother had pointed at the empty peg. 'She makes noises to herself, babbling, just like this.'

'Really, dear?' James poured out another drink as the second movement came to a close. Moira, with another of her flights of fancy. The sooner she left that silly job, the better. Not as if it were a real job, either. He gave her a glass of sherry, as if it were medicinal.

'I'm boring him,' she thought, looking into the yellow liquid and thinking of fishes, while the music continued into its storm.

Sally Flood Whose Justice

Thru' the iron grating –
I looked at your face
Thru' the meshed wire
no way of whispering encouragement
or touching your fingers
no soothing words could break the glass between.
The peaked cap shadowed on the wall
dried the tears that spoke.
I listened to the noise
    that grew like thunder
As last goodbyes
    were shouted and you joined the lost legion
        of youngsters.

So young – so vulnerable
the ways of law unfathomable.
And I, helpless,
    a stranger to justice.
I looked at this man
    who judged you by your accent
the policeman – who saw promotion
the jury – who wanted lunch
and learnt the bitterness
that comes with knowledge
that justice is outweighed by power.

Jan Revell
A Right Time for What Was And What Could Have Been

Don't you sometimes feel that you're just doing things to pass the time until you die?

A depressing, even a morbid thought? Yes, maybe, but it was one that had passed through Lily's mind often, over the years.

Why did it always take a time of crisis to make her appreciate her life?

People began to pile slowly out of the crematorium and form small, chattering groups. Lily stood away from them, alone, almost symbolizing the situation she now felt. It was mid-March, an early spring day, the air was still and the sun was warm on her, yet as a puff of smoke rose from the chapel chimney, a chill edged its way slowly through her body. 'This is it, then; Ted is dead, what now?' she thought to herself. 'Was it only two weeks ago that I was celebrating my sixtieth birthday and looking forward to doing all those things that the so-called freedom of retirement promises?' She heard her name being called and turned to acknowledge the person, in one sense annoyed at the interruption of her solitude, but in another sense relieved that she wasn't to be left alone and her thoughts allowed to become morbid.

It wasn't the right time yet.

A hand rested lightly upon her left shoulder: 'Are you okay, Mum?' She smiled slightly, and it crossed her mind that she wasn't entirely alone. It was her son, Jamie. She was thirty-six when Jamie was born. His father, her husband, hadn't wanted children at all, and made no bones about telling Jamie what an unplanned mistake he was. He had resented Jamie, and even at the age of twenty-four years, as Jamie now was, Ted had insisted on calling him 'boy' in a very patronizing and derogatory manner, that ably conveyed this resentment to Jamie. But to Lily, Jamie was her son and, for all his faults and shortcomings, she loved him and needed him, now more than ever.

People started to make their way over to the lone pair, shaking Jamie's hand, patting Lily's shoulder and generally offering their condolences.

Lily was pleased that the funeral was over, the last week had seemed a nightmare, but at last she was to be left in peace, to be able to go home and be alone with her thoughts.

'Mum,' said Jamie, 'come on, we've got to go now, the car's waiting to take us home. Everybody else has already gone back to the house.'

'Okay,' she said quietly, yet as she walked towards the car she felt her whole body screaming inside: 'No! No! Why can't you all just go away and leave me in peace?'

She knew they all meant well, but the thought of having to be polite and pleasant for a couple of hours more, was almost more than she could bear. The car journey home passed too quickly for her liking, and soon she was back in her own home.

'Jamie,' she said, 'look, I'm sorry, love, but this is more than I can cope with right now, you just go in and thank everyone for coming and give my apologies, but I think I'll go up to my room for a while.'

Lily entered her bedroom and sat on the wicker chair by the window. She sat staring, her eyes not focussed on anything in particular, just waiting for the onslaught of morbid thoughts to enter her mind, now that she was alone.

It's the right time now, she thought. But they didn't come. No breakdown, no tears. Instead, she found herself thinking about her retirement celebration and all the things she and Ted would have been doing and planning. She felt angry and cheated. Suddenly, it seemed that everything she had spent her life striving for was to be denied her, and she wasn't going to let that happen.

Downstairs, Jamie thanked everyone for attending, and explained that his mum had gone to rest for a while – she'd had a tiring week with all the arrangements, etcetera. Everyone nodded in agreement, and the small, chattering groups of the crematorium re-formed. Relatives and friends eagerly collected as much information as possible about the missed years of their lives together. After endless cups of tea and sandwiches, people began to leave in ones, twos and small family groups.

'See you at Leslie's wedding,' seemed to be the parting comment.

The days, weeks, months, went by. Lily had picked up the threads in her life and carried on. But still there was no breakdown and no tears. It was still not the right time. She spent her time dreaming of what her life might have been after retiring, the holidays, their caravan by the sea, their new car, refusing to accept what it now was.

One year later, almost to the day, Lily's mother died. She was ninety-two and had been ill in hospital for three-and-a-half years. The thoughts of a year ago had re-occurred, but Lily was not alone this time. She had her younger sister (by three years), and together they shared their unspoken emotions. Yet in their silence, Lily shed her burden of all that she had kept bottled inside her for the last year.

After the funeral she went home, and found herself sitting yet again in the wicker chair, staring out of the window. Only this time, there was no anger, no feeling of being cheated, just tears, endless tears and uncontrolled sobbing and suddenly, she knew this was the right time, at last, to cry for what was. The time for what could have been was over.

Nan Dalton Last Swim

Once more here,
dread time of year
watching, watching
the sea.

The knot of fear,
once more here
as a wave curves
into the shore,
sending an invitation
on rainbow-coloured spray
and I watch them running barefoot
into the sunlit bay.

Marooned on my picnic island,
I shield my eyes and search,
but bobbing heads all look the same,
as they swim among the surf.
Panic grips my senses as I
lie helpless on the beach.
Do they know there's an undertow,
that a freak wave lies within reach?

Mouth dry, heart beating fast
I shut my eyes and pray,
till suddenly they're beside me
glistening and wet with spray.
Their skins are cool to my hungry touch
as they tell me how good it's been
then eat as though they'll never stop
as I force hot tea through my teeth.

All packed up, time to go,
just one last look at the sea,
knowing that next year
will find me
once more here,
dread time of year,
watching, watching the sea.

Eileen Shaw From 'This way up'

Hatred dies down, given time, they say; it fizzles out like a
firework, a faded red and yellow cylinder gradually disintegrating
into the muddy November lawn, trodden down to mingle with
the worms and the soil and the beetles and the cold, sleeping
roots.

At the hearing, when Dorothy and Frank got divorced, my
granny attacked Frank with her umbrella. He lied his boots off,
and I kept thinking, 'When are they going to stop this farce?'
Dorothy sat, stupid and stunned, too awed to say a word. But
when my granny rushed at him, as if beating off a mangy dog
from a dustbin, we came out of it, and Dorothy ran forward,
unable to suppress a smile. I wanted to cry, the silly bravura of a
single thwack on his shoulders, Granny's way of rounding off the
day; and he cringed forward, didn't look back, made off with his
soldier's march. That's when the hatred should have stopped.

His parcel of crimes was grubby and mean, wrinkled brown
paper tied with string and left at the railway luggage office.

Within a week, it starts to smell, and the attendant calls the police. When it is opened, it is found to contain a human heart, Dorothy's heart, broken, naturally. A pedestrian little parcel of hopes and dreams and the ribbons of romance, shrunken and mangled and ripped into shreds. Dorothy's true heart, beating still, with a dumb, suffering thud.

Still it goes on, though she has nothing to do with it, not even a cat to stroke or a child to comfort, not even Jesus any more.

We went to Granny's flat for a cup of tea afterwards, and Dorothy played some old records to cheer herself up. I could feel her brain working in her head, wondering what she had done to deserve the treachery, passivity like a lump of porridge in her working, clogged-up brain. Then came Ally in a new car, banging on the door and frightening my granny. She's never done anything wrong in her life, never owed a penny, never stolen a farthing, but she still expects retribution to strike, waiting for that final knock. I went with him, suddenly excited by his glamour all over again, telling Dorothy I'd be home by eleven. I didn't come home for six days that time; we went to Wales and lived in a tent, and when I got back Dorothy had sunk into her own despair, like a bog closing over her head, sucking her down. The more she struggled, the deeper it pulled her down.

We didn't fight him, Fighting Frankie, neither of us; we let him arrange things, let him rule us, just so the small moments of escape would be possible, while we kept body and soul together on his money. It was easier for me of course, I wasn't chief cook and bottle washer, just a minion, a scullery maid. An invitation to go with Valerie Lambert and her wonderful mother and airforce father to visit their relatives in the country, was one such moment of escape.

When I think of how I looked up to Valerie Lambert, I am amazed. I was like some snotty-nosed kid gazing at a princess, because she did everything right, she had everything it was possible for me to want: a piano, a Morris Oxford van, a record-player, a quiet, neat, well-ordered house, a pretty brown-haired mother, perfect poise and generosity, the peachy skin and gleaming teeth of good health, the small, neat-boned face of a television newscaster, a skirt in nasturtium, the season's colour, so yellow-orange, vibrant, describing the perfect sunny day of her existence. There she is, in my memory, in some enchanted glade where we stopped for a picnic lunch. Scramble-down crags and hollows of feathery grass, and the sky a back-drop of blue and white and gold. She never sulks, her father never shouts, and her mother has the happy innocence of a Sunday School angel.

Then tea in the farmhouse, a white table-cloth spread with luscious temptation, strawberry jam and melting sponges, crumbling, golden pastry and yellow butter cream, and I know I must not take another but I can't resist, hardly daring to lift my head, trying to restrain the urge to cram food into my mouth, enough for an army, I think, enough to feed hundreds, oh, they surely must mean me to eat it, anything else would be torture! And nothing is said; the relatives are kindly people, bewildered by the lumpish child in the dress too-long and the broad, uncertain face; there is the merest hesitation in their manner.

'Frances writes wonderful stories, doesn't she Val? I've never known such imagination in a little girl.' The gentle eyes rest on the greedy child who is suffocating with a mouth full of butter cream, can't say anything, can't talk, even if my mouth were empty, and I have the hollow sensation of being a curiosity on display, though I couldn't blame them; my behaviour, by their standards, is bizarre.

Valerie Lambert had a kitten and a bicycle, and a father who exhibited interest and amusement when he spoke to her. They moved out of town and I lost touch, though I did visit once. They lived on an estate with identical, semi-detached houses, each one as neatly and lovingly tended as a stately home, they lavished love on their gardens and their paintwork and, to me, suburbia seemed like a glossy magazine picture come to life, charming and scented and put up for the photographer.

Valerie seemed grown up. She wore lipstick and had her cardigan on back to front, jiving with her friends at an end-of-term dance. I sat like a sack and watched her, and my mean nature now suggests to me that she wanted me, lumpish and wide-eyed, for an audience; to stare with wonderful concentration, like a snotty-nosed kid at a princess.

When the boys called to Valerie Lambert, she giggled and ran away. She wouldn't talk to them, she had this hysterical effervescence that I interpret now as fear and a middle-class, self-preservation instinct, though at the time I merely thought she was stupid. She thinks they have something contagious, I thought, and stumped after her with private disdain.

One, in particular, calls to her; David Webb, with the curly hair and the broad, flat wrists and the acrid smell of a man. Neat though, like her, as if made all in one piece and not thrown together with odd-fitting limbs like the rest of us. It is obvious that they are made for each other, and I can't understand the running away, my heart beating fast and melting for her, oblivious to danger. David Webb looks and waves, waves and looks, and Valerie Lambert flies.

One afternoon, I see David Webb, lying down in the grass over the beck. I am there picking flowers, mooning about, the inside of my head peopled by images; a teacher who scolded me, a girl who loaned me her new red pen, Mrs Fontaine, next door, who said I had lovely eyes. I see the unmistakable blond frizz, lit by bleaching sun, and it lifts until he sees me. He's much older than me, sixteen or seventeen to my twelve, and he's somehow complete and definite while I am unfinished, undefined. If Valerie were with me, we'd be running now, but on my own, my legs are made of lead. He's almost big enough to be a man, David Webb, a local heart-throb, Dorothy said, with her ironical throaty laugh. I stand paralyzed, staring, my images are gone, like a curtain coming down at the theatre.

'Here, come here,' he says with urgency, but not raising his voice. I don't even think of disobeying, though I know it's wrong; he shouldn't even be speaking to me, he loves Valerie Lambert. I go through the long grass, sun spraying down its suffocating heat like an aerosol. Somehow, I lie beside him, and he puts something into my hand. He is impersonal, not looking at me, locked in some compulsion of his own. I say nothing, subdued and sweating, and the thing is pale and smells hot; it is flesh-coloured but sallow, like something that got locked up some time ago and never got any air to it, but it doesn't threaten me. I feel detached and connected both, and he's breathing fast; is this it, then?

He hasn't touched me, just given me this long, warm sausage thing to hold, moving it with small jerks of his trunk so it's only my sticky inert hand that is necessary, the rest of me a superfluous lump stuck on the end. And now he moans, I can't look at his face. The sound excites me but I don't know why; a bitter, thrilling shock runs through me. There's something warm and itchy on my fingers, like a tickling insect, and he takes the thing from me in one polite movement and says, 'You mustn't say anything,' in his funny hoarse voice, 'you know that, don't you?'

I get up, walking quickly away, shock tingling through me. Now I run, throwing away the flowers, afraid to look back. I held bluebells all the way through. Did he sound scared? Should I be scared too? I thought they were supposed to kiss you? I start to feel frightened, a choking sensation in my chest, wanting to cry. I won't tell anyone. Ever. As long as I live. I don't cry, I feel guilty and blot it out from my memory. Even now, I don't admit to myself that it really happened, pretending that it's just a figment of my famed imagination.

But it did, it happened. You heard the unholy screech of the sawmill in the distance, and you see it now, that light blossom of curls in the grass, and the cabbage whites alighting on clumps of thistle. He was there, and he gave you his warm sausage thing to hold, which you blindly took and serviced with grimy nails and a bunch of broken bluebells. Laugh now, at the crushed green stems and the witless girl.

Margot Henderson Birthday Cloud

(After Chernobyl)

Saturday third of May
rounds his second year
spent dreamlike
in his element
he counts the bright beads
timeless in the belly of a shell
while we look, wordblind
into the eyes of clouds.

Till struck
the flicker of a flame
dances on a fruit-filled plate
a light his mother softly folds
into the corner of her drawer to keep.

Caught in the cry
of children's games
we pass around
the ice-cream and the latest counts
as through a shrinking window
the same mad sense
of placing unescorted children on a train
out of Kiev.

Susan Evasdaughter A Wumun's Work

In 1967, when I left school, the secondary modern was still considered an acceptable place to send working-class kids, to train us in skills that would be useful for our future rôles as factory workers and housewives. In Huddersfield, the Yorkshire town where I grew up, most of the products of these second-class educational institutions were destined, in those pre-recession days, for work in one of the numerous local mills.

I had resented being sent to a secondary modern school, and I resented even more the idea that I should go to work in a mill. My elder brother, having just scraped through the Eleven Plus exam, had flourished at grammar school, and was later to earn a scholarship to Cambridge. He had slipped through the net which is intended to keep the classes separate, whereas I had been firmly caught within it.

When our class, 4A's, turn came to visit the Youth Employment Bureau for what was misleadingly known as 'careers advice', I said that I would like a job working with children. I thought that this would be a less alienating alternative to mill or factory work. I had already established with teachers that, to be a vet, or anything else that sounded vocationally exciting or had

231

interesting prospects, necessitated the possession of the kind of exams that were only available to pupils at the grammar school.

The Youth Employment Officer suggested that I work on a factory production line, packing teddy bears into cardboard boxes, but the connection with children being too tenuous, I declined. My request for a living-in job met with more success and I was soon found a place working in a hotel. To say that my homelife, since my father's remarriage two years earlier, was difficult would be an understatement, so the prospect of leaving home had great appeal.

Had my father still been a widower, I would probably have stayed at home to look after him and my two brothers, but as things were, my stepmother was intent upon me following in her footsteps as a weaver so that I could help to support the new baby. On a brief visit to the mill, I had found the noise of the automated looms deafening and the stench of engine oil mixed with lanolin from the wool and dye from the adjacent sheds, sickening.

By leaving home, I would escape my stepmother and my future as a mill-girl, but I would also lose contact with my dad and my brothers. Not having been welcome at home during the past two years, it came as no surprise that, if I left, I would never be welcome there again. 'If you go now, you go for good, my girl,' was my stepmother's stern warning.

So, just after my fifteenth birthday, my bridges burnt, I set off for Clapham, a tiny picturesque village in the Yorkshire Dales, and the New Inn Hotel that was to be my home for the next nine months. Here, despite the newness of everything, all the hard work, the beauty of the surroundings and the sheer relief of getting away from home, I felt very alone in the world.

Hotel work was hard. My day began at seven with early-morning teas and breakfasts, which I delivered to the guests' bedrooms; then there was my own breakfast in the bleak staff dining-room at the back of the huge kitchens, followed by breakfasts served in the restaurant. I was also responsible for all the hotel cleaning: bar floors had to be Hoovered or mopped, depending on whether they were intended for use by the local farmers or the tourists and wealthier villagers; fireplaces had to be cleaned out, re-laid and, in the case of the cocktail bar, the red-brick fireplace had to be polished, and the dining-room halls and stairs needed hoovering. The bedrooms were just kept tidy until guests left, when, of course, they were cleaned out and the linen changed. Aside from the expensive food available in the kitchens, the guest rooms offered one of the few opportunities I had for 'perks' in that job. I would try out the guests' various expensive perfumes as I tidied their rooms, and collect forgotten soaps and shampoos they left behind them.

The job I hated most was sorting out the dirty linen which gradually built up over the days, as greasy kitchen towels, stained table-cloths, wet bar cloths and used sheets and pillow cases were thrown onto the bare wooden floorboards of the staff bathroom. The staff bathroom, which was always overheated because the hot-water pipes for the whole building seemed to converge in its cupboards, was an incongruously scruffy place in the midst of all the wall-to-wall carpets and plush furnishing of the public rooms on that floor.

The piles of dirty linen added to the contrast. On my first day sorting the dirty laundry, I was quietly counting through the items and marking them down on the list in the little blue laundry book, when, to my horror, the whole stack suddenly came alive with huge black crawling things. I rushed down in some distress to the bar manager, my immediate boss, asking him to do something – but I soon realized from his reaction that there was nothing to be done, and that it was quite normal for the laundry to be found in this condition. Thereafter, I managed to sort the laundry by half-looking the other way as I picked up the offending items of linen between finger and thumb, holding their very outer corners.

After serving and clearing lunches, there were three hours in which I was free while the bars and restaurant were closed. I would take the boss's labrador and roam the nearby hills and fields. About once a week, at this time of the afternoon, the bar manager would give me a lift in the boss's huge Wolsey, into Settle, the nearest town, and I would wander round the shops until it was time to meet up with him again for a lift back. Those trips to Settle were the only time I got away from the village, but I didn't really feel that I was missing anything. Fashion, discos and mixing with other young people weren't an option for me, so I didn't seem to miss them. The only concession I made to the existence of that other world was to buy the occasional hit single on those visits to Settle, although I didn't possess a record player on which to play them.

Back on duty by six, in the blue overall and red pinafore that I always wore while I was working, I served evening meals until around ten. While I was working in the dining-room, I had to learn Silver Service, which comprised serving food from stainless-steel trays held in one hand, with a spoon and fork held in the other, plus a number of little extras, like filleting fish, mixing steak tatare, and setting fire to various exotic dishes prepared over a flame at the customer's table. Usually, I coped quite well with keeping my mind on the proceedings of about six tables at once, but once I remembered that a table had ordered wine with their main course when I was serving their sweet.

Myself and a boy from a nearby village were the only regular dining-room staff. We both got the same wages, but I was the only one who did any cleaning, he was strictly a waiter. Our wages for a six-day week were just under five pounds, most of which was made up from tips, which we had to put straight into a tin. The contents were divided into named sections so that it could be checked to see that each person had been putting in their share. When tips were low, so were the wages, but no matter how generous the customers were, our wages never rose above five pounds.

At busy times like Easter, two or three extra girls would be taken on, and it was at such times that the owner of the hotel chose to take sexual advantage of his powerful position. In the midst of the lunchtime rush, we girls were ushered into the private dining-room at the back of the main restaurant. Once there, this small man of about fifty-five, with dark, greasy hair, beady eyes and a thin moustache, his well-rounded belly protruding from the dark waistcoat of the dowdy suit that comprised his usual apparel, told us to remove our uniforms.

As my workmates stood there in their underwear, I felt a small sense of victory for having worn my skirt under my uniform. I think I murmured something about having a cold or 'the time of the month', as he proceeded to douse us all with cheap Eau de Cologne. His explanation for this little ritual was that he liked to have us smelling nice for the customers! Although it only took place once during my time at the hotel, the idea of this frightening and degrading scene had worried me ever since my interview for the job, when I had been warned about it by an older wumun who frequently visited the hotel and seemed to be having some kind of relationship with the owner. Looking back now, it seems surprising that he dared, and even more surprising that we felt obliged to comply. I had warned all the new girls of the probability of it happening, and we had all agreed that we would refuse to take our uniforms off, but when the time came, we were all too scared to resist.

Another of the boss's unpleasant habits was spying on people, 'Watergate style'. No one ever discussed what was going on, but Chef used to shout into what looked like a small speaker on a shelf in the kitchen, and I would hear strange sounding voices sometimes before taking in the boss's early-morning tea. Later, I found out that he had receivers planted all over the hotel, including one that I spotted on top of the wardrobe in the bedroom that was usually allocated to honeymoon couples.

Just before Christmas, without any warning, to me at least, the hotel was sold and the new owning family moved in. The new boss wanted smartly-dressed waiters in bow ties and black and white uniforms, and I was given a week's wages in lieu of notice. I was unsure what 'in lieu' meant, but when the new owner explained that I had to leave right away, I set off for my grandma's in South Yorkshire.

Jane Toms
How I Sat In A Social Security Office – And Remained Dignified

---

I had moved house, and had to visit the social security to discuss the matter and to obtain a rent rebate. I did not have to make an appointment, but felt that would have been easier for me. I arrived at 11.50 am into a smokey atmosphere, which made matters worse. I took my ticket – number 23, which meant that seventeen people had to be seen before me. After calculating

seventeen times five minutes for each person, that equalled 85 minutes. So I settled in for an hour and a half stay – maybe less, if I was lucky.

A young girl, who I gathered had just left grammar school, did the interviewing. Only once during the day did another person help her. Number 22 – the man before me – was impatient; he had had a little to drink and was smoking nervously. He told them to hurry up and press the button. At least we could hear Plymouth Sound, which was being piped throughout the building. The smoke was getting me down, so I went out on to the landing and looked out of the window. Then I went for a ride in the lift – to the ground floor and back again. I saw that number 17 was being interviewed. Good, I thought, only seven to go. They had been interviewing number 17 for twenty minutes.

A little girl walked out and said to her dad with a sigh: 'Oh, dad, we can go home now!' By this time I was feeling jittery and wishing I were a smoker so I could have some relief. Other people were looking jittery, some were smoking. It was now 1 pm. I wished they would hurry up, before someone exploded. Still number 17. I should have taken a packed lunch. A phone call or a letter would have done for what I wanted to see them about.

The News at One – Plymouth Sound. The Queen visiting Plymouth, having lunch at Manadon College. On the menu: trout, strawberries and cream. People laughed. Looked hungry. You couldn't even buy a drink or a sandwich here. Still number 17 being seen . . . must be their favourite number. People came in, mostly in twos. I wished I'd brought a friend with me, like visiting the dentist. The bloke before me went up – number 22. He looked very annoyed, his language didn't sound too good. They pressed button number 18. The time – ten past one. Five to go before me.

One or two people were falling asleep. Next time, I'd bring my knitting. I could have knitted a jumper by now. Plymouth Sound were playing a record by The Carpenters, light relief. It reminded me of times gone by, happy times.

The door opened to the Inner Sanctum, letting someone out, and was then locked behind them. Still number 18. More people were arriving, looking fresh. They wouldn't be looking so calm and bright-eyed when they left. Plymouth Sound was telling us to go on a boat trip. If we ever got out. The smoke was getting in my eyes. I went outside. I came back again. Still number 18.

The impatient man went up to the girl again. Twenty to two. He shouted: 'Ridiculous!' I won't say what else. He was coughing and spitting on the floor. He lit up a fag and spat again. My stomach didn't feel too good by now. It was the longest couple of hours I'd spent for a long time. Should I spit, too, I wondered? He went up to the interviewer and threatened to be sick all over the carpet if she didn't hurry up and see him. Luckily, he decided to call it a day and go home, shouting as he did so: 'I'll be here, first thing Monday morning. I am sick and tired!' I was glad he had gone, but at the same time I felt sorry for him. Plymouth Sound was still shouting out: 'Larry Speare for carpets and beds – hooray for Larry Speare!' Which reminded me of an interview I had heard with Larry Speare and David Bassett recently. He told us how poor his parents had been – their six children, at one time, had had only one pair of shoes between them and could not go to school.

Plymouth Sound time – nineteen minutes to two. Someone was eating crisps. I felt hungry. I heard a newcomer saying: 'Oh, they have a radio in here now!' It sounded as though they came here regularly. I could have gone shopping and come back again. I'd been waiting this long for five minutes of their time. Number 19 went in. Some people left before their number even came up. The man with the little girl had come back. 'What, are you still here?' he said. I saw the officer. She told me to borrow my rent money until my allowance came through. I'd borrowed enough money already. I'd heard that's what they normally said. The rest of the information she gave me sounded as before, like a recorded message. I left at 2.30 pm. It was nice to get out in the fresh air after two and a half hours inside. I felt like crying. I hope I do not have to go back for a while.

Violet Verlaine Carole

(for my friend who died of cancer)

> She was such a beauty, I remember her well
> Now all I have left are photos to tell
> Of radiance supreme and a voice that was clear
> Never again her sweet voice I will hear.
>
> Just twenty-nine years old, a wife and a mother
> So easy it was to respect and to love her
> A queen she was, with features so fine
> How ravaged by scalpel, pain, and time.
>
> Yet her spirit remained in eyes full of feeling
> And into her room I found myself stealing
> To look through her window in childish delight
> As together we shared a wonderful sight . . .
>
> . . . a rainbow she saw, and this gave her hope.

Margot Henderson For Rosemary

In the picture house
you began to lose
your life-blood
and your child.

Down the main street
and through the close
straightforward and secret
you found yourself home.

In the living-room
you bled discreetly
not wishing to offend
your sleeping father
in the set-in bed.

In the early hours
home from the nightshift
my father found you wrapped
in bleeding sheets.

The close women of the tenement
with whom you shared
the bluebell china
and the kitchen talk.
They came and went.
Then the Egyptian doctor
who from both
heredity and practice
was bound to be familiar
with such passing
in and out of life
and who since confessed
his faith restored
by your observance of last rites
and your refusal to commit
your unmade child to flame.

Instead, my father made
from his good watch box
a peg-sized coffin
for your first misborn
and took you after
to the grave dug in the glen
long since the witness
of your early love.

Di Mason Screaming in a Bucket

'And why did you go after Daryl like that, Mary?' The trick cyclist peered over heavy, dark-rimmed glasses at her, small and insignificant in the opposite, uncomfortable armchair. She shifted restlessly in her seat for a moment and scowled, wanting to shout and swear at him for his lack of understanding. If these boys were supposed to know everything, this one was falling down on the job somewhere. He didn't know nothing about the pain of being two-timed, in care, and surplus to family requirements. It was tough at the Home, and only the strong survived.

'He went off with somebody else, didn't he, and I wasn't having that. I took him for a walk last Friday, he thought I wanted to make up with him, but he didn't know I had an iron bar down the leg of my jeans,' she laughed. 'He won't be doing that for a while, nobody messes me around and gets away with it!'

But Daryl had messed around; she felt sick and the room seemed to throb before her eyes. She laid back in the chair for a moment, her spiky, burning bush of orange and green hair clashing aggressively with the restful pastel decor of Doctor Wendel's office.

'It wasn't a very nice thing to do, though, was it?' He shook his head. He had been treating her for that bad temper since she was taken into care at the age of twelve. There was a history of drinking and family violence that seemed to be inbred in this one, and she was still only fifteen. She lit up a fag, taking three long drags, tapping the ash deliberately onto the ten pounds-a-square-foot pile carpet. The doctor blanched. No, he wasn't going to lose his temper, that was what she wanted.

'So, what d'you want me to do about it?'

She felt better now, sensing the good doctor's unease. It took her mind off the lack of periods for three months. Daryl deserved to be in intensive care, her only remorse was that she hadn't settled him for good.

'You very nearly killed him, Mary! You could have gone to prison, and what about Mrs Harvey? Surely there was no need for that?'

'That old cow!' She took another drag on her cigarette and laughed. Mrs Harvey was deputy matron at the home. They had one pound fifty a week pocket money, every Friday. Mary had spent hers on cider, with a bunch of mates she had outside the Home. They were all eighteen and older, so it was easy to blend in with them in pubs and that. A lot of the kids spent theirs on glue, getting it with the optional free plastic bag from that pillar of the community who ran the local general store. She sniggered; he ought to ask whether it was business or pleasure, every time he sold the stuff. She didn't like glue much – booze was a lot more effective.

The incident with the old woman had happened after a Friday night drinking session. They were supposed to be in by nine o'clock, but she'd strolled in with an empty cider bottle at half ten, feeling merry and good humoured, might even let Mike have his way tonight, providing John (that wimp who slept in, to supervise them at night) wasn't too active.

It was all too good, though, and when that woman stood there, bristling like a yard broom, demanding an explanation, it had got her back up. She could remember hitting out with the bottle. Mrs Harvey fell back on the tiled floor, and she'd just carried on hitting. It took three people to drag her off. John looked shaken, and dived off to the toilet, after he'd phoned for an ambulance. She couldn't remember anything after that, must have been the drink.

'I think we'll leave it there for this week, Mary.' The doctor wiped his glasses and looked defeat in the eye. He wasn't going to make any breakthroughs this week.

She always spent weekends at home, what a joke that was!

Mum had died an alcoholic and Dad was useless – when he was there, that is! This week, the journey seemed never-ending. The bus clattered and jolted and she felt like throwing up again, knowing she'd have to mention the lack of a monthly at last, anticipating the reaction.

She got off the bus feeling stiff and sticky, like a discarded toffee wrapper. Dad rolled up, face reddened with lunch-time hospitality. It was an unusual occurrence. He was normally in the boozer, at the bookie's, or knocking up Glenda, the divorcee he was having a thing with. There was never any grub in the house, and sometimes she found herself looking forward to Mondays, just to eat. Perhaps she should have killed Daryl after all and gone away for a nice long time. It'd solve all her problems, no need to worry about getting a job or eating, then. Momentarily, she cursed her lack of foresight.

'Hallo, hen,' he flopped over her like a puppet with cut strings as the familiar smells of whisky, cat's piss and Old Holborn shrouded her. He had a dog and three cats, none of them house trained. They were left to their own devices while he went to work. The house was a right mess. It looked as if a bomb had exploded in the middle and worked its way out. The curtains hung in rags from three hooks, the cooker was blackened from a chip pan fire, the back door was kicked in and nobody ever cleaned anything up. All it was, was a glorified doss house, and it seemed suspicious that the old man should be so welcoming.

'What d'you want, Dad?'

'Just come to see me daughter, and look who else is here.' Surprise, surprise, she sneered, might have guessed it'd be her, Maggie, the lucky one. She got herself a fella young, and moved in with him at sixteen. She had two kids now, done alright for herself. One of her kids was only two months old.

Mary thought back to her treatment by the two young lovers when she was eight. Steve, Maggie's old man, had been a long-haired art student with a motorbike then. He used to give her fifty pence and tell her to bugger off. If she wouldn't go, he'd add a few kung fu kicks for good measure. She still thought he was a shit, even though he now had short hair, drove a car, carried a briefcase and called himself a graphic designer.

'Say hello to your Aunty Mary.' Maggie picked up the howling bean-bag of human life and held it out for her inspection. They stood silent for a moment, like two kids weighing up prize conkers in the school playground: 'Mine's a tenner, what's yours?' Mary turned away at last with a mumbled hello. She felt the flutterings in her own belly. It made her feel sick, anyway, the thought of looking like Maggie had done, covering her deformity with the virginal purity of pretty print maternity habits from Mothercare.

At last the reunion was over, and Father had a sensible idea.

'Let's have something to eat in Woolworths.'

'Yeah, good idea!' What she was about to tell him would soon put him off his fish and chips.

'So, how's everything going at the Home, Mary?' he sounded bored already, now the drink was wearing off. 'The social worker phoned up and said about Daryl.'

'Oh, him,' she picked her moment, 'Trouble is, I got him too late, think I might be pregnant.'

He barely flickered an eyelid. Mary felt cheated of her big moment, she thought at last the family were going to respond to her, but there was nothing. Maggie looked miles away, face dreaming of newly-born babies and how wonderful it would be to compare notes on nappies and brands of babyfood. Terries versus disposables. Mary hoped it wouldn't be too late for an abortion; disposables would have to win this time. She wasn't walking round with a great, fat gut for anybody.

'I'll help you look after it,' Dad nodded grudgingly, 'No daughter of mine's going to have an abortion!'

'Mary, that's wonderful,' Maggie beamed, face full of maternal radiance. 'You're going to be a mummy!'

'That's what you think!'

Mary was right about the length of pregnancy, nearly four months gone now. She'd gone to a clinic in Bournemouth with the social worker, been prodded and poked like prime fatstock, and violated by a big bloke in a white coat, pounding into her with cold pink stuff over a clammy rubber glove. It had made her bleed a bit and it was uncomfortable to piss for a couple of days, but nothing she couldn't live with.

'You'll have to start thinking about contraception, Mary,' said the nurse. 'When this is done, we'll put you on the Pill.'

'I'm not taking that, it gives you cancer!' They weren't getting rid of her that easily.

'It's slightly trickier aborting after three months, we'll have to give you a miscarriage.'

'OK, whatever you like, just get it done quick!'

She admired herself for that. No, it wasn't her style, asking if it would hurt or not, 'course it'd fucking hurt, like everything else in life.

She thought back to the conversation as she sat waiting, the hard plastic seat cold to her bare bottom through the split in the tie-back white gown. The bustling feet of nurses and brisk instructions echoed down the hospital corridors. Somewhere, someone screamed. She patted the formative bulge, and bit her lip. It'd soon be safe, screaming in a bucket for a few transient seconds of breath between the sureties of life and death. Mary smiled wryly to herself. She was still screaming in her bucket. Perhaps one day she'd punch a hole in it and someone would hear.

Sue Moules Nature Study

The first badger I ever saw
Was dead, cold, turning high.
Never have I seen living moles
Stoats, weasels:
But when dead
Carved into the countryside
I admire their soft coats
And ancient forms,
Shy away from
Their stark reality
Unwieldy as corrugated cardboard
Giving up their life's sheen.

Heather Milne-Gordon Highland Croft

She heard the small bleating. Pausing, the icy wind flapping the long coat against her body, she located the sound. The lamb was tiny, lately born, standing weakly beside the dead ewe. She first looked carefully at the ewe, its blood staining the light covering of snow. A loss, and the lamb probably no profit. She took up the lamb without tenderness or roughness and held it under her coat. She walked back through the two fields to where a small light showed the cottage. A woman past her prime, but strong.

The sister preparing supper saw the lamb and pulled out the box from under the kitchen table, a box kept for lambs that needed the warmth of the kitchen range. The woman put the lamb on the straw. She brought a rough towel and rubbed the little body dry. She heated milk. With a little coaxing, the lamb took a small amount. 'We lost the ewe,' she told the sister. 'The lamb will die, too,' the sister replied.

At nine o'clock, the sisters read from the family Bible. They ended, as always, with a prayer for the benefits a loving God had bestowed upon them. The cold March wind chilled the stone cottage. The fire-light from the old range glowed kindly upon the shabby room, giving a degree of cosiness. The sister rose and banked the fire with coal dust. At dawn, she would rake the still-hot ashes, re-lay and light the fire. The women were careful to tend the fire; warmth was the only lover they would know.

The lamb stirred and bleated, the woman heated milk, the lamb took half a bottle. In the morning the lamb was still alive and took the bottle. March became April.

The sisters continued the busy routine of their lives. Thirty ewes with their lambs on the hillside, the goats, givers of milk, in the home fields, the hens, with their generous gifts of eggs, contentedly pecking and murmuring in the spring sun. The garden planted, tended and productive. The sisters, born in the cottage, working the croft together now, the parents in a Highland cemetery set bleakly on the hillside. No church, the towering mountains keeping eternal watch over the eternal dead. The sisters had known no other life. The woman who fed the lamb had a broad man's face, reddened by Highland winds, a thick body, dour by nature, even as a girl. The sister, born with one leg shorter than the other, wore a raised club shoe. Strong glasses shielded her defective eyes.

May came, the burn running sweetly, blossom and bird song, the gentle mantle of spring blessing this sombre place. The lamb, now getting its living from the land, rich with spring grass, did not run with the flock but kept to the home paddock and the kitchen door. Sometimes, the woman would give it milk if some, left over, would be soured by morning. A small indulgence. To the lamb, no pet name was given it, the woman was its mother.

That year, the market was good for the selling of lambs. The truck came one gentle May morning. Forty-seven lambs were loaded on the truck, the one by the kitchen door made forty-eight. The woman, dressed in her decent black, climbed into the seat beside the driver.

She would drive the twenty miles into the small market town, but would have to take the market bus back, walking the last two miles across the fields to the cottage.

At three o'clock, she stood with the other passengers beside the railway station, waiting for the bus to take her home. Cattle were being driven from the auction market to the station – a short distance. The woman watched some fine beasts, she thought; good profit, there. She stood, giving slight nods to faces she had known all her life, discouraging all tentative gestures of friendliness or grace.

Lambs were being driven by shouts from the shepherd, harried by the two dogs, jostled together, terrified by new surroundings. A bleating lamb, fighting its way from the flock, running to the woman at the bus stop, pressing its body against her black skirts, its mother found, all would be safe. Some of the women passengers murmured sympathy, wanting to touch the frightened creature. The woman, outraged by the attention focussed upon her, kicked the lamb away from her, kicked it again, shouted at the shepherd to order his dogs to do their work. The lamb was soon among the flock, its childish cries muffled by the terrified bleatings of its fellows.

The bus came. The woman settled herself by the window. She

opened her purse and selected two silver coins, noted with small satisfaction that twenty-eight were left. Clouds, driven by the wind, moved across the sky. The May afternoon darkened. The woman sat silent, expressionless, clutching her purse, waiting for her journey to end.

Lizzie Demdyke
Is There Something In The Coffee?

I bought one of those magazines today,
you know, the type that appeals
to women who decide to have children
or don't decide
but have them anyway
I read it and wondered
where am I?
Amongst all these women
where do i fit in?
With neat little categories of
CAREER WOMEN
POLICEMEN'S WIVES
SOLDIERS' WIVES
ANYMAN'S WIVES
GIRL GUIDE LEADERS
WOMEN WITH BOYFRIENDS
WOMEN WITHOUT BOYFRIENDS
MIDDLE-CLASS MUMS WITH CINDICO TRAVELLERS, PERSIL
AND THE HUMPTY DUMPTY CLUB
what's my slot?
I read the lists of women wanting to get
'In Touch' for 'coffee and a natter'
well, I don't drink coffee
and I thought natter was a male fallacy – invented
to diminish women's words into frivolity
but perhaps I'm wrong
perhaps it really has something to do with the coffee?

I went through the readers' survey
but it didn't apply to me
I looked at the ad for an endowment policy
for the kids
but if they're to have £5,248 each in 16 years
(and after all, what will that be worth then?)
they're going to have to starve until they get it
so I didn't bother
I looked at the article on healthy eating for children
but my children are too healthy to eat flesh
I read the article on how to save your child's life
but they didn't tell you how
to handle what happened when it didn't work
so what did I spend 75p for?
well
    I wrote
    Please put me 'In Touch' with someone like me:
    lazy, unattractive, striving anarcha/feminist
    lesbian (25), a daughter and a son, a dog and
    a cat. Disenchanted with motherhood, scared of
    dying in the nuclear holocaust.
    INTERESTS: trying to save the world
                    tea and conversation
write care of M&B address on page 3

Phoebe Nathan Heartbreak

I lay in bed, I turned, I was going to curl up and put my arm around her, then I realized she wasn't there. I clenched my fist, the tears came, I could not believe it. She would not be beside me anymore.

Am I dreaming? No, the empty space tells me that, it must be a nightmare, I open my eyes, and feel the empty space. What can I do, I cannot speak to her, I cannot hold her, or lay close to her.

My mind is in torment, no matter what my brain tells me. My thumping heart tells me she has gone.

I move to the empty space. My hand goes over the empty space, I roll over, am I going mad? It's pure hell, I loved her so much, so very much, she did not die, she did not have another lover. But she killed me inside.

I walk like a zombie.

I cannot cook.

I barely get shopping.

I just lay and think and think. My sanity is at stake.

The doctor calls, the Welfare calls, and others. What are they going to do with me? I hear them talking, but don't realize they are talking about where to put me.

I carried on with different pills. They sent 'meals on wheels', because I wouldn't cook. The time passed, weeks, months, years.

And maybe I was lucky. I often wonder, was I? The doctor gave me a new tranquillizer, every night I prayed, Please God, let me wake up well.

The one morning came, I'll always remember, I woke up and felt NORMAL and all the throbbing I'd had over my body all the time had stopped, I felt wonderful, I was OK again and then I began to live again. When I think back, I marvel at my recovery . . .

Pat Angove Bless This House

Susan showed all the qualities of a born leader, she gave her orders clearly and precisely.

'That brick should go there.' She pointed to the spot where she wanted Tom, her seven-year-old brother, to put the brick.

'Where shall I put this?' asked Colin, her five-year-old brother, dragging a long piece of two-by-two towards her.

'Ah, that can be the door,' she said, giving Colin a hand with it.

'I think it should be the window,' stated Tom, finishing with his brick and wiping his hands down his shorts. With all the patience of a saintly mother, she explained to him why the wood made a better door than it would a window. Her head, with its thick mass of mousey fair curls, bent towards her brothers. Although only nine, she was shooting upwards, long, thin and at least four inches taller than him. He was impatient to get on with their house, and argued no further. He sauntered off to the wood pile to select a piece of wood for the window.

Susan adjusted the bricks, they weren't straight and they had to be, for theirs was going to be the perfect house. Her head bent in concentration. She was wearing her only dress, a thin cotton, flowery thing, given to her mother by a neighbour. It was a bit frayed around the collar and it was most definitely grubby, its better days lost and gone forever. Susan didn't mind about the dress, though, her mum was ill.

Her mum suffered from asthma. She was always having attacks. She had had one that very morning, sitting in the kitchen, struggling for breath and squirting stuff into her mouth. No one took much notice, it happened so often, but Susan would watch her mother out of the corner of her eye, afraid, afraid that she might not recover. Her mother always seemed so isolated with her gasping and heaving, and Susan longed to go to her and put her arms around her. She never did, though, and kept her distance, longing, but never daring, to show her love and her fear.

She was just coming back from the bottom of the garden with two large stones that she had selected to mark the entrance to the front door of the house, when she spotted her father standing in the back doorway of their real house. His bald head nearly touched the top of the doorway. He was very tall, very tall and very thin, to her he was like a skeleton with skin on. She pretended that she had not noticed him, and went over to her own house. She stepped over the two layers of bricks that made the walls, and knelt down to concentrate on the house. Concentrating on the house was better than on her father's eyes which she knew were on her back, burning into her. 'Of course, it's Sunday,' she thought, 'he is always at home on Sunday.' To her, Monday seemed a lifetime away.

'Susan,' her father snapped, 'your room is a disgrace, go upstairs at once and tidy it.'

At those words, Susan felt as if she had swallowed one of her bricks. She felt the sick rise from her stomach and into her throat, she swallowed hard to control her desire to throw up, she didn't want to be sick inside her house, even though it hadn't given her any protection; six-inch walls were obviously not enough, but that was not the house's fault. She could not speak, her feet felt as if they were in lead shoes and her legs felt as if they were made of paper. One of her brothers spoke, she could only just hear what he said, it sounded so far away.

'Oh, Dad, we're building a house, all of us.'

Her father's voice broke through her haze, like a knife cutting gauze.

'She's too big to be playing games with you two, she's got work to do.' He turned to her. 'Come on, you lazy bitch, get going.' He stepped aside for her to pass him in the doorway. She managed to whisper, yet knew the answer,

'Where's Mum?'

'She's in bed, she doesn't feel well again, as well you know.' The accusation was clear. 'She's ill because of me,' she thought to herself. 'Why, what have I done to her, how have I made her ill?' Suddenly, the thought struck her with all the horror of finding a spider in the bath: 'She's ill because she knows, yes, that's what's making her ill.'

She climbed the stairs slowly, her father following closely behind her, pushing her with his body. She felt as though she was drowning. She opened the door to her room, her domain, her space.

She was pushed roughly against the wall, his hands every-where, pushing her, fumbling her, invading her. She looked away, away from his contorted face, away from his body, and stared at the rug they were standing on, the rug that he had made with their old winter coats. It was a deep red house within a deep red frame, a little path ran up to the house, so welcoming. He was so clever with his hands, her father, so very clever with his hands.

She managed to tear her mind away from the red house in the red frame when he disappeared into the bathroom. The sound of running water seeped through to her, she was left standing there against the wall, her legs wet and a damp patch on the rug, her rug. She felt dirty, she felt totally alone. Her brothers' voices reached up to her through the window, but they sounded far, far away. She listened to them arguing about the design of their house, and who was going to play the mummy and who the daddy. She felt very old, far too old for their games.

She walked her hurt little body to the bed and lay there, staring up at the ceiling. She heard her father go downstairs, heard him in the garden with her brothers. She heard him tell them that they would, together, build the best house in the whole street.

Her thoughts went to her little church, the church Aunt Phyllis had given her last Christmas. It had grey plastic walls, with little grey plastic pews, a grey plastic spire at one end and a beautiful red plastic roof. All the bits clipped together, and Susan had put it together herself. She could look through the windows and see the little pews. The doors at one end of the church were on hinges and, when opened, she could see the little altar with a cross above it. She loved that little church. Every night, she would put the church reverently onto the floor of her bedroom, open the little doors wide, kneel down low and pray. She would pray and pray until the church would be bursting at the seams with her prayers. She would then close the doors as fast as she could, so that all her prayers were trapped inside. Her Sunday school teacher had told her that God lived in churches, that they were houses of God, so he must obviously be in her church, too. Shut away in there, with all her prayers, nobody else's, just hers. He couldn't possibly fail to listen to her prayers.

Every night, without fail, she would breathe her prayers into her church, until one night her mother caught her doing it. She told her never to do it again, because it was a very evil thing to do. Her mother called it 'idol-worshipping'. Susan didn't know what idol-worshipping was, but she didn't think what she was doing was wrong. She was allowed to pray inside the Sunday school church. The only trouble with that was that there were always so many other people praying there at the same time. God would be too busy hearing all the other prayers to get around to hearing hers, so what chance did she have of getting any granted? She could not, and would not, stop praying into her church. There, she had God's undivided attention; it meant far too much for her to stop.

The next night, Susan reckoned that, as she had put herself to bed every night since she could remember, and as Mum coming up to say goodnight was such a rare thing, she would take the chance of discovery, she needed to pray, she had a lot to be forgiven for. She had only just got the little church half filled with her prayers when her mother opened her bedroom door. Although Susan pleaded with her mum, and even tried to enlist her father's help, the church was taken away from her. It was given to her brothers. It lasted for two days. For two days, Susan watched the slow destruction of her church. It was used as a garage, its doors were wrenched off, the steeple broke in a tug of war between the two brothers as they argued over it. The end finally came when one of them rode his tricycle over it. The church was swept up and thrown in the dustbin, along with the contents of the carpet-sweeper.

She lay on her bed, feeling so alone, so very alone. God was too busy listening to other people to listen to her and, anyway, why should he listen to her? She was wicked and sinful. The tears that had been threatening for so long, came at last, but she stopped them immediately. She could hear her mother stirring. Whatever happened, her mother must not catch her crying, she might ask questions and Susan could not look into her mother's eyes, nor answer her questions. She swallowed continuously, until she had pushed her tears well down into her stomach, then she got up, found her knickers, put them on, and began to tidy her bedroom. As her mother's footsteps approached her bedroom door, Susan began to panic. She dived under the bed and pretended to be searching for something. She hid her face so that her mother would not see what was there. Her father was always saying that if Mother found out, Susan would be thrown out onto the streets. The thought of being alone with nowhere to live terrified her. She tried to calm her breathing and to give all the appearance of being 'normal'. Her mother's footsteps passed, they went slowly and quietly down the stairs. She lay on the floor, with her head still under the bed, and let the relief flood through her body. She felt a strong desire to laugh. She relaxed and revelled in the relief, the laughter and the silence.

'Come down, you lazy bitch, and help your mother with the dinner, you know she isn't well.'

With a sigh that was older than the hills, Susan got up, brushed down her dress, and went downstairs to present herself in the kitchen; business as usual.

June Burnett Night

I was just about to read a poem,
'Anne Frank Dreams at Bergen Belsen'
when I stopped.
The shout, 'No!' ended in an animal moan.
I winced,
convinced the woman in the next-door flat was dying.
The poem's theme and her continual screaming,
met together and putrified in the clamouring night,
compatible companions.
I rose, to shake the babyish sobbing from my head,
and couldn't.
Later, I heard him laughing with her,
and should have been relieved,
but wasn't.
My open page of horrors and his imagined performing of it
tied conjugally together,
lashed out at me lying alone,
with little inhumanities trickling,
and scouring the channels of my brain,
to form a torrent.

Ali Raven A Promised Land

Sometimes I stop and wonder
where it is we're going.
This promised land –
a lesbian feminist vision.

Do working-class dykes play there,
with our children growing there,
solid with our culture,
knowing our oppression,
knowing our strength?

Can I grow in this vision,
learn in this land,
with no assimilation
to a middle-class norm?

Will we all be new womyn
or just some of us?

Sylvan Agass Holding the Baby . . .

A woman wrote in her diary:
                              Mum-in-law to stay.
A daughter-in-law writes in her diary:
                              Richard's mother to stay.
Got talking 'olden' days.   Babies. Women's talk.
              'You're never going to leave it there?'
Women's talk.   Woman lying in the dark with her baby
                             So many voices.   *So many voices.*
When can we stop telling lies?
    Making noises, not sharing.
Which voice am I?   And which am I?
Which is my story?   Which voice? Which
Which mine is the?   story?
Which?   Mine which? witch . . .
    The woman's hand lays heavy on the dead baby.
    Fifty years of darkness. She regrets not looking. Letting it go
    without knowing. In the dark she wonders now how they'll
    recognise each other . . .
So many voices.   Fell asleep.   Woke . . .
Beginning.
Not her fault.
No one's fault really.
    Her hand lies heavy like lead on the dead baby. Heavy. In the
    dark you'd think it was sleeping, the baby. But for the crackle
    of newspaper under the shawl. The body bred. Or bleeding.
    Breeding dust. For all that, the baby was taken without her
    permission. It was still a gift, the gift of her body. This body.

256

Clumsy.

Wincing.

Stumbling out of bed. Already, the tops of your legs chaffed raw from the gauze pads. Cotton wool pads that couldn't hold all the bleeding.

The misses don't count, really.

That's what the midwife said. And she should know.

A blessing, really.

I've seen some little mites, perfect-looking like this, but that damaged inside, their own mother'd gladly swop places with you this day.

They don't count, really, the misses, just so long as you don't name it. Save it for the next one . . . There's plenty more where that came from. You get your rest now . . . the baby's asleep.

At some time in the night, she got up to go to the baby. It was crying. She touched it. It was cold. Yet it called to her, pulled the mother from her dreaming.

Babies cry.

And mothers,

even mothers whose hips cradled to term nothing more than a bundle of rubbish, wrapped up in yesterday's newsprint, enfolded in a shawl,

mothers rise,

they get up in the dark, stumbling in the dark, arms and heart ahead of head and legs.

(The knowing begins here, the forcing of the mind upright onto leaden legs.) Waking from that thickened sleep, she'd known at once that it was dead, but for all that, she got up and went to the wailing baby. Her outstretched hand willing life into the baby, her mind telling: It is done. Finished. And the midwife (not unkindly) saying:

Do you really want this baby?

We might be losing this one . . . The misses don't count, really.

Her hand lying broad and heavy on the baby's back, her mother's hand, as broad across the palm as the breadth of the baby's fragile ribs, her crinkled wash-worn fingertips stroking the place where the many-wrinkled baby neck met the downy shoulders she would never see.

Bodies make their own demands. Bodies programmed to go on with the plan, as arranged. She leaves the child and takes her sore breasts back to bed. Thick yellow stuff oozing out of her nipples. The smell stuck to her nightie. The drip matches the cramps in her belly, mocking her labour with mock-labour pains. Full, round, useless breasts, straining under the cotton nightgown. A fine figure of motherhood still. Her hand, for all it's so heavy, ugly even, has ever had a light touch with the cradle, the fretting, the teething, the tears.

. . . Getting out on the wrong side, stumbling from one wrapped parcel to another, the stiffened gauze pads bundled ready for burning, the baby . . . the creak of the newsprint inside both parcels . . . and the utter silence of the baby in its woollen shawl. Her hand, warm upon the wool, willing life into the parcel, her mind saying: Finished. It is done.

She wanted very much to take the baby back to bed.

Then she wanted more to take the baby to the window, to uncover its face and, in the lamplight from the street outside, look on its tiny shadowed features. In the yellow light, the skin would not look blue. Just as if it were sleeping. But the parcel wasn't hers to handle any more. She went to bed.

In the morning, she carried the baby's weight into the other room, and stood framed with it in the window. The same view as from the bedroom, to the end of the block, then the corner. She hummed under her breath as she waited, the baby juggling in time to the tune, so that once, absent-minded, she almost dropped it. The shawl fell away from the newsprint face, but she scooped the wool fringe back, without looking. A long wait. The crook in her arms stiff with waiting. The ache in the small of her back was so like the last dregs of pregnancy that she almost forgot the time was past. She waited.

Waited till the bike turned the corner.

Still waiting till the bike turned the corner of the road, wobbling a little as it goes out of sight. The last glimpse to be had was of the energetic pumping of the midwife's lisle-clad legs working the pedals, and the baby in a weathered wicker-basket swinging from the handlebars, squeaking on the leather straps . . .

Josephine Zara The Burning

Nearly forgotten was the grey day of moving-in. The cold house, its peeling wallpaper, cracked sink and stone-flagged floors, looked like the other houses we had lived in – well, nearly.

The fire shone on the silver and lace we had rescued, our coloured and embroidered cloths covered the shabby furniture, our curtains hung to hide the grimy street beyond. My mother sang her sweet, gentle songs again.

But upstairs, anarchy reigned. Glorious freedom from the rigorous tidying, sweeping and dusting of our everydays. Today, we were going to decorate; tear from the walls the multitudinous layers of the years, and replace with the inevitable, passionate paper flowers of my childhood.

Huge lumps of soaked paper lay about the floor, wetter lumps were gleefully pulled from the walls, tiny determined-to-stay-forever pieces were scraped off with forbidden knives. Water and happiness seeped into our clean dresses.

'What are these, Mum?' my sister asked. 'What are these little brown things on the wall?'

'Don't bother me,' my mother said. 'Can't you see I'm busy?'

'These little brown things, round and fat and running about,' my sister persisted.

Our neighbour's curlers edged round the door.

'Eh up, luv. 'Ow yer doing? Ee tha's got sum right good kids. Look at 'em pulling them lumps off. In't it a mess? Nay, soon be done. It's different when there's a man, quicker like. Thee's never done it afore? Poor lass, thas'll 'ave to learn a thing or two. Them little brown 'uns? Ee, luv, them's bed-bugs. We all 'ave 'em. Nowt to worry abart, gies yer a nip at night, but it's nowt. Best thing is, not to paper but to get some distemper. That soon kills 'em, well, fur a while, any road. Get your lasses to burn 'em up first wi't candle. 'Ere, Josy, come and get some candles. Your mum looks a bit white, needs a rest, 'appen.'

I came back with the candles and proudly lit them. We were going to burn bugs! No one I knew had ever burned bugs, no one.

Tomorrow, I would tell my new teacher and all my friends at school.

Jenneba Sie Jalloh
All You Need To Win

For my mother, Helena Hunt

When I think of my mother,
sitting there with nothing, after all these years of working
struggling to bring me up on a pittance, I feel like crying.
But I know that what I have to do is to
take that energy, that hate, that disgust,
and put it into fighting.

I know you think you're clever,
you just break us with your measures
but hundreds of years of the same technique
has produced in us a fighting streak.

You cannot see your mother and father
crushed by this so-called 'free and democratic system'
still fighting to maintain a so-called 'decent standard of living'.

I know you believe that all of us,
all the living products of your inhumanity
will be easily tempted away from the fight
by your materialistic commercials on TV.
But we don't all conform to your right wing, fascist philosophy,
we're not naturally greedy.

It will be easy for you, harder for me,
but the final fight is close at hand, as you will see.

I am bombarded with the same old fiction –
that all you have to do is work hard and well,
and you will eventually be rewarded with all the things you
    tell us
through your adverts and plastic dreams makes life worthwhile.
And some of us believe your fiction and your fairytales

for some of us have no other choice in this your 'wonderful
  and free
society' . . . or so you claim.

But let me ask you this:
After all those years of work and struggle,
and living on existence level,
where is our reward, this claim we feel we have,
lauded by you, so high above?

A book, a pension, a pittance
does it balance with all those years of sacrifice?

Never tell me, and don't tell my children.

Don't say it again, because this lie is wearing thin,
that consistent work (when and if you find it)
is all you need to win.

Gill Newsham We Have It All

Well, we have it all, don't we? 1987 and Britain is a Feminist
Paradise – a woman monarch AND the first British woman prime
minister! Is this what our sisters struggled and campaigned for
over the last two decades? The female face of the 1980s – an
un-proud heritage of reforms, reactions and reach-me-downs,
second-hand ideologies and second-class lives. 'Oh, to be a
working-class woman in 1988 . . .' Is this an Ode to the
Unemployed?

This generation, my generation – what do I know of the
Working-Class? . . . Visions of lines of men, ten thick or more,
rebelling against the Torys' stringent assault on their communities – strong, proud, etc, etc . . . Or is it, perhaps, these same men
denying power en bloc in their unions, and the same, perhaps, at
home, to their wives, their sisters and their daughters? Is this
working-class unity?

Male power, patriarchy, men – they have given their name to

the working-class movement and at the same time, made *woman* invisible. At best, she is exceptional.

I got my first thrust of strength, of support, through feminism – but feminism does not cross class-boundaries, it does not cross political backgrounds – it can try, but it is not automatic.

Woman-Power may not mean power for all women – we can see this through the destructive effects of Thatcherism, of most women at the top of the tree.

It is all too easy for working-class women to be swallowed up in the women's movement, just as they have been in the various men's movements we are expected to support. Maybe it is only through exploring, thinking and writing about class and women, that we can forge a new autonomous identity, and band together as working-class women to demand the rights and benefits that have been repeatedly denied us by those too secure to share their power.

CLASS PRIDE AND CELEBRATION
– the voices we carry within us

Though our pride is fierce, this section was one of the most difficult to put together. Pieces celebrating our class identity were few. The reasons for class pride are elusive, slippery and difficult to express. From birth, we face less opportunity and choice and for most of us, life is a continuous struggle.

And yet, none of the hundreds of women who sent us their writing spoke of wishing to be other than working-class. We may not be able to say why, but all of us are glad, proud to be who we are – with our resilience and energy, our capacity to survive, to hope, to be creative, to maintain a sense of humour and a vision of beauty.

Women, here, remind us of generations of unrecorded voices – voices we hear in yarns, fragments, tales by the fireside. Some assert their class with confidence and wit, others describe a gradual dawning sense of themselves as they lift their heads high and feel their class identity running 'deep inside [their] blood . . . like fire' (Anne Cunningham).

Along with all women, we celebrate different ages and periods of our life, our capacity to stretch ourselves and juggle a myriad of different activities, responsibilities and skills. Sometimes we just take pleasure in a moment (though usually with an eye to the practical), or in the sheer beauty of a triumphant struggle – 'the thrill of fighting against the fists of the ocean' (Sarah Hunter).

Just as we're almost overwhelmed by the drudgery, the greyness of our days, we find unexpected enjoyment in the rush of starlings or the scent of a lavender flower. In 'Weekending', Julie Cotterill's razor-sharp wit graphically exposes middle-class pretentions, and Jenneba Sie Jalloh charges the privileged and complacent to question the way words define and condemn.

Faced with a view of ourselves as inferior, we not only survive we also struggle to overcome obstacles, we climb high mountains, yet in the midst of the effort, there's a reaching out for 'the rare blueness that eases our pain' (Theresa Verlaine).

These days, being working-class doesn't necessarily mean unremitting poverty or a total lack of higher education. But, for working-class women, nothing comes easily, without effort and difficult choices. In a poem not included here, one of our contributors sums up this particular experience:

> '. . . in this empty space there's freedom
> to feel your assumptions
> about me, the world –
> your knowledge that the sun shines for you.
>
> Me – I know that if the sun does shine,
> I've got on a ladder and heaved and heaved
> to put that sun in the sky . . .'

> Ali Raven, from 'Differences'.

Jeanne Wilding

Kitty Fitzgerald Voices

A reaction to male literary critics

I come from generations of illiterate women
whose tales were told,
not on paper
but in the lilt of a song
or among fireside company
when a long working day was done.

Those are the voices I carry within me,
shades of greenery
from field and plough,
red knuckles twisting watery sheets
in sunshine, frost and snow,
scratched legs from gathering peat.

You say they're valueless as a tradition
to work from and
build onto inch by inch.
You say their songs and tales
are nothing more important
than the echo of a banshee wail.

I cannot take your droning seriously.
There is no spirit
nor any magic
in the tongue of history
you insist on lashing.
Go back to your mother's knee and hear Herstory.

Anne Cunningham Power Play

Rebel,
refuse to be a victim.

Long grey years,
hauled or
hauling myself through
misdoubt mistrust misfit.

I was a 'good' child.
Born late,
an afterthought or accident.
My mum,
exhausted by the needs of seven children,
needed me to be 'good'.
I learned early,
behaved,
tried to help her
and sought her love,
by suppressing my own needs.
I learned early to
take up little space,

not want,
not shout,
not demand.

She knew some things,
my mum,
and despite the odds against her
and at what cost to herself,
taught me
about injustice as she saw it,
'one law for the rich,
another for the poor',
she'd say
seeing quite clearly
on which side of the fence
she stood.
But in her hopelessness
she also taught,
'to survive,
just be good,
don't make a fuss
and keep your head down'.

And I learned good
for a very long time

a very long time.

Now,
gradually, painfully,
I'm teaching myself
to lift up my head
high.

Long days, nights, weeks, years
exhausted

or

pent up with rage
that has nowhere to go

or

sick and wanting to be cosseted
instead of looking after others

or

wracked with guilt
because my anger and frustration
burst onto my children
who I love fiercely
but society tells me
I shouldn't have anyway
without a man
and the money to keep them.

So when you ask
how I know my class
I am speechless to describe
how I feel it
deep inside my blood
running like fire.
It is my experience
my life
the knowledge of my struggles
and my mother's.
A deep vein
that knows our gains have always been denied
and we are called
stupid/thick/rough/dirty/loud/ugly.
And I know that nothing's changed
And I know that when the lines are drawn,
and they are constantly,
which side I am on.

And there is nowhere
I can turn for strength and validation
except myself,
and witnessing the enormous leaps

of courage
other women make
when they take hold of their own strength.
It can seem such tiny things
but the bravery behind that stepping out
makes me gasp,
and love intensely
that sad–sweetness
that is a woman
fighting back.

And I know it's not simple
for them,
or me,
or any of us.
So, rather than deny each other's power
we could
celebrate
that awfulness agony,
the isolation craziness
that is the price of our strength.

We could learn from each other
tactics of survival,
share our doubt,
our weaknesses,
our loneliness.

But above all,
recognize
we are all the same.
There are no strong women
or
we are all strong,
no exceptions
no special cases.

I am
big loud working-class lesbian mother woman fighter

but still
I am afraid
too many painful times
there have been
behind the words

and will be again

They are a raging river
I must constantly cross
and re-cross
without ever finding
a place of safety.

Janice Galloway Two Fragments

I remember two things in particular about my father: He had
ginger hair, and he had two half-fingers on one hand. The ring
finger and the middle one fastened off prematurely at the knuckle,
like the stumpy tops of two pink pork links, but smoother. They
were blown off during the war. This was a dull sort of thing,
though; my mother had another story that suited my child-need
far better.

It started with the usual, your daddy in the pub. I could've had a
mint of money today if he hadn't been a drinker, by the way.
Anyway, he'd been in there all night, and he came out the pub for
the last bus up the road, but by the time he staggered to the stop he
was just in time to see it going away without him. He chased it,
but it wasn't for stopping. He'd missed it. There was nothing for
it but to start walking.

He had to go along past Piacentini's on the corner, and that was
where he smelt the chips. It wasn't all that late yet, and they were

still open. The smell of the chips was a great thing on a cold night, and with all the road still to go up, and he just stood there for a wee while, soaking up the warm chips smell. It made him that hungry, he thought he had to go in and get some, so he counted all the loose change in his pockets, and with still having the bus fare he just had enough.

He was that drunk, though, he dropped all the money and he had to crawl about all over the road to get it all back, because he needed every penny to get the chips. That took him a wee while. And by the time he finally got in, Mrs Piacentini was just changing the fat and so he had to wait. That was alright, but the smell of the chips was making him hungry by this time. Just when he was about to get served, a big policeman came in and asked for his usual four bags and because he was in a hurry and he was a regular, he got served the chips that were for your daddy. So by the time he was watching the salt and vinegar going on to his bag, his mouth was going like a watering-can. He was starving. The minute he got out into the street with them, he tore open the bag and started eating them with his fingers, stuffing them into his mouth umpteen at a time and swallowing them too fast. He thought they were the best chips he had ever tasted. He was that carried away eating them that it wasn't till he went to crumple up the empty bag and fling it away he saw the blood. When he looked over his shoulder there was a trail of it all the way up the road from Piacentini's. He was that hungry, he'd eaten two of his fingers for chips, with salt and vinegar.

My granny had a glass eye. She was a fierce woman. A face like a white gingernut biscuit and long, long grey hair. She smoked a clay pipe. And she had this glass eye.

My grandfather was a miner, and the miners got to take the bad coal, the stuff with the impurities the coal board weren't allowed to sell. She built up the fire one day and was bashing a big lump of this impure coal with the poker when it exploded and took her eye out.

But my granny was the very stuff of legend, so there was another story about that, too, centring on other great truths. Again, it was my mother's: I was much too feart for my granny to ask her anything.

'Your granny could be awful cruel sometimes. She drowned cats. She drowned the kittens, and if the cats got too much, she drowned them as well. There was one big tom in particular, used to come up the stairs and leave messes in the close. Gad. Right outside your door and everything. Stinking the place out. I don't like tom cats and neither did your granny. She got so fed up with the rotten smell and its messes, that one day she decided she was going to get rid of it. So she laid out food, and when it came to eat the food she was going to sneak up on it with a big bag. It was that suspicious, watching her the whole time while it was eating: your granny staring at the cat and the cat staring back. It was eating the food in the one corner, and your granny was hovering with the bag in the other. High Noon.

Anyway, she waited for her minute and she managed to get it. Not right away, though. It saw her and jumped, but it went the wrong way and got itself in a corner and she finally managed to get the bag over it. By the time she got into the kitchen, with the cat struggling in the bag, she was a mass of scratches. The cat was growling through the bag and trying to get its claws through at her again, so she held up the bag and shook it to show it who was the boss. Then she didn't know what to do next, till she clapped eyes on the boiler. A wee, old-fashioned boiler, like a cylinder thing on wee legs with a lid at the top.

She got a string and tied up the top of the bag and then she dropped the cat right into the boiler drum. It was empty, of course. She was going to keep it in there till the boys came back (that's your Uncle Sammy and Uncle Alec), and get one of them to take it to the tip and choke it or something. She was fed up with it, after all that wrestling about.

She got on with her work in the kitchen, and as she was working about, she could hear the cat banging about in the boiler the whole time, trying to get out, while she was getting on with the dinner and boiling up kettles of water for the boys, coming home for their wash. When they got in from their work, the first thing they did was get a wash: there was no baths in the pit, and they never sat down to their tea dirty. Your granny wouldn't let them.

So they came right into the kitchen when they got home, and the first thing they noticed was this thumping coming out the boiler. Alec says to her, what the hell's that, mother? And she tells them about the tom cat. Just at that, the thing starts growling as if it's heard them, and our Sammy says, I hope you don't think I'm touching that bloody thing; listen to it! And he starts washing at the sink and laughing, like it was nothing to do with him. Even our Alec wouldn't go and lift the lid. So she got quite annoyed and rolled her sleeves up to show them the scratches, to tell them she wasn't feart for it and she would do it herself. So, after she'd gave them their tea, she got them out the kitchen so she could get on with it.

She had thought what she was going to do. First, she got two big stones from the coalhouse and the big coal bucket from the top of the stairs. She put the bricks at the boiler side and filled the big bucket with cold water at the sink. The cat had stopped making so much noise by this time, so it was probably tired. This would be a good time. She got the washing tongs, the big wooden things for lifting out the hot sheets after they'd been boiled, and went over to the boiler, listening. Then she flung back the lid, reached in quick with the tongs and pulled the bag out before the cat knew what was happening. The minute it was out the drum, though, it starts thrashing about again, and your granny drops the bag and runs over to the sink for the pail, heaves it over to the boiler and pours the whole lot in.

She filled it right up, nearly to the top. The bag was scuffling about the floor, so she waited till it went still again. Then when it had stopped moving, she gets hold of it with the tongs, quick, and plonks it straight into the water, banging the lid down shut and the bricks on top.

She went straight into the living-room to build up the fire and tell the boys she'd managed fine without them, quite pleased with herself. She would just leave the cat in the boiler till the next morning, to be sure it was drowned, and get the bucket men to take it away. Sammy was a bit offended. He said she was a terrible woman, but they didn't do anything about the poor bloody cat, so they were just as bad. There was no noise in the kitchen when they went in for a wash before they went to their beds. It was a shame.

Well, it was still the same thing the next morning when your granny went in to light the kettle. Nothing coming out the boiler.

That was fine. She got me and Tommy away to the school, and your Uncle Alec and Sammy were away to the pit, and our Lizzie was out as well. So that was her, by herself, and she started getting the place ready for the disposal of the body. She put big sheets of newspaper all round the floor and got the tongs ready. It would be heavy. She shifted one of the bricks off the boiler lid and listened, to make sure. Nothing. She shifted the other one off and lifted up the lid.

There was a hellish swoosh, and the cat burst out the boiler, soaked to the bone, its eyes sticking right out its head. It must've fought its way out the bag and been swimming in there all night, paddling, and keeping just its nose above the water, and the minute it saw the light when your granny lifted the lid, it just threw itself up. It shot out, straight at her face, and took her eye out – just like that. Your granny in one corner of the kitchen, with the eye in another, and the tom cat away like buggery down the stairs.

> Fingers for the army.
> An eye for the coal board.
> A song and a dance for the wean.

June Burnett
A Letter from my Treadmill

Dear Jeanne,

Going back to the old chestnut often raised by those in the middle classes who, for some reason, feel guilty about it:

'Why do you call yourself working-class?'

I went to a party recently and got into conversation with a couple of women there. They told me something of their lives and I told them something of mine. I was quizzed at some length about our collective, and did my best to explain what we were about, but the moment I mentioned 'working-class identity', what had been a fairly boozy, lighthearted conversation suddenly took on a different hue. I felt I'd been nominated for the MENSA test, or had unwittingly put myself into the 'Mastermind' seat, where the audience wait spikily for abject failure on the part of the contestant.

I was quite unprepared for the rising note of hostility in the woman's voice. Her name was Jennifer and I suppose she was thirtyish. I imagine that if you wanted to apply an unpleasant label, à la Jilly Cooper, she could go down as a 'spiralist with a right-hand thread'.

'What exactly do you mean by working-class?' she asked in a voice obviously reserved for bolshy upstarts like myself, the tone disguised and softened by well-modulated, sugary patronage. She smiled at the end of the sentence, her lips closed and she raised one ginger eyebrow. I groaned inwardly, wondering yet again if it is a basic insecurity in some middle-class people who seem to be quite clear about their own place in the 'great design', and have no trouble admitting to being middle-class. However, the moment a working-class person says they're working-class, without lowering the voice or genuflecting, they tend to go on the defensive. As intelligent beings, you'd think that if history didn't remind them we were a class-ridden society, instinct would. Although instinct is probably why they go on the defensive anyway, poor souls. Just as chronically blinkered as those who cling to the myth that there's no North/South divide, or even worse, no poor, redundant or out-of-work people, simply because they haven't met any.

'Well, I suppose I define myself as working-class because my family were working-class and I grew up with and identified with working-class people: Our hardships, sorrows, humour and, largely, our aspirations, were the same.' I replied. 'After years of unrewarding factory jobs, I realized an ambition to be a teacher. I imagined being a teacher would give me automatic entrance to the middle class – of course, it didn't. My accent hadn't been mutated and I had been heard to say "bloody 'ell" in the staff-room. I didn't wear the correct dress, and laughed too loudly. In a word, "common!" I saw Jennifer take a mental step backwards, even though her face still wore the smile.

I couldn't help thinking how, at one time, when I was younger and dizzily impressionable, I'd have given at least four fingers to possess a posh voice, live in a real house instead of furnished rooms, and be equipped to pose as anything except what I was. But, as you know, I have yet to receive the little 'windfall' from a deceased relative enabling me to have that holiday in St Lucia or Mustique, or to convince the bank manager I am a safe bet for a personal loan – to begin my own little business in town, selling health-food luncheons to business men accustomed to calling everyone in a frilly pinny 'sweetie'.

Although her friend kept quiet, Jennifer came right back at me with, 'Oh, for goodness' sake, June, how can you possibly categorize everyone like that. Surely everyone these days is working-class?'

Well, I guess I should have expected that predictable volley, but I could see what was flummoxing her: I didn't fit. I'd been a teacher and had exhibited my paintings, so what was I doing, insisting on this ludicrous claim to be working-class? I wasn't anything like the stereotype she'd been fed with. I couldn't be working-class and be anything close to articulate. I'd been ex- posed to reading matter other than the obligatory romantic pulp magazines and books, and it was more than clear that I refused to sit for hours in front of the TV, being slowly lobotomized by glitzy soaps, designed to anaesthetize the majority of the work- ing class against their real problems. I could see she was having real trouble about the whole concept of someone who had had any education after the age of sixteen and could still consider them- selves working class without a flush of shame. Nor did she give the slightest thought as to how hard-won that education had been, without the benefit of privilege in the form of money or connections, which the middle class provide for their children, as of right.

To tell the truth, I began to feel I'd survived ritual exposure, only to be confronted by Jennifer and made to account for myself, as an educated member of the working class – and one who showed no sign of abandoning my working-classness in favour of a longing to 'better myself'. A deviant of the worst possible kind!

Suddenly I was visited with a sense of ease, and I felt consider- ably better. I had, I suppose, 'bettered myself', but on my own terms and without surrendering the identity I had matured with.

'There's no real answer to that, Jennifer,' I remember saying, through a glass of vodka fumes. 'But if you call yourself working-
276

class with Daddy being head of a private school in Surrey, and Mummy having half a share in a racehorse, then so, I'm afraid, is Mrs Windsor, Queen of this Parish – right?'

Well, that was where the incident ended, as most of them do – in polite little smiles and gulps of gin all round – a disengagement without bloodletting, not even a scratched psyche. Makes a change from trying to remember when Spencer Tracy's going to come up in a Trivial Pursuit question, I guess.

All I was left with was an unpleasant feeling that sooner or later someone would take it into their heads to get slightly miffed that, instead of attempting shame-faced invisibility, and assuming a shuffling gait, I could still be as proud to admit, in a voice above a whisper, '*Yes*, I'm working-class'.

love, June.

Annette Kennerley She

She pushes a buggy down the dirty street
She works behind the cash register at the superstore
She does her washing at the laundrette once a week
She cleans the offices when the staff have all gone home
She cooks the children's tea every night
She watches TV with a cup of tea
She drinks with other women in a bar on Friday night
She walks for hours alone in the park in the pouring rain
She drives a taxi through the busy streets
She does the housework in the midnight hours
She runs to catch the crowded moving bus
She is taking a sick child to the doctor
She is putting her arm round a friend in need
She is singing aloud in a long hot bath
She is a million different things
She is a working-class woman
And she is a writer

Mary Haylett Brenda on Holiday

I was sitting with me husband
in me one-piece by the pool
when two women going topless
sat beside us looking cool.
My discomfort was apparent
I felt hot and couldn't speak
'course that pleased him even more
he's got a vicious streak.
They were smooth and slender
I was plumpish, he was staring
he inferred that I was frumpish
and never had been daring.
I was just about to leave the pool
when I must have changed me mind
cos I stepped out of me one-piece
and rubbed me own behind.
His face it went quite purple
get dressed, I heard him croak
his mouth was hanging open
I thought he'd have a stroke.
I strolled towards the diving-board
like I was in a trance
and when I reached the very top
I did a little dance.
Three steps for me stretch marks
three for being caged
and before I jumped I shouted
this is ME, I'm middle-aged.

Carole Smith
Thoughts on a Wet Sunday

Drizzle, a wet Sunday,
the roast in the oven.
New time at my disposal
that I have never had before,
like new clay
in the hands of the potter,
must be shaped, moulded,
made good use of.

Sarah Hunter
The Witchery of the Ocean

She said,
From girl-hood
a desire
to explore
the underworld
flailed my blood.

Time hung heavy
for fifteen years,
but afterwards
exploration
became a reality
and the witchery of the seas
astounded my eyes.

While diving under
tremendous cataracts
of water,

I beheld
a measure
of the ocean-bed
stippled
with every shape of shell
in existence.

Although my face-mask
was water-smeared,
I knew I was under
sharp scrutiny of fish
swishing and vaunting their tails
with the authority
of old residents.

Still cutting through
the watery catacombs
I alighted upon
the shattered hulk of a ship
whose sides were alive
with barnacle.

Time was waning
but I was determined to return
mostly to explore the ship;
I did go back
but found nothing worthy
of preservation.

Yet the thrill of fighting against
the fists of the ocean
was a sensation
which, for me,
can never be equalled.

Honor Patching The Starlings

One day, as she sat on the lower deck of a number forty-nine bus, the constant voice in her head stammered and fell silent.

It was the misogynist that caused it, of course, suddenly barking at her like that. Normally, she had no truck whatsoever with her fellow passengers. She would sit, unnoticed and unnoticing, apparently staring out of the bus window, although her gaze did not penetrate even as far as the grime on the glass. Her attention would be wholly engaged by the voice in her head, which might be analysing relationships, or speculating on the hidden characters of her friends, or the real state of their marriages. In a more intellectual mood, she might be assessing the political situation, or mentally reviewing books she had read. On the best days, when her mind was in its fullest feather, her imagination would take off like a bird, to soar and dive and ride on the thermals of fantasy.

Sometimes, the voice would divide into two, and she would have the most delightful conversations, such as the one she was having today with her grandmother. When the old woman was still alive, she and her granddaughter had hardly conversed at all, beyond everyday phrases concerning the price of beef, perhaps, or the next-door neighbour's sciatica. But now that Grandmother was dead, the two of them frequently indulged in long, intimate talks, generally about other members of the family.

But the misogynist spoiled it all.

'Bloody women!'

His voice cracked out with the force of a rifle shot, tumbling her into the present in a confused heap.

For a few seconds, she was so muddled she wasn't sure if this new voice was inside her head or out. Then she noticed a man, small, puckered and intense, with grey raincoat and bushy eyebrows, who was sitting next to her.

'All they ever do, women . . . yakkety yakkety yak. Hark at 'em, clucking away like a load of old hens.' He cocked his head towards her confidentially, as though to indicate that the two of them were utterly superior to the other passengers. 'Always moaning, of course. Never anything cheerful.' He paused to let the aptness of his remark sink in, inflating his lungs in a significant manner and exhaling again with a sardonic sigh. 'No, never anything cheerful – look at their miserable bloody faces.'

Brought down from the realms of imagination, she stared at him, bewildered, like a bird that has been momentarily stunned. Which women did he mean? And if he hated the female sex so much, why was he talking to her? She decided to ignore him and turned to the window again, trying to pick up her conversation with Grandmother. What were they discussing? Ah, yes, the real reasons behind Aunt Lilian's divorce.

But another voice intruded upon her consciousness.

'. . . it was ever so painful . . .' It was a woman's voice this time. '. . . I've never known anything like it. But, do you know, I had to wait six months for an appointment up at the hospital . . .'

She heard a small, explosive snort from the seat next to her and was aware that the misogynist was trying to catch her eye, but, firmly, she looked out of the window. Where was she? Oh yes, Aunt Lilian.

Desperately, she fixed her eyes on the window-pane, trying to shut the bus and its passengers out of her mind, but the image of Grandmother had slipped from her inattentive grasp and was floating away, like a balloon with its string dangling just out of reach.

The bus, held up in traffic, came to a standstill between two huge, headless stumps of Victorian brick, twenty feet or more high, one on either side of the road. She remembered the delicious shade of the railway arch that used to stand there, a wide stripe of shadow curved over the road on hot days. Remembered running to stand underneath it as it rocked and reverberated under the shrieking, terrible load of a train, watching the sudden little whispers of dust shaken from chinks in the brick, thrilled by the scary thought, will it fall? This time, will the bridge fall?

Remembering her childhood, the talking voice almost came back for a moment, but like a doleful chorus, the women on the bus intruded again.

She looked at the factory on the corner, where her grandfather used to work, and noticed for the first time that all the windows of the vast oblong building were boarded up. It was shut in by a six-foot fence of corrugated iron, topped with barbed wire. The gate was padlocked and a sign bore the name of a demolition company.

She tried to remember the factory hooter that always used to sound when she was getting dressed for school, and to picture Grandfather starting for work with his lunch-box. It was no use. Now she had noticed the women's voices, she couldn't ignore them.

On the opposite corner to the factory was the cinema where she used to spend Saturday afternoons with John Wayne, or Elvis Presley, or Donald Duck, the upholstery of the seat abrasive against her thighs as she sat in the stuffy darkness. The old cinema was plastered with signs and peeling posters. BINGO! EYES DOWN – SIX NIGHTS A WEEK! Then, papered on top of the first layer: BINGO – LAST BIG NIGHT! On top of that, PREMISES TO LET.

The engine roared and the bus wallowed and pitched forward again for a hundred yards or so, to the next stop, opposite a window full of Bargain Buys. Plastic bowls and scrubbing brushes adorned with bows of paper ribbon: SPECIAL OFFER THIS WEEK.

A woman in a tight blue coat was running for the bus, waving her arms in a hopeless, restricted sort of gesture. The bus-driver sat and watched her. Just as she reached the bus-stop, he closed the doors with a hiss and swung the bus out into the line of traffic. The woman stood panting, fanning herself ineffectually, her face red and sweating and resigned as she watched the bus draw away.

The cemetery was in sight now. Grandmother was buried here, somewhere among the gloomy rhododendron bushes that glistened, greasy-wet in the drizzle.

They passed a department store. A group of people on the pavement were watching a young man who had his head between the swing doors. He stood, white-faced, perfectly still, his hands at his sides, propping the door open with his close-cropped head, staring at nothing. Visible behind the glass, overalled assistants and suited store-detectives inside the shop, watching. They were waiting for the young man to do something, she decided, preferably something loud or violent that they would know how to deal with. But the youth just stared and propped open the door with his head, and the bus moved on.

At the next stop, the man with the fierce eyebrows got up to leave the bus. On the platform, he turned to the rest of the passengers with a ferocious scowl. 'Smile!' he shouted. 'Why don't some of you bloody well smile?'

Someone retorted, 'Smile yourself!' but the misogynist only scowled all the more as he alighted.

A brief silence, then the talk resumed.

A disabled man was crossing the road, infinitely slowly, like a tortoise crossing the Sahara. Apparently oblivious to the traffic which roared and hooted and ground its gears all around him, he made his way, step by slow, shuffling step, across the wide expanse of tarmac. Leaning heavily on his stick, he kept his eyes fixed on the oasis of the opposite pavement.

Though the man was crossing directly in front of the bus, the driver did not attempt to slow down. He made no more concessions to the pedestrian than the latter did to the traffic. Slowly, slowly, looking steadily ahead, the man crept across the road. The bus was twenty yards from him, then ten yards, then ten feet. He still concentrated on the pavement ahead. What else could he do, she thought. At about five feet away, the driver finally cursed and slammed on the brakes, and the bus juddered to a halt, inches away from the man. All the bus passengers were hurled into the back of the seat in front. The disabled pedestrian gave the bus-driver a cursory glance through the windscreen and continued his slow, determined crossing.

The silence then lasted for nearly a minute.

They came to Grand Parade, where the huge old elms hold out branches full of wrinkled, browning leaves against a darkening sky.

And there were the starlings.

First, the sound of them: thousands of excited, shrill squeaks, transformed into a whole choral symphony by the mere force of numbers. She craned her head to look at them through the grimy glass. The enormous flock of birds was like a storm-cloud in size and density, but it wheeled and turned and spiralled, now near, then distant again, now like a great dark umbrella opening and closing in the sky, now like a column of smoke rising and billowing and flattening out, now like a humming top or a cyclone. The chorus of sound filled her ears and resounded in her head, vibrating like some great, transcendental mantra.

I must be the only one who likes these birds, she thought, with her face pressed to the glass. The Council was constantly consulting experts to find out how to rid the town of the starlings. They had tried shooting, poisonous pellets, bird-scaring explosions, even playing tape-recordings of birds in distress. Nothing had succeeded. The starlings still flocked to those trees in their thousands at that time of year.

A woman saw her looking and leaned forward to speak. She was bound to say how filthy the starlings were, how the Council ought to do something about it.

'Beautiful, aren't they, those birds,' the woman said.

'Beautiful, that's what I say.'

She was too surprised to answer and could only nod and stare at the window and back out at the starlings.

The bus had stopped. A rowdy contingent of birds swooped down towards the window, wheeled up again and over the top of the bus, their cries and the soft, feathery flappings multiplied a thousand times, filling the bus with the sound. Heads craned to watch them go on the other side.

Everyone's face was right up against the glass, watching the birds as though their lives depended on it. Half-a-dozen people got onto the bus and everyone saw at the same moment that their clothes were scattered with fresh white splodges of bird-lime. Their hats, their hairdos, their suits and jackets and handbags were liberally dolloped with white, like so many plates of lettuce doused with salad-cream.

Now there will be ructions, she thought.

But, no. These people were laughing. They were looking at their clothes and gingerly feeling their heads and shaking out their jackets and *laughing*. And now the whole bus full of passengers was laughing. Someone said: 'That's supposed to be lucky, that is!' And everyone nodded and giggled and guffawed and wiped tears of laughter from their eyes. Even the driver had an approximation of a smile on his face as he took the fares.

And she was mentally up with the starlings, wheeling and turning and squeaking and dropping good luck on people's heads.

The talking voice in her head had started up again.

Lori Gatford Travel And Change

We look for a path
that leads to another place,
an endless strength travels with me
over stony paths, painful to tread.
We are alone in the lingering fumes of the city.
Shrouded in its poisonous fogs,
and painted with its dust and grime.
Wading through its waste,
dodging the canine edges of broken glass.

I can still hear the cry of melancholy,
but at the roadside there are thistles
the hardier specie flourishing on spiny ground,
stretching far over the horizon,
to the scent of the lavender flower,
to the blowing primroses.
And to a woman walking by the sea cliffs,
stepping through marshes in wellington boots.

Barbara Ponton
Sometimes at the Social Club

(for an old acquaintance)

While the music throbs and grows
thrust and flow,
Imogene will celebrate the Tango:
proud head tilts on brown arm
which curve must grace a throw.
Wadjet's eye confirms her kith in Pharoah:
bragging sandals swoop and glide,
trawling knees,
and sensual entirely she does entirely please.

The chi-chi music skybound
as her beckoning fingers tease.

But tempo styles passion
(this, women know)
especially when rhythm strides the crescendo.
Lost in a silence,
from cloud nine dropped low,
Mrs Lee panicking,
backs from the show.

Jenneba Sie Jalloh Untitled

WITCH PURE   MAGIC EVIL
WHITE   BLACK
SNOW GOOD   BAD WITCH

You have been charged
on the following counts:
1. HAVING A BLACK HEART
2. BEING A BLACK LEG
3. ISSUING A BLACK LIST
YOUR CHARACTER HAS BEEN BLACKENED
AND FROM HENCE FORTH THERE WILL BE
A BLACK MARK BY YOUR NAME
HAVE YOU ANYTHING TO SAY?
Well,
    Blacken my character,
that's the way it should be
Put that black mark
by my name,
makes no difference to me
I'll be that black mark . . .
    I AM THAT BLACK MARK
On your landscape
so white

and so terribly, terribly pure and clean.
Look at me,
I'm the
Black Sheep
the
Dark Cloud
   (with that lining so bright)
my Black heart is as Black
and as proud
as any Black heart could be
AND THEN . . .
   Everything went BLACK
And if you take that to mean
that what happened was bad . . .
                    THINK AGAIN

Kate Hall My Mother

I am
the daughter
of an amazon
she
survived
violence
pain
abuse
worked
hard
all her life
no
she's not
a six-foot-tall
warrior queen
she made
mistakes
felt weak
even

collapsed
occasionally
but always
rose again
phoenix-like
from
her life's
disasters
'life goes on'
she says
and
so it does
I am
the daughter
of an amazon
I
have
her
blood
in me.

Rene Carrick −18p−

Her genius she gladly
proclaims as her ingenuity
saves her pence,

those so badly needed
to hang together the nylon threads
that cover a woman's legs

And hold her life together.
A penny on the tea,
a penny on the butter.

He doesn't know the prices.
Gathering enough,
she buys the nylon threads

that cover a woman's legs
and hold her life together
she grins her triumph.

Jenneba Sie Jalloh The Promised Land

A stranger to Africa,
I know that upon reaching your shores;
Africa, my spiritual home . . .
I will find a culture different from the one I'm used to,
A music different to the one I'm used to hearing
A people who see me as apart, not a true African born.

But as an African, born in a foreign land
I must have something to dream in – something to believe in
I must feel there is a safe place,
Even if I never reach there myself . . .
                                    AFRICA

A stranger, an 'English Person'
But while I'm here, Africa, land of contradictions,
Suffering, starvation . . . first and greatest civilization . . .
                                    Hope . . . my father's land

Give me something to dream upon.

I may, eventually find . . . disillusionment,
But for now, in England, so cold, so unwelcoming
Let Africa be . . . THE PROMISED LAND

Dedicated to Dennis Brown's 'The Promised Land',
and to all exiles in a foreign land, who dream of, or remember a safer,
better place.

Theresa Verlaine Reaching

I want to reach for the sky
and pull down the rare blueness
that penetrates and eases my pain
to ease it more.

I want to reach out the window
and kiss the space that cushions me
from a cold and cynical world
that wasn't cold before.

I want to get drunk on happiness alone
like I did in the innocent days
when all I knew was nature's touch
as the moon beckoned.

I want to wave at the sun
and feel her kiss upon my face upturned,
knowing I can rest forever,
not merely a second.

Julie Cotterill Weekending

We had settled down to tea and lardy cake, when I saw the spider scrabble four or five repulsive inches up the fireplace surround. Because I was in polite company, I decided to give it a dirty look, hoping it would mooch towards the window, maybe toss an apology over one of its shoulders on the way out. It stretched to its full span and pumped up and down, plotting.

'How's the lardy cake?'

Dora's voice cut like a stylus into the reverential silence. The clock chimed five.

'It tastes of lard,' I said, still trying to commit insecticide with my right eye.

'Marvellous,' her family chorused, and Matthew added: 'Joe hasn't lost his touch.'

The spider spitefully tickled the surround with one of its legs. It was about to make a run for it.

'So tell me, Janet, how's the job-hunting going? Matt tells me that . . .'

'Someone's going to have to get rid of that bastard, right now,' I said, climbing on to the sofa in anticipation. Four pairs of eyes looked at me, and followed my shaking finger towards the spider, which had by now trebled in size and was under starter's orders.

'Get it!' The request was emphasized with a kick in the thigh to Matt, who laughed manfully and explained that spiders don't hurt you. I told him to repeat that statement the next time a jumping, red-kneed tarantula went for his jugular. By now, I was on the arm of the sofa and heading for the dinner table. Dora was eyeing the footprints I'd left on her oatmeal Chesterfield.

'I really do think Janet's feeling a little uncomfortable, darling,' she said to her husband. 'Scoop it up, would you?'

'And shut the window!' I shrieked, as he reached for the yogurt pot. 'The little buggers follow me about.'

This was my first encounter with the middle classes made flesh, and within ten minutes I'd blown it. The plan had been to assimilate.

Matthew and I did the journey from London to Cambridge by bus, the blazing July heat melting my Poppy-Red pout, nerves dissolving my stomach. Matt was the epitome of ragbag Oxfam chic from head to ankle. The feet were encased, as always, in solid, sensible, hardwearing, handmade leather shoes. Brown.

Dora met us at the bus station. She had short, dark blonde, practically-styled hair and a face scrubbed to a wax finish. She stretched an Indian-print sleeve out of the car window.

'Dora, this is Janet. Janet, my mother, Dora.'

'You call her by her name?' I said, shaking her hand.

'What's wrong with that?'

'My mother's name's Rosie, but even my dad calls her Mum,' I said, explaining my surprise.

'Delighted,' said Dora. She sounded like she'd just eaten the proverbial horse.

Home was a 400-year-old converted barn, nestling in half-an-acre of ordered chaos that, I later learned, kept the freezer stocked. Passing through the stripped pine, aga-warmed kitchen (it was here that I discovered how common eighteen-piece matching dinner services were), we entered the sitting-room: all elegant poverty – an upmarket jumble of sturdy antique leather, scattered rugs, a nod to Habitat, a monument to good taste. A portable, mono television set stood in disgrace over in the corner, its existence justified by the carafe of rough-cut, home-grown roses it supported.

The meals were endless. Supper (what I would have called tea, or dinner if I was trying to make myself understood to a Southerner) was taken around a huge, crowded table, amid noisy cross-talk; long and lazy breakfasts next to the aga; and then there was elevenses, something I'd grown up believing to be a figment of Enid Blyton's imagination. Tea, in the sitting-room, with cake and chit-chat; and lunch, a two-course affair, usually vegetarian. No wonder the middle classes can talk with their mouths full.

The class which demonstrates that good taste is symbolized by expensive understatement, sells to the plebs its fitted carpets, cocktail cabinets and wall-to-wall colour TVs, laughing all the while up its Burberry sleeve.

The unbreakable mealtime rules in my parents' house were, 'no elbows on the table and no talking'. We barely looked at each other, just ploughed through our food, cleared away the crocks and squabbled over who made the tea. Once, my youngest sister came to the table with two balloons packed inside her skinny rib jumper. She ate her meal, the false chest nudging her plate across the table like an ouija board glass and, while we siblings kicked each other and snorted into our hands, Mum and Dad munched silently on. It was only when we stood up to clear the table that Dad noticed. 'You're bloody daft, you,' he said.

Supper, chez-Dora, was a different matter, a lengthy process lasting more than two hours. An esteemed pudding was followed by coffee, which was drunk at the table. The talk was of politics, literature, family and friends; often it was about food – how a certain dish was made, whether it would have been better made with yogurt rather than cream. Each mouthful appeared to merit comment.

Dora, her politics hot off the *Guardian*'s presses, couldn't decide whether to ignore my background or acknowledge it. Ignoring it, she would speak conspiratorially of 'posh people', thus assuming that I didn't regard her family in this light. Acknowledging it left her with the uncomfortable feeling that I was lacking something. Culinary expertise, maybe? 'Have you ever tried smoked salmon?' she asked me, after I'd objected to her speaking about nasty processed foods in a mock Yorkshire accent. Some people don't have the gardens to fill the freezers, the freezers to save the money that buys gardens, that buys time, that buys choice . . .

She settled, often, for a mother's role, any sticky question of class hidden behind her billowing floral apron. 'You really are a fool for smoking, Janet. Give it up.'

'I've tried.'

'Well, try just having one after meals.'

'Don't think I could manage thirty meals a day.' She thinks I'm a little scrubber, I said to Matt.

Sunday found us on a drive out to the Cotswolds, and the country retreat of Uncle James, who was hosting an afternoon soirée to celebrate forty years in show-business. James's name was unfamiliar but, to my annoyance, his face was not: he'd played second lead in countless television soaps and featured in commercials for banks, supermarkets and the sort of convenience foods his wife would never consider feeding to her family. The dining-room was scattered with stars of peak-time viewing, heaping their plates with salads and dips, bleating after children called Sam, Jack and Sarah; dropping names, singing praises, twisting the knife. It was easy to remember who the adults were: they all answered to Darling.

'Darling, pleased to meet you. I'm James.' James poured more sangria into my nearly-full glass.

'Janet,' I corrected, covering the rim. An orange wedge splodged between my fingers.

'Janet, darling,' James said, addressing a space about six inches above my left shoulder. He was still pouring. 'Marvellous.'

'Absolutely,' I said, inching away to find a serviette.

On my way out, I heard James's mother describe her son's home as 'cosy'. It had four storeys and an extension on the kitchen. A mezzanine. Two receptions. A floor for each child. Matt, I said, your family is incredibly rich. Matthew had been kicked in the street-credibility and was hurt. 'My father has a thousand-pound overdraft,' he offered. 'If my father had a thousand-pound debt, he'd top himself,' I said..

Spot the difference.

Dora insisted that she didn't spoil her children, making them wait until birthdays and Christmas for the things they wanted. She listened to their problems, financially bailed them out, made a point of memorizing their friends' and colleagues' names, the smallest details of both her sons' lives. Matthew cherished an ambition to be a pop star and plucked painful, tuneless and talent-free jingles on a three-hundred-pound secondhand, dark cherry Gibson that Dora had given him to help him along. He thought a set of keyboards might conjure up an ability to write songs, and the Easter Bunny obliged. His brother, Alex, a similarly un-gifted musician, was equally indulged. They often forgot her birthday.

Matthew, then, was not surprised when his mother asked: 'Can you bear to get the bus back to London?'

Bear it? What was the woman talking about? All we had to do was get on the bus, sit there, and in an hour or so we would be in Victoria.

'How do you mean?' I asked, but Dora was looking at her son.

'Can you bear it, darling? I mean it's so bloody uncomfortable. And it will only take me a couple of hours to run you back.'

A lift back? From the Cotswolds to London? Wasn't that just a touch out of the way?

I was about to protest about petrol, inconvenience, my discomfort, even at being chauffered about in this way.

But Matthew pointed out, as we headed for the car, that my bag was rather heavy. And it was raining.

For Judith Morris and Mike Sawyer with love and thanks for all your encouragement.

Mandy Dee
Event On An Andean Mountain

Five rockmen
(average good men all)
kitted with the best
that money could buy;
crunched defeated through the ice-field.

Steadily upwards,
nearing them,
came an old man
(. . . beyond fifty . . .)
with a patched blue
anorak
and
cracking better–day
boots.

Astounded . . .

The rockmen
halted
to view this apparition
and were only just
underway
when

The woman
young
strong
but undoubtedly

too small for
(almost) anything
came around
the shoulder of
the mountain.

Determined
to prevent
inevitable disaster
the rockmen spoke firmly
'Go down, go back'

The steam was rising from their open mouths
as into view hopped
the man with tin legs, last of the three.

Metal struck metal struck rock
in sounds unfamiliar to their ears
as his blue and black-handled
crutches (National Health)
came
suddenly quiet
to the soft snow edge.

Overwhelmed,
their brave expectations
rubbed to bleeding
by these three eccentric fools,
the rockmen
bundled themselves

off
away
fast
down
the rock slopes

Later the three
at the summit
saw
what five had never reached

and came back
to talk
not of their impossible feats
but of laughter
on the mountain.

For Jonathan, Sue and Purdy.
'In from the cold' 2nd or 3rd issue
taken from a story by Norman Croucher, who was the man with tin legs.

SURVIVAL AND RESISTANCE

This final section attempts some definitions and challenges. Defining ourselves and challenging stereotypes is the first step in resisting exploitation. But until we organize together, create networks of support, refuges, resistance etc, that fight will be no more than it often is here – individual statements, angry letters, witty remarks to keep the pain at bay – private solutions.

Originally, some of us wanted to produce a book in which we, as working-class women, explored the boundaries of class and the relationship between class, feminism, race and sexuality. We wanted to arrive at our own definitions and come up with some strategies for action that would bring working-class women into coalitions and allow us to move forward.

Our early publicity was vague and invited contributions from working-class women on more or less any subject. We were inundated with material – letters, poetry, prose – from women who had been silenced, unpublished, or denied recognition as writers. The majority of these described the pain, the damage that we suffer, and few had begun to analyse our experiences.

Frequently the analysis we did receive was contained in correspondence. Sometimes it was angry, sometimes good-humoured, but however expressed, it was only a beginning. So, directed by the pieces sent in to us, a different, but powerful book has emerged and the original project has had to wait.

Two of us in the Common Thread have already agreed to co-edit a second book in which we will seek out land where we, along with other black and white working-class women with different experiences, sexualities and ages, can come together to explore our identities and the links we might forge.

In the meantime, our voices need to be heard everywhere, and the avalanche of words has to gather momentum and remind us of our roots and our strengths. As Alice Walker wrote:

> They were women then/My mama's generation/Husky of voice-Stout of/Step/With fists as well as/Hands/How they

battered down/Doors/And ironed/Starched white/Shirts/
How they led/Armies/Headragged Generals/Across mined/
Fields/Booby-trapped/Kitchens/To discover books/Desks/
A place for us/How they knew what we/*Must* know/With-
out knowing a page/Of it/Themselves.

These were not only black women – they were working-
class women, and they fought for us to have the right to
know.

Jeanne Wilding

Rozena Maart Brave Soil

The ground, she claimed was ready
the roots, it had to grow
the soil was dark and strong and bitter
but ME
she had to sow.

The reaping soon was over,
clenched teeth
and yet no cry.
A roaming moan alone was present,
on this eventful dawn.

When above the earth I showed,
a grey and crowded sky appeared,
my flowers dark
my siblings near
sprouting beside me without a fear.

The winters made us sway,
the summers made us dear,
in autumn we lay close by,
in spring we were so clear.

In later moons my petals changed
a deformation
I heard them say
they tried but failed
and later said
she's changed too much to save.

She'll wither or die
or dwell or stray,
her roots will no longer
belong.

Instead
those very petals extended
and grew
much more.

At home the talk continued,
at play it did not stop,
for me as flower,
the revolution
within has started,
and could not
could not, stop.

My petals enjoyed its
new environment,
my roots,
pulled at my breast,
for my roots was planted,
in black soil
that could not,
feared not, rest.

Hania Dolan Curly Cabbages

Working-class, feminist, lesbian, whatever the labels we choose, they can mean something different for each of us. What does it mean for me to be a working-class woman? I have only recently begun to ask this question, raising the lid on childhood memories repressed for years, allowing anger and past hurts to surface, making connections between strands of my life and with those of other women. Looking for answers meant looking back as far as I could remember, recording my working-class childhood, writing it as therapy.

One of my earliest memories is of being taken by my dad down to the allotment beside the railway line. We lived in a small terraced house with a tiny back yard, so Dad was lucky to have an allotment less than half a mile away. I loved going there, on a summer evening or Saturday afternoon, fascinated by the neat rows of huge curly cabbages, not much smaller than me, and the higgledy-piggledy shack on each plot looking as though it would fall down at any minute. I was in my element, pottering about talking to the gardeners, watching the mysteries of cultivation unfold, playing with the soft earth. The ultimate treat was when the woman who kept hens on the next allotment gave me a warm, newly laid egg to take home. It was always a speckly brown one, and the giving and receiving of it and the safe transporting home of it were accompanied by much excitement.

It didn't seem to matter here that we didn't have much money, that the vegetables my father grew were a necessary contribution to the housekeeping as well as something he loved doing between shifts at the asbestos factory. It didn't matter that my parents were immigrants, the children of peasant farmers, both having left school at fourteen. It didn't matter that Dad was Polish and did not speak English very well, or that Mum spoke with an Irish accent. These were simply the facts of our lives. The street was a friendly place, neighbours chatted at front doors, which were often left ajar. The older children of the street took care of the younger ones, taking them to the nearest playground, and people treated each other with respect.

All this changed when I was three and we moved house. Our old terrace was demolished a few years later, and by then we were living in a road of three-bedroomed semis with long back gardens. I don't know how my parents managed to buy this house, as my dad's wages were very low. But Mum had been working and carefully saving for about ten years before she married, and Dad won £300 on the pools, a lot in those days. When Mum came over from Ireland, she first worked as a machinist and then as a clerk in the office of a grocery wholesaler.

Meeting the mortgage repayments became increasingly difficult, especially when me and my sister, who was one when we moved, were joined by two brothers. We might have been happier if we hadn't moved, with money less of an issue and cause for argument between my parents. As it was, every penny of the housekeeping was accounted for each week, and Mum made a lot of our clothes, knitted and baked to stretch the budget, as well as taking in lodgers and later doing part-time jobs.

Several of the houses in the new street were occupied by middle-class snobs, who evidently thought we lowered the tone of their environment. The atmosphere here was very different – distrust, 'what will the neighbours think?' and 'keeping up with the Joneses' – if you could. Our immediate neighbours were pleasant enough, but two families who lived opposite and were related to each other, were particularly prejudiced. We couldn't really avoid them, as we went to the same church, where one of the families always sat in a prominent position to show off their expensive clothes. We went to the same school, too, sometimes being offered lifts in one family's car. We didn't have a car and were the last family to have a TV, and were made to feel that this lack of material wealth was somehow shameful. Few opportunities were lost to convey that our family was in some way inferior to theirs.

There was another family who would deliberately cross the road or turn away if we passed them in the street, although they would make a great show of being friendly with those they thought worthy of their attention. I remember Mum raging when they would stop to let their dog piss or shit against our front wall. This was more than being looked down upon, it was actual harassment. One morning we woke to find the magnificent six-foot-tall sunflowers which Dad had grown in the front garden, completely uprooted and dumped, wilting, on the pavement further up.

Mum was very ambitious for us and saw education as a way of ensuring better-paid jobs for her children. So for months before the eleven plus, she would give me extra homework, with me often in tears as she pushed me to try harder. I surprised my primary school teacher by passing it, and the entrance exam to the grammar school run by the Loretto nuns. My mother had been educated by nuns in Ireland and found them tyrannical. In her childhood, the priests used to humiliate poorer families by reading out at mass the amounts given in the collection. This seemed to be the spirit in which the nuns ran my school.

Mum was really proud that I'd got there, but it was a struggle to buy all the uniform.

We were always being asked for money, for school funds, raffle tickets or collections 'for the poor'. My mother said bitterly that we were poor, and that the nuns didn't have to worry where the next meal was coming from, but she would always try to scrape something together to save me humiliation. Others were not so lucky and were openly derided for lack of charity. A favourite cause was that of 'heathen black babies of Africa', and I wonder now what the few black girls in the school felt about this. As Catholics, we were taught to regard ourselves as superior to everyone else. But we could only make the grade by being, or pretending to be, middle-class. We were being educated for Catholic marriage and motherhood, and to be the 'wives of successful men', to quote the headmistress.

She was a particularly vindictive woman, whom I grew to hate. I remember at age twelve feeling desperately angry, but sickened, by her authority as she ruthlessly humiliated a girl in front of the whole class. This girl spoke with a broad Lancashire accent and was made to try and repeat words in a pronunciation alien to her, until she was crying with embarrassment at her failure.

It seems ironic, in these days of media hysteria about political indoctrination in schools, to remember the head telling us to persuade our parents to vote for the Tories, who supported Catholic schools and valued family life.

Later, at university, I became conscious of my own accent and the fact that most students came from very different backgrounds to mine. Class differences seemed much more obvious than at school. I studied for one year in Oxford and found myself trying to hide my Manchester accent from some people. This memory generates deep anger – anger at having to deny part of myself in order to feel acceptable.

As a child, I could not articulate the anger; the feelings of being devalued, the confusion. In my sixth year at school, I found expression for some of this anger by becoming politically active, but there was no space here for my personal feelings. I didn't think anyone would understand anyway, and it was quite a shock and revelation, years later, to hear other women talking about being working-class. This happened for me in a women's support and discussion group, tutored by a working-class woman, and in a CR group where two of us were working-class.

When we talked about our backgrounds I was overwhelmed by the strength of emotion rising in me as I allowed myself to remember and voice some of the anger and pain. Starting to talk in the CR group was a breakthrough, releasing energy which for years had been expended in 'forgetting', and forging an increased pride in being working-class. Once I'd allowed myself to remember and write about the hurtful things, I could move on to look at how I coped with the prejudice our family faced, and what a positive learning experience that was.

Strangely, it was religion with all its own oppressions which helped me to rationalize and understand what was happening as a child. We were unjustly treated, and there were many to identify with in the scriptures. But surely Jesus would be on our side, if there were sides.

Much confusion was caused by hypocrisy and double standards. Those neighbours in our street were not humble or charitable, and yet were very well in with the parish priest. I knew beyond doubt that their treatment of us was wrong and was somewhere being marked up against them. I knew as a child, too, that the prejudice we encountered was because we were different, and that this was not solely a class difference. As a Polish/Irish family we were 'other', foreign, and what we experienced was racism as well as classism. Of course, there were times when I wished we were like everyone else, but mostly, being different was exciting and positive. We were unique and special.

Our family history was much more interesting than other children's and we had relatives all over the world. We got to do things like Irish dancing, winning medals at the feis and parading in our costumes at the annual Catholic Whit Walks. We had a rich cultural heritage on both sides, and although the Irish influence on our up-bringing was stronger, I knew that both nations had a long and proud history of struggle against oppression. My mother was a powerful woman, sensitive and courageous. As I got older, it was through her that I gained insight into the unjust nature of our society, and particularly the position of women.

Her reaction to anti-Irish attitudes helped shape my first under-standing of racism. She identified strongly as working-class, always voting Labour, always wanting more for herself and her family, but never at the expense of other people. She had deter-mination and a vision which carried her through the struggle to rear a family and to meet the personal goal of becoming a qualified teacher. This she achieved just eighteen months before her death from cancer at age fifty.

Getting an education did not distance her from her class roots or change her politics. For me, too, having a university education and lots of qualifications does not mean that I stop being working-class. My sister also went to university, now works as a carer, and feels the same. Neither of our brothers had any higher education and they have contrasting attitudes to class. One is a firefighter who has not lost touch with his roots. The other now contributes to the system of oppression as a Tory-voting police officer. He says he knows that Mum would have hated the politics of what he does, and maybe it's to numb that thought that he drinks too much.

I still feel 'different' and unique, and am still putting the pieces together, exploring possibilities in my life through writing. I have been teaching for several years, but that's another story.

Hania Dolan is a pen-name, used because I cannot be out as a lesbian at work, but refuse to be made invisible as a working-class lesbian in my writing.

Nanette Herbert The Working Class

The popular (i.e. media) definition of the working class goes like this: The working class is loud, vulgar, it murders and gets murdered, the women stay at home and get pregnant endlessly, their husbands beat them up, steal and go to jail. Working-class people work in factories and shops, have parties (where they play records like 'The Birdy Song' and 'Viva Espana'), go to Spain for their holidays, allow themselves to be manipulated by the media (the TV they watch consists of soap operas, game shows and 'Carry On' films) – they like going to the cinema to watch sex and violence, films like *Rambo*, they wear the latest clothes, buy chart compilation records etc, they read *The Sun*, play bingo and do the football pools, take drugs, sniff glue, smoke twenty fags a day – they're pretty stupid.

But who's to really say what the working class is? The dictionary definition is: 'Grades of society comprising those employed for wages, especially in manual or industrial occupations'. By that definition, the millions of unemployed (of which I am one) aren't working-class – I guess they'd just be called 'poor'.

Each class seems to have rigid boundaries and its own rules, attitudes, history, tradition and language. It's difficult to go from one class to another – for instance, someone who's working class, would probably feel uncomfortable being in the same room as the upper and middle class – they'd feel out of place. Many working-class people would also resent the middle and upper class – they've had it easy and they don't know what the real world is like. Unfortunately, the people who rule us – the politicians, law-makers, judges and solicitors and the greater part of the media – are middle and, upper-class. I would love to see Mrs Thatcher try to live on unemployment benefit in some damp little bedsit. Maybe then she would see what it was like and try to change things – instead of trying to make it worse for the unemployed by deliberately making the DHSS as complicated as possible and gradually dismantling the Welfare State. Of course, Mrs Thatcher has private health care and is employed, so the lack of a Welfare State wouldn't bother her.

I wish that there were no class barriers. Sometimes people do break through – in the Sixties it was fashionable to be working-class – and some working-class people got rich by becoming pop stars, photographers, fashion designers etc, gaining economic power. It's rare for the working class to advance through education, because education is designed and run by the middle and upper class. The working class get overcrowded schools, poor teachers and materials. And they wonder why kids play truant.

The higher up the education scale you go, the more dominated it is by the middle and upper classes – and by men. Maybe, one day, there won't be any such thing as class. We will all be equal. Maybe . . .

Theresa Verlaine People like me

'People like you' she said
indignation choking the plums of her ever-full mouth
'People like you' she said
rage and anger flushing the already-rouged cheeks
'People like you' she said
spitting the words from a lipstick sneer and folding fur-coated arms
'People like you' she said
trailing off into a nose-in-the-air high and mighty silence
'People like you' she had said
looking me up and down with a contempt reserved solely for people like me.

'People like me' I said
looking her squarely in her hoity-toity middle-class eyes
'People like me' I said
'will rise up in their millions one day and wipe
People like you,' I said,
'off the face of this bloody earth.'

Jeanne Wilding
The Power of Letters and Articles

In 1983 I wrote a letter, published in a national women's liberation newsletter, calling on working-class women to organize together. At that time, it mattered little to me whether we organized a conference, series of workshops or meetings, or produced a collection of our writings. I simply wanted an opportunity to be with, and work with, working-class women who, like myself, felt that class was an important issue on which to focus. I had no idea, then, what a trigger that letter would be.

Over the last five years we've seen, and been part of, a lot of changes – working-class women's newsletters have been produced, more working-class women's groups have sprung up, more working-class women have started speaking out and writing, more have been published, we in Common Thread organized a series of readings of working-class women's words, participated in conferences, published articles and developed a film proposal about working-class women's lives for Channel 4 . . . and, of course, we put together this book. So, between us, we made sure that 'the voices of those too often silenced, ignored or . . . revised' were at last heard.

Before 1983, little had been written and published by working-class women about our experiences of class exploitation and oppression, or our sense of ourselves. There had been a few American anthologies and pamphlets, and some particularly inspiring writings by black women, which dealt, almost in passing, with class. In this country, two articles appeared around the late 1970s/early 1980s – both very different in style and approach, and both focusing on the women's movement. Despite the different ways in which they attempted to draw attention to class issues and the effects of classism – one raw, punchy and at times bitter and hostile, the other more conciliatory, more 'carefully reasoned', restrained and probing – both pieces were saying much the same, and were received by many middle-class feminists with either stony silence, a yawn, irritation, a dismissal or annoyance and defensiveness.

For many working-class women they spoke the unspeakable, challenged myths and stereotypes and encouraged us to assert our identity with pride.

Evelyn Tension's pamphlet, published in 1979, *You don't need a degree to read the writing on the wall*, seems a bit dated in parts, but much of the anger and analysis still has a resonance today. She describes her working-class identity as 'basic to who I am, how I think, talk, respond, behave, my aims (or lack of them), standards, what I expect, what I see, what I eat, drink, what I do, how I enjoy myself (very important that). The point of discussing class is not to make middle-class women feel guilty, and it's not to glorify the working-class . . . It's middle-class women who do that, with their flamboyant poverty and groovy working-classness . . . you don't glorify it if you've lived it . . .'

Much of what Evelyn wrote about her family and background rang immediate bells for me. Although having no middle-class aspirations, her parents, like my father, were keen for their daughters to get 'edgecated', and make a better life for themselves. They had no idea what that better life would entail, any more than Evelyn did. Our parents at least supported the idea of education, if not the day to day reality of it, and wanted us to pass exams – they didn't want us to be the kind of person we had to *be* in order to do so.

'Class distinction at grammar school was rampant. It was there that [Evelyn] first felt the sense of shame that goes with being working-class . . . It was there, too, that [she] first encountered a role now familiar . . . unco-operative, too emotional, hostile, crude . . . never heard of working-class culture until [she] found the women's movement.' She wondered what it was, but wasn't going to ask – 'most of my life in the East End [or Hunslet, Moss side, Falls Road, Liverpool 8, Brixton etc] and I didn't know what working-class culture was! No matter, there were plenty of experts on the subject. They glorified it, us having to make something out of nothing. So, it was communal and it was spontaneous! It was also the culture of a class who are powerless, who lived with over-crowding, damp, bad sanitation, poverty, enforced ignorance – and who have been repeatedly culturally raped. Working-class stereotypes are as much a creation of the ruling class as female stereotypes.'

In one section of the pamphlet, Evelyn describes how our relationship to the women's movement is characterized. Working-class women are seen as 'out there. Where they're safe. The stereotype is of the inarticulate working-class woman who can't help herself and can be used by middle-class women to boost their own egos and comfort themselves with their own reasonableness and charity. There's a tradition of working-class and middle-class women working together alright: the tradition is that the middle-class women are the leaders, managers, helpers. That's the trouble with people who can help you, they want you to stay down, so's they can go on helping. And those who "give" help, whilst keeping control of it, can always, if they disapprove or feel threatened, withdraw it . . . [well, working-class women] want equality, not sympathy, not patronage.'

Evelyn has a lot to say about communication and language – and about 'being nice'. She's adamant that ways of talking come from our material position in society. 'The middle-class indirect speech, full of innuendos and possibilities, perhapses and maybes, this day, next day, sometime, never, their lack of urgency, are a product of time. Working-class women are always running to catch up . . .'

In a letter to one of the leading exponents of revolutionary feminism some years ago, frustrated at her casual disregard for economic class, I wrote – It's no coincidence that the women who are most able to get their ideas into print are predominantly women who earn their living in the realm of ideas, research, lecturing or whatever. It's no coincidence that very few of our theoreticians are women with young children, women who work in occupations involving long hours, physically draining types of work. (She had told me to stop whingeing on about class and do as she did on gender – write about it.) Well, working ten hours a day, and bringing up a child without help, does actually limit the time and space you have for doing other things! And to cite the exception does not challenge the general rule. It seems incredible now, that I should have been forced into a defence of working-class women, who were somehow being caricatured as less serious, less able, lazy or a distraction! When I re-read my copy of that letter, and many others I wrote challenging women on their classism, I'm struck by how polite and 'nice' I always tried to be, even when angry!

Evelyn argues that 'being nice', or using verbal niceties, is one of the insidious ways that those with power and privilege control their 'inferiors'. Not that she's advocating that we should all be as nasty as possible – and although she believes that working-class people are more honest, less hypocritical and mannered, she doesn't delude herself that 'relationships inside working-class families are . . . more candid, generous and warm, with everyone saying what they think and feel. Another middle-class romanticism – those are the characteristics of a future society, not of the oppressed class in a class society.'

Along with Evelyn Tension, when I've tackled people on their behaviour, language, assumptions and their classism, I've frequently been advised to 'moderate the way that I talk. Otherwise, I would alienate people and they wouldn't listen to me. Great stuff! It's the refinements of language that make it most difficult to challenge the actions, attitudes and dominance of middle-class women. Out come the clichés, defences, justifications, all glued together with moral superiority . . . As soon as working-class women begin to talk we're told we're not working-class because we're articulate.'

The image of us as inarticulate allows others to continue to determine what's good for us, '. . . to extend their tolerance and expect our gratitude. The mistake is to assume that any articulate woman is middle-class because of the middle-class assumption that working-class speech is a lesser, ungrammatical version of their own: diminished and diminishing!' All of us in the Common Thread, at some time or other, have been greeted by pernicious portrayals of working-class women – the scenario so graphically described in the words, 'Oh, you're not a real working-class woman'.

'Real working-class women wear iron curlers, have a bottle of stout hanging out of our pinny pockets, like Florrie Capp,' Evelyn writes. 'And we're all the same, too, which is nice – means they can see us coming a mile off. If we're standing next to them and talking about feminism and classism – well, we can't be working-class, can we? Feminists are middle-class! There's an educated middle-class argument and circularity for you . . . In particular, they tell a working-class woman who's been to university or college that she's not working-class any more. Too bad about the twenty-odd years that went before . . .'

The pamphlet is useful, in that it lists and details the many denial tactics used to maintain middle-class women's advantages, and our dependence and silence.

'Some middle-class women go through every detail of their lives to prove that they're not middle-class at all. They suddenly find a long-lost working-class relative, who is produced like a rabbit out of a hat. Hoping to blur class lines, avoid change, and preserve their own position. Some . . . try to deal with class guilt by having a working-class friend or lover . . . Guilt is one of the best smoke-screens there is . . . they wear it like their Sunday best . . . If they feel guilty, they think it's enough.

'Then there's the divide and rule tactic. It goes, "but you're different, it's possible to talk to you, you're reasonable . . ." Working-class women, of course, are not reasonable – we're over-emotional nitwits . . . There are certain ways of talking, more acceptable than others. Controlled/controlling "rational" speech which, on no account must be interrupted . . . [otherwise you're] bad-mannered or hostile or . . . unsisterly . . . not making the right connections (theirs) and uneducated . . . Almost the worst are the women who try to explain us away: "Yes, so-and-so's a bit hostile, but she's had a hard life . . . she can't really help it . . . not really responsible, bit weak in the head . . ." I saw a hoarding outside a church: "The Lord is gracious and merciful. He is slow to anger and filled with steadfast . . ." Ah well, I thought, even the Lord is middle-class – no help there . . . How about this one: You tell us when we're being classist so that we can stop doing it. Putting all the responsibility on us. Hoping we'll tire ourselves out?' The list of denial tactics is endless.

For Evelyn, one of the solutions is for working-class feminists to organize together and struggle 'for our own consciousness, to understand how we've learned to hate ourselves and (some of us) our own class, to break with the need for middle-class approval . . . that's difficult. I don't know if we give the impression of being brave and strong and fearless, but I don't think we are. Sometimes, the noisiest people are the scaredest people'. She

315

admits to being full of fear, doubt and disillusion, but she still wants to build a working-class women's movement.

Marlene Packwood's article, published originally in *Trouble and Strife* in 1983, covers much the same terrain. It's worth reproducing, not just for itself, but because of the reaction it aroused.

It has been the policy of the Common Thread to include work from working-class women only. One extremely patronizing letter, published here in response to Marlene's article, is from Hilary P., who defines herself as middle-class. This would seem to contradict Common Thread's policy, but the letter was included

a) as a vehicle for the debate which followed and

b) because, while the collective would not wish to define women's class for them, it rejects Hilary P.'s definition of middle-class as 'educated, articulate and able to use the media'.

Kate M's criticism of Hilary's letter and Marlene's last word completes the section.

Marlene Packwood
The Colonel's Lady And Judy O'Grady – Sisters Under The Skin?

Being working-class has its trials and tribulations, no less in the Women's Liberation Movement than elsewhere. The disgruntled noises of rebellion and dissension have been heard for some years now from working-class women such as myself, yet they remain ignored by the majority. This paper began when I asked myself why I got so angry with the coarse rebellion of working-class women which occurred from time to time in the WLM. Was I looking for a more refined insurrection? A more genteel revolution? This became my starting point. A stone which, when I turned it over, revealed the middle-class values I had absorbed, and a mentality which states 'don't rock the boat'. I had learned my lesson well in the middle-class grammar school I had attended, along with a small number of working-class girls from poor families: bright girls from 'dim' homes. Perhaps others will recognize the symptoms – the fermenting working-class anger placated by the carrot in front of the donkey's nose.

In the women's movement, working-class anger sometimes comes out sharply and with jagged edges . . . The resentment and hasty conclusions of these confrontations are that middle-class women are complacent, comfortable, unable to recognize the everyday struggles for money to pay the rent, to find a decent place to live without being able to afford a mortgage, finding a job – any job, paying gas, electricity, phone bills, or finding the price of a bus fare into town. Issues I call 'basic survival numbers', of which the middle classes appear to be unaware, cause desperation and despair. Yet these merely concern money. They do not encompass the deeper attitudes which cause feelings of inferiority and loss of confidence – lack of a good education and the luxury of having words that spring to mind for use in argument or debate; articulateness with the whole of the English language and not merely that section of it which the working class is seen as fit to consume in schools. (Despite this, I think working-class women are more articulate than middle-class women in using a combination of language, anger and emotion in order to be understood.) Perhaps this is why the reception we get when we lose our tempers with middle-class women in the heat of an argument is one of passivity, cold-shouldering, back-turning, snubs, coy snobbery, or fear and tears, none of which is conducive to discussion and debate.

As a result, many women are reluctant to declare their class origins openly. Many's the time working-class women will try to pass as middle-class by disguising their accent or (lack of) education, or by buttoning their lips. Other women will not reveal that they are middle-class, fearing to appear oppressive; or not question privilege . . . One thing is utterly clear – one class is subordinate to the other, and each fears the other for reasons which are power-laden.

It's my contention that middle-class women will have to acknowledge the advantages they have gained by virtue of their class (by birth and circumstance) . . . In a country where over eighty per cent of the population are working-class, that should also be the class composition of women in the WLM. However, this is not the case. The foundations of the movement originated through middle-class ideals, hopes and aspirations, via women in universities and the male left in the late Sixties . . . this class power base has not shifted to accommodate the new women coming in [and there hasn't been an] acceptance and incorporation of working-class women's values . . . Working-class women's culture, ideals, hopes and plans for a feminist future are as valid as anyone else's, even if our tradition is often more verbal than written. Perhaps some of our voices are so loud because, even up until very recently, working-class women were ridiculed as worthy of only pity or charity, or amusement.

Mrs Mop, with her views on the British Empire, or the harassed housewife stuck in a tower block, on the verge of a nervous breakdown – both are stereotypical images . . . of working-class women . . . How strongly the middle-class media has attempted to trip us up – through our lack of education – which they are so greedily preventing us from having access to. Working-class women who do manage to achieve any higher education are immediately reached out to by the middle classes, in an attempt to absorb them. Hence, education can only be a middle-class phenomenon and the working-class woman who escapes her traditional, allotted place in the hierarchy is penalized through a denial of her roots.

Middle-class education has always had within it a sense of callousness and the selfish hoarding of information, which is at the root of what undermines the confidence of working-class women. This attitude is often unrecognized and unacknowledged in feminist meetings and is a prime bone of contention, for it means that some women are 'in the know' and others are not.

For instance, until recently, there were few 'great' women novelists and writers, but the contribution of working-class women to literature has been non-existent. Never allowed to read and write until the turn of the century, and then only in small numbers, our experience has had to rely on a verbal tradition, mother to daughter, sister to sister, or be rendered invisible. Even today, the methods of teaching literacy remain middle-class and so a great number of working-class people remain either illiterate or semi-literate. By this, I mean they may be able to read and write but find it hard . . . to express themselves in what can appear to be an alien language. Such a situation cuts across all the races and cultures which make up this country, and thus racism and classism become interwoven. Following on from this, even when working-class women can write, they are discouraged from being heard (i.e. published), unless they conform to the established principles of traditional writing and literature . . .

But to speak about literature, or theatre and film, is to open up not only 'culture', but also the arena of the most influential image-makers in this country; such illusions of grandeur project far beyond most women's experience. Historically, this situation has changed little over time. Working-class women have been actively prevented from making their mark, or furthering images of themselves as positive, determined, intelligent, softly spoken, perceptive, caring, supportive and angry. For the record, current images show working-class women as ignorant, dominating, gossipy, unaware politically and in relation to current affairs, loudmouthed, insensitive, uncaring and selfish. Both television and the press are responsible . . .

All of this goes some way to describing the lack of validation working-class women live with daily. Bombarded by imported American materialism via soap operas such as 'Dallas' and 'Dynasty', and devoid of strong heroine figures, it is hard for us to find any images of peers who have risen without rejecting their roots. Our anger and resentment at women who seem to succeed on their own, while we do not, who have space to pay for (working-class) babysitters and au pairs, comes out sideways . . . The images which are presented via the media, TV, magazines and the gutter press, reinforce our roles in life, our lack of advantages and low horizons. *The Sun* tells us how profitable it could be if we took our clothes off and sold our bodies to men . . .

Our confidence is weak, our voices quiet, and our demands ignored against those who [took for granted the] benefits of a university education . . . working-class women are forced into the narrow spheres of servicing others – modelling, hairdressing, serving in shops, working in factories, nursing, striptease, prostitution. In fact, any servile job which guarantees a steady income.

As Carole Hanisch pointed out in *Feminist Revolution*: 'Raising working-class consciousness – our own and others' – would do

319

two things: build a working-class movement which would be in our interests as workers, and help change men's consciousness on feminism . . .' This means we need to explore how Socialists and working-class men have also been instrumental in keeping working-class women down, and from defining their own culture and history . . . And middle-class women, too, whether inside the movement or not, do play a part in rendering invisible working-class women.

Classism today is the culmination of this situation. It represents a specific oppression where the rules, values, mores and ideals of one class are imposed upon another . . . within feminism it filters through from middle-class to working-class women, denying us a language, banning us from self-expression, labelling us as ignorant, stupid, coarse, bombastic, rough, uneducated and ineffectual . . .

In these times of financial hardship, middle-class women appear to be consolidating their positions in their careers. If these careers are not opened up to working-class women, this causes even more suspicion, snobbery and secretiveness, as do salaries which are two or three times those of their sisters. Money may be the root of all evil. If there is no opening up and honesty about what women do own and control (as well as what they do not), a situation of secrecy can only be perceived by working-class women as one of snobbery, prejudice, greed and guilt. Time has come for a long-overdue discussion and implementation of income-sharing, as well as on inherited wealth, and where this came from and how it was made. If we are serious about any Socialist principles which women's liberation is supposed to hold, then there has to be a dialogue about the redistribution of wealth . . . As a whole, working-class women have less chance of going to college or university, less chance of fulfilling, creative work than ever before . . .

The issue of the way we as women support each other has never been without complications, yet such support and solidarity is the very fabric of our movement, of living and learning. It is part of our process of achieving change as well as our long-term goal: the constant creation of a political movement dedicated to radical change for women . . . The issue of the laying-on of middle-class values when working-class women try to organize,

320

or even the ways in which we communicate in meetings, must be treated more seriously, and with respect – it must not be given the sceptical, objective distancing which . . . working-class women have been subject to for so long.

Reply to Marlene Packwood – from Hilary P.

Marlene Packwood . . . I am sure you are right that middle-class women often are complacent, patronizing and unimaginative, and do sometimes use their articulacy and education as a weapon rather than a bridge. They often don't realize their own advantages, and, yes, they often do resort to ignorant stereotypes. But . . . You mention the working-class women's culture, ideals, hopes and plans for a feminist future. Here you had a good opportunity, in a long article, to at least sketch out where these differed from those of middle-class women, so that we could see and discuss the differences, and find areas where perhaps both groups were missing out. (You obliquely referred to one; the middle-class fear of displaying emotion or getting angry.)

Like lots of middle-class women, both I and my husband are of working-class roots, a generation back. All I tend to mean by middle-class is 'educated', articulate and able to use the media. I totally agree that using one's bootstrap for a ladder and then pulling it up behind one is an unlovely thing to do, but I have certainly never felt that the middle classes were greedily preventing access of anyone to it. More, I would say that they are constantly preaching and lecturing and trying to impart it to people who, as you say, they then absorb. I don't think you can simultaneously accuse the same people of both excluding and absorbing.

I agree about the non-existent contribution of the working class, but not as a shocking new fact. It simply follows from my own definition. The people who dominate the media, write the books and make the images, simply *are* the middle class. And Marlene Packwood, trenchant, articulate, highly verbal, is too . . . It is now infinitely easier to be listened to on the media with a regional, low-status accent than it used to be – people don't have to deny their background as they used to.

I don't really understand the bit about 'denying working-class women a language' by the use of elaborate phrases, academic jargon, and the rest. It happens, but I haven't noticed it in the feminist press . . . In any case, I see no difference between the way you write, presumably with this problem in mind, and the way I am doing. How many working-class women do you know who could define 'catalyst', 'misogynist', 'validation', which you have used in several places? How concerned were you that working-class women would be able to understand your piece?

Where I do say, 'Yes, amen', is the so-often, barely-disguised patronizing of the working classes, the stereotypes you discuss, the cosy ignorance of money problems, the emotional coldness and 'sceptical, objective distancing' which you describe so well. These often result in hostility and rudeness from the 'other side' which is only too understandable, but makes it difficult for any one individual to stop the rot. But you are right that those who have most of the advantages should be making all the gestures and holding out more genuine offers of sisterly support. I wish, though, that you could have offered to the (mainly middle-class) readership a slightly less doleful view of the working class – if, as you tend to suggest, their attitudes consist of resentment about what the middle classes have and they haven't, then it is hardly surprising that people deny their roots once they gain these goodies.

As a child, I used regularly to visit for holidays an elderly aunt in the heart of Failsworth, a working-class area of Manchester. I was always sorry to leave, and in many respects have only realized in adulthood what that community had which the one I live in now doesn't. It would probably sound patronizing of me now to try to describe their culture, and anyhow this has been done many times over in books like Richard Hoggart's *The Uses of Literacy*. Next time, Ms Packwood, please try to make *us* feel jealous of what they have which often we haven't; it might be a more effective way in the long run of making us listen. A lot of women sometimes feel they are prisoners of middle classness.

And a reply to Hilary P. from Kate Monster.

The most enraging letter I came across, and the one that finally prompted me to reply, was Hilary P.'s 'What is class?'. What, indeed? You could almost be forgiven for thinking that you'd made the whole thing up, and the history of industrial capitalist society had been a bad dream, when you read that all she intends to mean by middle-class is 'educated, articulate and able to use the media'.

She seems to want to confirm a romantic notion of what it's like to be working-class (which, she says, she learned from visiting her aunt in Manchester), else why would she demand that working-class women present a 'less doleful view' of our position than Marlene Packwood did?

To say, as she does, that people don't have to deny their backgrounds as they used to, is a blatant lie. It totally sidesteps and denies the reality of many women's attempts to bridge the gulf between assumptions that are made about who you are when: 1. You're an 'educated' woman with, perhaps, a well-paid job, and 2. The woman that you know yourself to be, irrespective of your financial circumstances.

It is not with nostalgia, but anger and pain, that you consider your ma's varicose veins and your dad's fascist or left-wing politics. Over the years you see your brothers' and sisters' horizons become more and more limited. You watch them take their sense of worth from new and useless goods, foisted on us all by the advertisers. They may gain their pride from a car, a telly or a garden full of builder's dirt if they're lucky enough to get one of those council houses on a new estate.

Keeping body and soul together while working a lifetime away for these prizes is no easy task. Any passion for art, music, books you may be moved to describe as literature, must be firmly contained, if not suffocated, and your total energy channelled, instead, into the precarious business of staying alive. The fear is that if you relax this tight control, your spirit will scream with rage until they carry you off to the loony bin. And for many, many working-class women, this is exactly what happens.

It is not always long before you sneer contemptuously about earlier dreams and ambitions. By the time you get 'careers' advice . . . you've probably already recognized the great myth (that you can do anything if you work hard enough) for what it is. If you give up at this point, the feeling of defeat may never leave you. If you fight on, the responsibility is enormous. What it must be like to struggle through the British education system, hanging on to a notion of 'bettering yourself', I can hardly imagine. But when I try to picture it, it seems to me like an unending diet. A constant curtailing of your needs to fit in with some professor's notion of a broadminded individual.

Oh yes, Ms P, we certainly must deny our backgrounds, and our whole lived reality as well. I meet 'successful' working-class lesbians every day, who testify to the harm that does us.

Ponder, if you will, the implications for us all, when working-class women emerge out of college, with sociology degrees (three years of middle-class men's class analysis) and a brave new vocabulary with its carefully tailored, yet inevitably ill-fitting Queen's English accent. What are we to do with our dislocated histories – community work?

Writers who struggle to reconcile this kind of experience are a brave few who truly seek the meaning of integrity and offer it to us as a living word in a living language. As such, Marlene Packwood has my respect, even if I disagree with aspects of her politics. How dare Hilary P. bait her, and the rest of us, with suggestions that we cannot define words like 'catalyst'.

Despite platitudes about feeling a prisoner of middle classness, Hilary Ps' complacency is apparent throughout her letter. She says that illiteracy is one of the things by which she defines class, not a shocking or new discovery, and goes on to suggest that Marlene change her writing style. She says it might be a more effective way of making them listen. I say that this attitude betrays her patronizing arrogance. My mother would say it reflected on her upbringing, and I suppose that just about sums it up.

And a final word from Marlene:

Please don't force me into the middle-class mould . . . I don't want to go into it, nor do I feel a part of it. In fact, I am very much in limbo right now, with a working-class background and life-style, resisting middle-class absorption, trying to create a new space for working-class women. I expect to be here for the rest of my life. I can't feel 'jealous' of what 'they' have (as you say), for I honestly don't know if it's any good to me. I have enough to contend with right now, exploring working-class women's existence.

Annette Kennerley
Under The Bedclothes . . .

My mother had to read under the bedclothes, at night, by
    candlelight.
It wasn't considered 'decent' in those days –
Only the idle rich indulged in such a pastime.
Education came hard in those days to my mother.
A snatched, guilty luxury.
It came easier to me.
I read books, I worked at school, I went to university.
But I kept my class roots hidden under the bedclothes –
It still wasn't considered 'decent' in my day to be
    working-class.

Letters to a Working-Class Women's Magazine

In 1987 a new magazine/newsletter was launched. It was called
Working-Class Women's Voice.

The editorial was confused and, in part, simplistic, but on the
positive side it contained a paragraph prominently headed
'CLASS'; it made clear that class and classism were central issues,
and it stated boldly that the magazine was for working-class
women only.

Over the next few issues the confusion increased. The magazine's title changed to 'Black/Non-white and Working-Class
Women', suggesting that working-class women were all white,
and implying that the magazine was now for some middle-class
women – as long as they were black, etc. Blank pages were
introduced for black women, the two white women producing
the magazine threw out an invitation to black women to take it
over, and the section of the editorial headed 'Class' became 'Race
and Class'.

Frustrated that class looked like it was going to drop off the agenda altogether, and concerned that the editorial duo seemed to be disappearing under a morass of guilt instead of dealing with white racism unflinchingly, Jeanne – a white lesbian – wrote to the magazine asking for more information, raising questions on their policies, and offering support and constructive suggestions. She also wrote about white racism, and the magazine's policy of no personal attacks.

Thankfully, a number of women wrote, and, in particular, Maria Noble tackled the magazine's racism. These letters and criticisms were welcomed by the editors. As a result, the title eventually settled at 'Black and White Working-Class Women's Voice', the tokenistic blank pages, held in reserve for black women, and the confused editorial were scrapped, and the magazine became livelier and much improved.

We've included only extracts from two of the letters which contributed to these debates and changes.

Firstly, from Maria –:

Well, here I am, sisters. I'm uncertain whether I'm going to end up feeling like the token black voice in your magazine (assuming you're not into skin politics, because these days it seems that if you're light-skinned you're not black enough to claim that identity – but that's another story!).

I'm not a woman of colour – that, to me, is just another way of lumping together anyone who isn't of white European origin. Perhaps I'm not working-class enough because I earn a good wage, and yet I think to myself, how long has that been in coming, and how long will it last when the powers that be realize I won't sell my soul for the pennies, nor sell out my community? Maybe it will all come to an end when black people/equal opportunities cease to be flavour of the month.

My commitment to writing this piece stems from a belief that Afro-Caribbean and Asian women in this country need to actively work with black/working-class struggles. Whatever our family and economic background, we can't escape racial or class oppression by trying to hide our origins or climb up the social ladder: we can't free ourselves without challenging all forms of oppression. In writing, I'm keeping in mind the need for black

326

and white women to find common ground on which to unite in this struggle.

There are so many things I want to say about this magazine. Firstly, I'M GLAD THAT IT'S HERE. In response to the letter from the editors in the November issue, I would say:

The two pages reserved for black women *were* tokenism, but changing the name of the magazine is not enough to make it a real voice for black women.

I don't expect white women to jump because I shout, but to have respect for my views and the experience that creates them.

To invite any black woman to take over the direction of the magazine is in itself racist. Black women vary in their politics as much as any group of women. Some of us are so deeply scarred by racism and class discrimination that we can hardly recognize what is happening to us and end up being carried along and used to work against ourselves and others.

Given that white working-class women have to fight against feeling inferior, just guess what it is like for black women, because every part of our culture and background, appearance and life is put down or made to seem exotic – e.g. black women are seen as passive, aggressive, ugly, stupid, sex-mad, vulnerable, crazy etc, etc.

I accept that men create the bulk of the problems for women because they have the power and they want to hold on to it. I don't see it as my role to defend or promote men's interests, but as a black woman I experience racism. My skin colour provides one of several excuses for powerful white men to divide and rule everyone else.

It is crucial that, even though I challenge them on various fronts, I stand with black men in fighting racism. Viraj Mendis is being deported as a black political activist. He is determined to fight back, and therefore the Government is determined that he should go. The police give black men a hard time because of racist ideas that all black men are criminals. I saw that, in the last issue, it was black men who were at the top of *your* list of male 'baddies'.

Why do you feel so sure that black/Irish/lesbian (some of us are all of these) women have other space to publicize issues which concern them?

You want to hear 'what racism means for black women'. For

this black woman it is too often about white women constantly wanting to tell me what racism means. 'It's *always* happening to me, don't be so sensitive' . . . 'I know just what you mean, I'm oppressed too'. . . 'Who me? I'm not racist'. . . 'Well other black women don't say that' . . . Perhaps worse are those who say one thing in support of black women, but in *practice* act against us.

My main concern at present is not about who the magazine is for, but about what black and white working-class women can say in it and how relevant it is to them.

You say that you will not print anything which attacks identifiable women. In doing so, you assume that every woman has an equal voice, has a chance to speak or a place where she can be heard.

Black women have not shied away from trying to make their voice heard or demanding to be heard and respected, but we don't generally have as much power and status as white/middle-class women. Surely you must recognize this, as working-class women!

There are many white women who pass themselves off as 'liberal' and 'fairminded', who are *racist* and use their power to damage individual black women. Can't black women at least make that behaviour public? One weapon that should not be denied to black women is the right to publicly challenge what we see as racism, and, where necessary, to make other women accountable. Assuming, of course, that there is a right to reply.

You have already denied that weapon to Black Women for Wages for Housework. Having spent an afternoon recently being inspired and soothed by Audre Lorde, the Afro-American lesbian writer, I was appalled to hear the same women who, moments before, had applauded her went on to hiss Black Women for Wages for Housework. To borrow Audre's words – 'For other women of all ages, colour and sexual identities who recognize that imposed silence about any area of our lives is a tool for separation and powerlessness . . .' – Please review your policy.

Yours in sisterhood,

Maria Noble

And from Jeanne:

. . . On your new title for the magazine – I'm not sure whether you mean by it *all* working-class women, or whether you mean black and non-white women regardless of class, and white working-class women. Reading through your editorial, it does sound as if, whenever you write 'working-class' you really mean '*white* working-class'. Maybe I'm reading it wrongly. I also wasn't sure who was non-white but not black . . . I think it's important to change the magazine's title – to name black and white working-class women, and to have an editorial policy on racism, but in your recent editorial the section, previously headed WORKING CLASS, has now been replaced by the heading CLASS AND RACE, and the specifics of both struggles are lost. The oppressions of classism and racism, though twins with much in common, are not the same, and should surely not be lumped together . . .

In response to your queries about whether black women identify as working-class – again, I don't believe that black *or* white women should be lumped together as if they/we had one view. I know of black women who don't identify as working or middle-class, and I know black women who see classism as important and insist that there are class differences within the black community. Come to think of it, I know lots of white women who deny class differences or won't acknowledge class as an issue, and I don't agree with black or white women who say they're classless. That doesn't mean I think we should put class before other oppressions like race, disability, gender, sexuality – alongside will do. But at the moment, classism seems to be universally denied – by the Right and Left, by radical and Socialist feminists and by white and black middle-class women, as an arena for struggle . . .

If I was producing a magazine for working-class women, I would not want it to be read by *any* middle-class women, *all* of whom are capable of oppressing me as a working-class woman. I can't really think of black women as any more classless than white women. But how black women define *themselves*, and how they relate to the British class system, is for black women to debate and decide. I know that deciding on an editorial policy is never simple, and being prepared to make decisions, and take responsibility for and stand by them, is easier said than done . . . It's a huge mess, which we've got into collectively as white women – the cycle of unthinking and complacent white racism, followed by denial, tokenism; followed by guilt; followed by resentment and anger against the objects of our racism, who never asked us to feel guilty in the first place!

Because all my life I've lived in working-class areas populated by black and white people of all nationalities, and because of the books which inspired the founding of Common Thread, most of which were written by black women (dealing with economic exploitation so graphically, and putting into words so much of my own anger), the notion of working-class being other than black and white is unthinkable. At the same time, I know from my own experience . . . that for many people, the term 'working class' conjures up stereotype images of the Barnsley miner (and his wife), Hilda and Stan Ogden, Flo and Andy Capp – all of them white. So, yes, I do think it's necessary to spell out who we include and exclude in the title or in the blurb . . .

Anyway, in case this sounds like a whole bunch of gripes, I'm looking forward to the next issue on women's experience of being working-class, and am really grateful for all the work you must be putting in to producing this magazine.

Yours in sisterhood, Nov 1987.
Jeanne

Jeanne Wilding Letters to a Bookshop

Last year, I had an argument with one of the workers in a feminist bookshop. They'd renamed their 'Working-Class Women's section' 'Community' and, as the following letters explain, their reasons were ill-thought out, defensive and classist. It was a lengthy and, for me, unpleasant debate. I was snubbed and patronized by the collective. After several letters from me, they finally replied – but unfortunately refused permission to publish. Their reply cast me in the rôle of gross and hysterical customer, and political simpleton. I ended up writing a final letter in a pompous tone, similar to theirs – which is a bit sad – and several other working-class women's groups, horrified at the bookshop's letter, and at the removal of the working-class women's section, also sent in letters of complaint.

The argument eventually led to a re-discussion by the bookshop collective, and as a result of the complaints, in person and by letter, the working-class women's section was reinstated.

Dear Sisters,

I wrote to you a month ago, after an argument over your removal of the Working-Class Women's section. On that day, you asked me to leave. You said that to discuss the matter with me in the shop would interfere with business, and that if I had any complaints about your stocking policy I should write in formally. In my letter, I explained how upsetting that incident was . . . I wanted to give you a chance to explain why you had behaved so defensively, so that we could move on to a proper dialogue about the need for a working-class women's section.

It's now November, and as I've had no reply, I'm wondering whether there's any point in writing again . . . Still – classism in the women's movement needs to be challenged and I'm fed up with working-class women being invisible and silenced.

When I asked you where the working-class section was, you referred me to the shelf now marked 'Community'. All of us live in 'Communities' of one sort or another, and to call the Working-Class Women's section 'Community' is to attempt to take the politics out of class oppression and exploitation, to patronize us and treat us as a quaint, 'folksy' object of study.

When I pressed you on where the Working-Class Women's section was, and you explained that, as a matter of fact, you'd stopped stocking it, you put the responsibility for that decision on to one member of the collective – the only woman in your collective, who, according to you, identifies as working-class. You blamed her three or four times, usually when you felt unable to justify your new policy, until I objected to your doing that. Your bookshop is collectively run, and you decide your policies collectively, and also, the woman concerned wasn't there to put her own point of view. I felt, too, that you were attempting a

331

classic 'divide and rule' tactic, setting one working-class woman against another, and using her to validate your own views and give credibility to your actions.

When I asked you if you'd reconsider your policy if two working-class women's groups asked for the section to be re-instated, you were resistant, and argued that you would only do so if we were prepared to 'define class for you' and actually do your categorizing! You insisted that it was impossible to say what class a woman was . . . As you well know, there have been debates within the black community around defining black, within the lesbian community around defining sexuality, debates amongst women with disabilities around defining disability . . . Those debates continue, but they do not prevent you having sections around these identities. Neither do you expect women from these groups to come in and do your categorizing for you.

You also argued that, unlike race and gender, class is not fixed. True – but then lesbianism and disability are not fixed states of being either, but you would not use that argument against a lesbian section and a section on disability. We would not expect you to define or guess a woman's identity around any of these oppressions, but would expect you to accept each author's own definition, and to use a range of indicators – including your own judgement. You also said you could tell if a writer was a lesbian from the subject matter of the book, and disagreed with my claim that not all of us, as lesbians, write only about lesbianism! I found much of what you said quite offensive.

Another reason you gave for ceasing to have a Working-Class Women's section was that there were so few books by working-class women. In the bookshop that day, there were several books on your shelves where the author was defined as working-class, but even if that hadn't been so, a relatively empty section for working-class women's writings would have been a constant reminder of our invisibility, how our voices have been silenced, and so would still have been worthwhile.

Fundamentally, your arguments, your policy, and your be-haviour that day were all indications of how class is viewed in the women's movement; that class oppression is not as serious or important as other forms of oppression. Your position denied the privileges you have as middle-class women, and denied our oppression and identity as working-class women.

This letter has been discussed and endorsed by the Common Thread – a group committed to producing a collection of working-class women's writing, and by the working-class lesbian group that I'm in. All of us feel that a working-class women's section is necessary in your bookshop, and hope that you will reconsider your policy.

Yours in sisterhood,

Jeanne

Dear Sisters,

I bitterly resented your reply to my letter. To begin with, you distort what actually happened last month. You say:

'. . . We are always open to suggestions from groups and individuals about how we can improve our services to all women. However, our goodwill begins to fade slightly when accusations are made and distorted accounts are given about what goes on in this shop. As shopworkers, we are trying to improve conditions here and this means *we are not prepared to keep open house for dissatisfied customers* who refuse to listen to explanations of why we cannot meet their demands . . .'

At no point in the shop, or in my letters, did I make accusations. I made political comments, raised questions, and, yes, challenged one of the workers – the white, middle-class woman who did most of the talking. I queried your abandonment of the Working-Class Women's section – I didn't refuse to listen to explanations, but I listened and disagreed with those she gave, and eventually lost patience with the entrenched classism they revealed. The above quote shows a complete refusal on your part to take any responsibility . . .

In addition, you say in your letter that class is not 'another form of oppression to be put on the equal opportunities list alongside race, sexual preference, disability' and that the working-class woman there doesn't 'feel "oppressed" by [her] co-workers at the bookshop, none of whom come from the white British class system . . .'

You have some nerve! I'm aware that it's all the rage amongst some Marxists to put down what they call 'identity politics', and to deny oppression as a 'bourgeois and self-indulgent' notion. It's this view which dismisses the power, strength, dignity and struggles of movements for Black, Women's and Gay Liberation. You are trashing those identities, forged as they were in opposition to racism, sexism and heterosexism. By putting the word oppression in inverted commas, you attempt to question or deny its existence and its effects. I think you well know that oppression is real and cannot be reduced to a feeling or subjective attitude.

Classism is unquestionably a form of oppression. It's the combining of economic power and prejudice to keep one class subordinate to another. It helps maintain, systematically, the economic exploitation to which you refer, and a global capitalism which does not, as you imply, end at Britain's shores.

Moreover, after attempting to dismiss equal opportunities, and struggles around identity, it's surely inconsistent and manipulative to then refer gratuitously to the various identities of the bookshop's workers. That most are not from 'the white, British class system' and that one worker does not feel oppressed by them, is deliberately misleading. It implies that economic exploitation, power and privilege only exist in Britain – and not in the United States, Australia, India, Europe, the Caribbean etc – thereby denying the privileges and power of the middle-class workers at your bookshop.

I was also disturbed by the dismissive tone of your letter, because it seemed to reflect a lack of accountability to the women's liberation movement out of which you grew, and which continues to help generate your profits. I support your attempts to have good working conditions, but such conditions should make it possible for you to engage in discussions with customers – dissatisfied or otherwise – and not be used to enable a classic 'we don't want to talk with you face-to-face, you must complain in writing' approach.

Over a month ago now, I went into your shop merely to buy a book. I left upset and dissatisfied by the way my enquiry was dealt with. I was angry, not so much because the Working-Class Women's section had been removed, but at the classist explanation you gave, and your reluctance to re-discuss and reconsider your policy if several working-class women's groups approached you. I'm pleased that the argument, and letters of complaint you've had, have now led to a lengthy discussion in the collective, and that the end result is a reaffirmed commitment to both bring back and improve the Working-Class Women's section.

Yours in sisterhood,

Jeanne

Dear Sisters,

We are concerned about the removal of the Working-Class Women's section in your bookshop. We are also disappointed with your reply to one of our member's letters about this issue.

We feel that, as a bookshop which grew out of the Women's Liberation Movement, you should be accountable to that movement – and that if women's groups make suggestions, requests or demands, these should be considered in a political light, and not as the rantings of a difficult customer. The group felt that your letter was pompous and dismissive. It is revealing that you see accountability to women as 'goodwill' which can 'fade' should women's approach to the collective not be quite as gracious and deferential as you would like.

The issues raised by our member were not dealt with in your collective response – it was a defensive statement reacting to the incident in the shop, rather than an explanation of your policy.

We are glad that the bookshop has now decided to include a bigger and better Working-Class Women's section. The Common Thread has put years of hard slog into producing a working-class women's anthology. Working-class women's words (in print) don't come easy. Our book contains the lives, feelings, thoughts, politics, joys and sorrows of many working-class women. It is no ordinary book. We feel it deserves pride of place alongside the work of other working-class women, all of whom are saying: 'We are here'.

Don't join the mainstream that tries to keep us invisible.

Yours in sisterhood,

Julie

pp The Common Thread

Jenneba Sie Jalloh Destiny In Custody

Dark, cold, no light
No hope, no future
Whose hand is my future in?

These hands that have to work, struggle to survive?
They are heavy, weighed down with existing

They take pain, racial abuse, sexism
Injustice, oppression from everywhere
From each side, everyway I turn
No turnings left

My future rests with others
Not of my colour, not of my sex, not of my class
They bear no relation to me
We are oceans apart
They have no idea of my life
My wants, my needs
If they did, someone like me would be
Sitting, discussing, decision-making with them NOW

My future is in hands which don't work
Are not fighting to survive
Fighting to be recognized, fighting for dignity
Unspoilt, unworked, cold white hands

A Black woman's destiny
In cold white male hands

Something is wrong
This cannot be, this must not be
We must struggle, not only to live
But to live with dignity and recognition
For what we are and who we are.

I will fight white man
I will fight you white man
I will fight to be in control of my own destiny
Because until that day, no-one, not even you comfortable,
  complacent white man
Not one of us is free
But that is all we share
And that is all there will ever be.

Kate Hall Dying Breed

I am a dying breed
a lost burlesque show
working-class hero
cockney
well almost
sparrow
enjoying overt crudity
crying
at the loss
of innocence
poverty
and cheap laughs
trying hard
to merge
a university education
and
a political consciousness
with a deepseated
appreciation
of glitter.

Sandra Anlin
'Women's Aid – The Effect Is . . .'

'Women's Aid – The Effect Is Shattering.' Slogan from a tee-shirt bought at a Women's Aid conference in 1977, when Jean had been living in a refuge for women leaving violent men.

She was having a good ol' sort out, because she was moving again. Out of London, this time.

Looking at the tee-shirt now, and looking back, she could afford to feel *lucky* that she had met Vic and been forced by his violence to go to a refuge. Lucky? But how else could she have left Jim? Jean had not been happy with Jim, having married him when she was still in her teens; and having no money she could call her own to help her leave him, she would probably still be with him now. God forbid. Jean shuddered.

Jim had been husband number one, a postman – and boring.

Vic had been husband number two, an office clerk and exciting.

After five years of Jim, she'd been bored stiff with being a daughter, a wife and a mother. So she'd been ripe to fall for Vic when he'd paid her some attention. The excitement of the affair had been all for herself. She'd felt wonderful. She'd also thought that Vic had better job prospects than Jim, who would always be 'just a postman'. Vic was ambitious, 'I might be a tin-pot office clerk now, Jean, but I'm going places'.

A few months later, Jim had left and Vic had moved in with Jean and the two kids. They'd been much poorer as a family than when Jean had been with Jim. They might be poor now, but they were happy, and Vic was going to be so successful in the future that he'd be able to buy Jean a big house and keep her and the kids well provided for. So Jean thought.

It hadn't been long, though, before Vic stopped being exciting and started being violent.

She hadn't fancied much getting married again. Vic, however, wanted the security of marriage, and as he was paying the bills, she hadn't had much choice. They married in secret. He wouldn't even let her tell her mum. 'How romantic,' said one of the witnesses they'd pulled off the street outside the Town Hall. Jean remembered the feelings of total helplessness as she'd sat with him and the witnesses waiting to be called in to get married. The same woman had wiped away a tear from Jean's eye. 'You must be so happy!' Vic's arm had been around her the whole time. If only they'd known the truth, she thought, they might have called the police to help me get away from him.

Jean had stopped feeling wonderful when he'd started poking her, shoving her, and even spitting at her. The slaps became punches. Then kicks. Bruising was not visible when he had repeatedly banged her head against the kitchen cupboard. Each time he was violent, it grew progressively worse, until he was punching, kicking and raping, all in one session.

Jean had appealed to Vic's mum for help with his violent behaviour. Mary had been glad he no longer lived with her, though, and all she'd had to say was, 'Well, Jean, even as a little boy Vic got very grumpy when he was tired, and, after all, as a woman, you should know how to keep him sweet.' Grumpy! Keep him sweet! Jean was talking about intimidation and injuries and fear!

After two years of living together, and being married only seven months, Jean had left him.

She'd packed, taken the children, and had made her way to a refuge. He found her there, the first night she'd left, because she'd been daft enough (in her organized panic to get away while he was at work, scared that he might come home suddenly to discover what she was up to) to leave the phone number and address by the phone. The women in the refuge had protected her, and had sent her the next day to another refuge in another London borough, where he wouldn't find her. She'd later learned from his mum that he'd scoured the streets on his motorbike, looking for Jean's battered old mini, every night for three weeks, taking a different section of the A–Z every night.

Jim had never been violent, although they'd had some terrible rows. Jean could be angry or disagree with him without being scared that he would hit her. She had been the same person in her marriage to Vic, as in her last; probably better, believing as she did, that she loved Vic so much more.

So, as far as she had been concerned, Vic's violent behaviour had not been her fault. Very few women feel as sure about that as she did, when they first go to a refuge. She soon learned, as she asked for help from various people, that not everyone felt the same as she did about what had happened to her.

The individuals that she'd encountered at the social security, social services, Homeless Families, Marriage Guidance, the police and the courts, all tried to lay some of the blame, if not all of it, on to her. At the social security office, when she was making her claim for Supplementary Benefit, she was asked by the Liable Relatives Officer, 'What did you do to make him violent?'

'Nothing,' she'd replied.

'You didn't provoke him?'

'No.'

'Did you commit adultery?'

'No.'

'I *have* to ask you these questions, because we must establish whether or not he is liable to support you and the children.'

'He's not the father of my children, and I don't want any money from him, and if you go asking questions where he works, it will make things worse for me.'

'That really is not my concern; DHSS regulations state that we must find a relative *liable* to support you – in this case, my dear, your husband. When we interview him . . .'

Jean could not bear to hear any more. What if they told him her address at the refuge? They hadn't done, but neither had they put her mind at rest. They'd believed her at the Women's Aid refuge, without question. When she'd told the workers how he'd raped her, amongst other acts of violence, the night before her arrival, there had been no need for justification. Just positive action as to how they could best help her to sort out some of the practical problems she was now faced with, and get back some self-confidence.

The refuge had been a slum. Old railway cottages due for demolition within the next two years. Not that it had been Women's Aid's fault that that was all they could provide for women and children. Property due for demolition is deemed good enough for women leaving violent men, to stay in temporarily while they wait for divorces and re-housing. Jean had put two and two together. Who was it that benefitted, if women couldn't put up with the slum conditions in refuges and had to return home? Who, mainly, decided what buildings could be made available to feminists taking up the battered women's cause? Men. Yes. Men.

'Mum! Yuk! Plaster's fell into my mouth in the night again from the ceiling. When will *we* get a new place?'

But Jean had been desperate and *had* to stick it out.

Here she was, holding the tee-shirt. Faded black cotton with the words printed on it in that plastic that burns when you accidentally run the iron on it. The plastic was crumbling and peeling off now, seven years on. Only fit to be a duster now – and that would only be possible if it was turned inside out. You can't dust with bits of plastic crumbling off. 'Women's Aid – The Effect Is Shattering.' She looked at the tee-shirt intently, as if she was waiting for it to speak to her.

Mind you, Jean thought, it *could* tell a tale or two. She wouldn't wear her political views on a tee-shirt now. She remembered the first time she'd worn it, having been in the refuge several months by then. Two of the refuge workers had taken Jean and two other women from the refuge to a party.

Jean's experience in life having been somewhat different, the workers had explained that most of the people at the party were middle-class (well, she could see that!) and belonged to a left-wing, Socialist, political party. Jean had been surprised, then, when a bloke came up to her with what she'd thought, to begin with, had been an original chat-up line. 'What does, "Women's Aid – The Effect Is Shattering" mean?'

'Well, it's an organization that helps women to make new lives after leaving violent men, and provides . . .'

He'd interrupted her. 'Are you one of those women's libbers, then?'

'Yes . . . I'm a feminist . . .'

Before she could finish, 'You hate men, don't you?'

'No . . .'

'Okay! Okay! Whoa! Only joking, love – trouble with you women's libbers – you're always so serious. Ha ha ha!'

The tee-shirt looked much more faded than it should have done, as Jean couldn't seem to remember wearing it that often, because of the ridicule it seemed to invite. If a woman has somewhere safe to go when a man is violent to her, then it takes away his power to control her. No wonder men need to put Women's Aid down, Jean thought. But it had taken Jean a long time to cotton on to the fact that some men are violent and commit rape and murder, but all men benefit from the way women are controlled by these actions. And why do most men go along with the idea that women ask for it? Violence, incest, rape and murder are punishable by law, and Jean had experienced three out of the four. Thank God for Women's Aid, or it might be four out of four. Why should I thank God? Jean thought – it's women that have done all the work.

Neither Jean's father nor Vic had been punished by law, though. Funny that, she thought. Funny, too, how when you tell 'nice' men that you have become involved with and supposedly trust, of all these terrible things that you've experienced, they tell you of incidents they've had, of being 'led on' or provoked by a woman and can, therefore, sympathize with men that get carried away, and are violent or rape. Funny that.

All sorts of memories came flooding back, of how she'd felt around that time, of living in the refuge. Naïve as a feminist she might have been, but some things she'd always felt were wrong with men, and how, in her own life, they had kept her down and in her place. Feminism was the term, new to her, that named all these injustices and how women could be strong together to fight them. She was consciousness-raising. And she loved every awakening minute of it. Right on, sister! We don't say that today, do we? Jean thought.

For the first time in her life, *she* existed. She spent time with other women, exploring her own identity, what *she* was about and what she could be capable of, for *herself*. The other women in the women's group that she'd helped to form had been mostly middle-class, married or living with men, Socialist and higher-educated.

Jean had brushed aside these differences because these women had given her the chance to speak (more so, than any of them) for the first time, about her experiences of childhood, marriage and, now, living in the refuge. She'd liked holding court, telling them about her life; but she hadn't liked it when she went out with them and was introduced to their husbands and friends as 'Jean, who lives in the refuge for battered women'. The husbands and friends were never introduced to Jean first. But she could cope with that. No problem. As long as she was able to be with women, learning more and more about feminism, she would be happy. On social security she might be, but she was more contented than she'd ever been.

After only ten months of living at the refuge, she felt that for the first time in her life, she was making her own decisions. She remembered telling Pauline, a worker at the refuge, 'I've never felt so clear-headed, 'cos no pig of a man is battering my body or my mind now. And I feel ready for a new start!'

Jean remembered these words now with slight embarrassment. Someone had described her as 'waxing on lyrical' at the time. But it had been real; she *did* make a fresh start. She was re-housed on a smart council estate (middle-class, the man at the housing department had called it). Jean would be kidding herself if she chose to forget that it had not been easy all of these years as a single parent, which is why she could look back with embarrassment at herself for thinking a fresh start would be wonderful. Now she could get it into perspective. These past seven years were better than *any* she had spent under the different tyrannies of her father or her ex-husbands. She had been just as trapped living with a boring husband as with a violent one. She had built up a home and her self-respect; both things that all these men had stripped her of.

And now . . . another fresh start. What would the future hold?

This tee-shirt is symbolic, she thought. What else must I remember, and learn from, before I lay this tee-shirt to rest (or to dust), like ghosts from the past? Can I exorcize the past? A good ol' sort out of memories to chuck out and make way for the new? But, more practically, how long have I been sitting here, supposedly having a good ol' sort out to move to the new place? How much time have I got left, before Jackie comes home from school? Jean decided to spread a few things around to make it at least look as though she'd been more busy. A few rubbish bags strewn around the floor will impress, she thought.

The front door slammed.

'Hallo, Mum!' As Jackie came up the stairs and into Jean's bedroom.

'Cor! You've been busy, by the look of this mess!' Jackie scanned the room quickly. 'I remember that old tee-shirt – bet you wouldn't even get into it now . . . give it to me and I'll bung it in the rag-bag when I go down.'

Jean handed the tee-shirt to Jackie, too stunned to say anything. Jackie twirled the tee-shirt round and round in the air by one of the sleeves, knocking the light-shade in the process. Dust flew everywhere. 'Be careful with that, Jackie . . .'

Jackie left the room, ran down the stairs and shouted back, 'Wanna cuppa tea, Mum?'

Ah well! I know where to find it if I need it again, Jean thought.

Annette Kennerley Judge Me Now

I was given the chance to try to make something of my life by a mother who had had to leave school reluctantly at fourteen to work in a shirt factory to bring in a wage to her family. I wanted more out of life than most of the kids on our estate had to look forward to in a small provincial town up North. Getting an education meant a passport out – a chance to see something of the world, to meet all those interesting people out there.

A lot of shocks came at eighteen. I began to realize how divided the world was – how most of the people I met at university were middle-class – the label came later, only at the time there was a vague sense of shame at being somehow different or inferior. This was partly due to my having a Northern accent in a Southern university, but, also, I lacked a certain kind of knowledge about the kinds of things their backgrounds had graced them with. I felt immature and naïve – in awe of their big homes and parental handouts, their tennis club teenagehood and experience of foreign countries. I kept my roots hidden as much as I could; after all, I just wanted to be one of the crowd, normal. So I mixed with them, but always as an observer, on the edge of a clique, an élite little world, sometimes a mascot, always distanced.

A brief romance with Oxford's élite followed. I was a shy, nervous girl, who couldn't cope with historic, cloistered colleges, antiquated traditions, boxes at the opera and extravagant country house parties full of dons, wine waiters and literary names. I'd gulp down a few glasses of the vintage wine and creep away to some far corner of the house and listen to the essential and daunting socializing going on. I wondered what I was doing there, and which was the real world. Henley Regatta, Pimms by the bucketful, ageing sports cars and double-barrelled names. Sons of titled old men, daughters of the landed gentry, clinging together in a vacuum.

I learnt a lot at university – much more than a piece of paper with a degree certificate on it could ever bear witness to. When I left, I went back to the North and worked in an industrial town for several years, mingling once more with the ordinary people who shared my background and experiences. I began to think about class and about the things that determine your class identity in this world. About how you become much more aware of your class identity when you mix with those of a different class and frequently end up either hiding your class or having to justify and prove it all the time. The class closet and the hassles you meet if you dare to come out. The guilt it disturbs in others, and the hostility. But, most of all, their total inability, maybe through fear, to even listen to you, to hear about your background, your experiences, your life. It is only seen as whingeing and being miserable. And then, time after time, they will leap on you: But how can you call yourself working-class when you have had an education, have a well-paid job (or a home of your own, a car, a smart pair of shoes, a large vocabulary, a video, a ticket to the theatre, a glass of wine in your hand, an avocado in your fridge, an Access card, a holiday in Turkey – the list goes on and on . . .). Such stereotypes are a middle-class hang-up. Strip us of the top coat of compromises, attempts to conform and assimilate, and listen to *our* story. I feel sure about *my* identity now, and it is something that no one else can define for me.

So, if I found myself at an Oxford society party tomorrow night (not something I imagine would happen these days, mind you), the once shy, nervous girl would speak loud and clear to the Joe Sainsburys and Iris Murdochs of this world, saying, you are no better than me because of who you are or what you own or control, and I am no longer in awe of you, or creeping away to hide, but proud to show you what and who I am.

Christine Hyde
Blue-Eyed Blonde Buying a T-Shirt

I was looking at T-shirts
the shop was empty
except for me
and the male shop assistant,
who said,
'Are you Swedish?'
I sighed and
ignored him.
He said,
'Are you Swiss?'
I sighed and
ignored him.
He said:
'German?
French?
Austrian?
Belgian?
or
Dutch?'
After having listed
every European country
he could think of
where blue-eyed, blonde girls
come from,
I said,
'No, Shepherds Bush, if you must know.'
And
that
put
him
right
off.

Jenneba Sie Jalloh
I Am At The End Of 85-Contradictions

I am a girl, and a woman, a daughter and a friend.
A lover, and a girlfriend,
An advisor, a supporter, a consoler
Independent and strong
Insecure, and sensitive
Excited but afraid of what's to come
In need of constant reassurance and love

A working-class woman, a Black woman
A woman of mixed race, conflicting heritage
A Londoner, not English . . . in Paddington, born and bred
A child of immigrants, an alien, an outsider
                    (an insider in my area)
A daughter of Africa, daughter of an African, a stranger to
    Africa

A student – a cynic (and worse) of 'student types' . . .
Playing with politics, theorizing on Real People's hardships and
                                    real people's lives
Textbook theories, textbook hearts
Parrot-fashion, slogan–swinging
Living in a different world from the one I'm living in

A believer in, and a serious critic of, the human race
Hater of the 'rat race', but harbouring no illusions
                    aware of my unavoidable place
A fighter for the oppressed, and through my life's experiences,
forced to be a fighter for myself
A believer in Socialism, sick of poverty
Dislike materialists, wouldn't mind a little luxury
Detest pretension and insincerity
Wary of 'liberals' (especially of caucasian variety)
A human being, a Black woman, an African . . .
With an alternate Irish heartbeat
A survivor, a fighter, and a West Londoner.

June Burnett
The Half-Black Woman's Memory Book 1960

All those frightened years
trying to 'vanish' or conform.
Be a 'nice' coloured girl.
Straighten your hair
and keep a careful check
on your blackness.

Remember the scouring oils
and skin-lighteners
which made us look like unwashed ghosts?
Every Friday in the bath
we'd punish our young bodies
with a pumice
in expectation of a miraculously
milky sheen we were not rewarded with.
We wore elastic girdles
to control betraying
African behinds.
And make-up,
made for white faces
which turned ours
into sickly travesties.

White girls now eat pills,
and gorge the Continental sun
to possess colour
we once denied, and perm their hair
to a dry-bone frizz
which we disowned.
My white-skinned daughter
dyes her African hair blonde
and waves two fingers
to the world at large.

Annette Kennerley About to speak

In my silence
I can be proud
And self-respecting
Keeping my thoughts and feelings to myself
In my silence
I can witness injustice
And ignorance
Keeping my bitterness and anger to myself
In my silence
I can understand
And value my experience
Keeping my culture and beliefs from your analytical claws
In my silence
I can define myself
My background

And my class
Keeping your language and your questionings from my ears
In my silence
I can remain calm
And acceptable
To your refined tastes
Keeping my strength and wisdom to myself
In my silence
I am like a mountain in the sun
And when that sun burns down
Look out for the avalanche
As I begin to speak my words

THE CONTRIBUTORS
The Common Thread Collective as the book went to press

June Burnett – born Liverpool, 1936. Mother white, father black, now lives in Stoke with her family. A working-class writer, her book, 'When the Singing Stops', was published by Hutchinson in autumn 1988. She believes in the magic of change, and that, ultimately, the human family will triumph over greed, destruction and bigotry. She hopes to go on writing.

Julie Cotterill – Thirty-one, white, able-bodied and heterosexual. Born and brought up in the English Midlands, although I now live in Brighton with my husband, Phil. My mother is an Irish Catholic, and my father an English Protestant – and I got stuck with a Catholic up-bringing which I think I've managed to shake off, finally. I work as a freelance journalist.

Annette Kennerley – I was born in 1956, and brought up on a council estate up North. I have worked as a reporter, and am now doing a degree in film-making. I have survived a relationship with a violent man and the hassles of coming out as a lesbian. I have a baby boy called Jack. I have kept a diary since the age of twelve and have always made the time to write, as a way of working through so many phases of my life.

Phoebe Nathan – I was born very young and weighed in at nine pounds. My father was a fishmonger and I have been a stinker ever since! I have reached the ripe old age of seventy-three. I am Jewish. I love women. I worked in a shop, then I worked in a factory for eighteen years on a 'man's' machine. It was hard work, dirty and low paid. I was afraid to leave, in case I would be out of work, which I could not afford to be. I am the greatest singer of all times – will challenge anyone. There will never be another like me!!

Jeanne Wilding – In my fortieth year, white, a lesbian mother of a smashing daughter, now eighteen and a stroppy feminist. A committed, but critical trade unionist, and a feminist myself, I've lived and breathed politics for over twenty years. I've had loads of different jobs – shop work, clerical, cleaning, spot-welding, driving, teaching braille, and a whole range of finance work. Grew up and lived in Leeds, Yorkshire, until 1984 when I moved to London, partly to get this anthology together and partly to make my fortune. Managed the former, still practising at being a Muppy (middle-aged, upwardly mobile . . .).

Viv Acious – Born 1955. Enjoys eating, drinking, talking about food and biting her nails. Works as a sound engineer, DJ, promoting women's bands and music, barmaid, etc. Ambitions: to inherit a pub by the sea, be the first credited woman sound engineer on television, and to live till I'm ninety-six – with my friends.

Sylvan Agass – White, middle-aged Londoner. Originated from a poor working-class home, where my mother (a hospital domestic) was the sole provider. My 'career' until '82 was in multiple and badly paid work. Attempts to document some of the frustrations and anger of this period led to writing and to ten years' effort to acquire an education with the Open University, then an M.A. in creative writing at the University of East Anglia. Now work as a PT tutor, and also do fund-raising for the NSPCC.

Jill Aldred – Twenty-seven, works as a housemother in Edgeware. At present I'm writing a few articles and am working on a book about my grandmother.

Pat Angove – I'm forty-two and have three children. As a child, I was sexually abused by my father over a number of years. I lived with constant fear and guilt, trying as best I could to keep out of the way, to be unnoticed, and as insignificant as possible. Writing, later on in years, started as the therapy I needed to release the pain, fear and anger, and to make way for the real me inside – strong, loving and beautiful.

Sandra Anlin – I am a thirty-five-year-old white woman, who also happens to be a radical feminist, a lesbian, a mother and a full-time mature student aiming for a first degree in sociology – hopefully as a route to further courses in feminism and women's studies. My piece is semi-autobiographical.

Joan Batchelor – I was born in South Wales in 1937. I have twice been divorced, now living with a caring, sharing younger guy. Was a battered wife in my first marriage and had to cope with an alcoholic, depressive husband and emotionally disturbed son. I am winning against Limbutrol withdrawal, am menopausal and have an anxiety neurosis caused by drug dependency. I have been a community arts worker, a nurse, shopworker. I'm now a caterer at a local college, and study in my spare time.

Jenny Bauer – Born in 1949 in Wolverhampton. I met my Austrian husband in 1970, and moved to Austria in 1972. I have worked as a bank clerk in England and in Austria, and at the British consulate, Vienna, until the birth of my son in 1976. In 1977 I had a car accident which left me paralyzed from the navel downwards. For the last eight years I have done my best to run my own household and bring up my son who is now eleven years old.

Mary Bird – I'm sixty-six, have been happily married for forty-six years, but unfortunately my husband is now in a home for Alzheimer's Disease sufferers. I have a loving daughter, who shares with me a great sense of humour. Hobbies include amateur drama and operatics and I've spent many years performing in musical shows. I'm now a retired senior citizen, spent six years in the National Fire Service during World War Two, worked in telephone exchanges, helped in a school and as a library assistant for twelve years.

Sue Buddin – Born in Hackney, London. Mother worked in a factory as a dressmaker, then at a printing works. Father, an Irish immigrant, who worked on the buses. He died when I was ten. I was brought up in Essex, on a council estate. I had polio when I was a baby, but it prevents me doing nothing. At twelve, I was declared 'word-blind', but learned to read with Mum's help, from cornflakes packets, newspapers and magazines, and haven't stopped since. I'm married, with two children, and work in a building society.

Chaucer Cameron – Born in Essex, 1954, and gradually moved East. I have two children, one of either sex. My main preoccupation is trying to raise a boy child in this society; a battle in itself. I see myself as woman-identified, feminist, and a mother. I have always written, and suffered the classic syndrome of self-deprecation, hiding my writing from the world for years. Finally, as I became more politically aware, my anger grew and, with it, my self-confidence. Working-class women should be heard and seen often – we have a lot to say. By the very nature of our standing in society, we have been forced to become strong. Words have a strength all of their own, and, as a strong woman, I have the right to use them.

Miriam Carney – I was born in 1954 in Maidstone, the county town of Kent, to an Irish Catholic father and an English mother. Both came from rural working-class backgrounds. Educated at the local Catholic school, I showed an early aptitude for writing and arts subjects. I have worked since the age of sixteen in various occupations, ranging from chalet maid to dental assistant, and, more recently, a civil servant. Work, or the lack of it, has always been the basis of my life.

Elizabeth Carola – Ex-New Yorker, came to London in 1984. Involved with feminist campaigns around violence against women, particularly incest and pornography, for seven years. I've published fiction and prose sporadically, and worked as a typist, proof-reader, baker's apprentice, art model and 'grill boy' in an all-night diner. I feel most fully alive when writing. It helps me process my experience, make sense of craziness, understand the world.

Rene Carrick – Born in Middlesbrough, 1956, and received a typical working-class education: one that prepares a child for nothing. Most of what I've picked up in the way of sense, intelligence and feeling has been derived from friendships, lovers, travel, self-exploration and lesbianism.

Della Chapman – Now in my fifties, I spent my childhood in a council house with my parents and two brothers in Luton, where my father worked in a factory. Luckily, got a grant to go to a London art school. Married. Now a printmaker, teach art and write about my childhood.

Kathleen Chell – I'm a widow – my husband, an HGV driver, died in 1983. I'm fifty-three, have one son, four daughters and six grand-children, and have had progressive rheumatoid arthritis since 1968. I'm now wheelchair-bound, in spite of twice having an operation for a knee joint replacement.

Barbara Collins – I am thirty-four, white and physically able-bodied, although my mind plays up. I am single and have three children. I write endlessly in my head but battle with even holding a pen to put things down on paper.

Anne Cunningham – I'm a white woman from a large Irish Catholic family, having been born and brought up in Liverpool, where I still live with my two children. I'm a single mother and lesbian. I've no formal qualifications and left school at fifteen, have been writing on and off for about five years, mostly poetry, and attend a women writers group twice a month.

Nan Dalton – Sixty years young, abandoned marriage five years ago and felt life just beginning. Born in London to working-class father, gifted mother. Secretary till marriage, three children. Followed husband to West Country in 1963, where women were still paid very low wages. 1966–70, involved in pressure group resulting in open visiting in local children's hospital wards. Compulsive walker, music lover, writer of poetry and articles, and dedicated to seeing women reach their full potential.

Mandy Dee – The doctors diagnosed me as 'spastic' from a birth injury. I am white, over-educated, rescued working-class. I went to a showpiece special school that I still dream about, and then became a teacher. I came out as a lesbian in about 1981 – the best thing that ever happened to me. Since about 1975, I have had undiagnosed multiple sclerosis. I was finally labelled as an MS person about four years ago. I live in a wheelchair-accessible flat in South London and am always looking for helpers. It is my ambition to live until I am forty.

Lizzie Demdyke – Born 1960, in Padiham, Lancs. Cancerian, lesbian, mother, white, pagan, temporarily (I hope!) celibate, not previously published, thinking about getting an education for when the welfare state collapses but still finding it too daunting. I poached my name from one of the Pendle witches murdered in the 17th century, as until recently I've always lived within sight of their hill.

Hania Dolan – Born Manchester, 1956, to Irish mother and Polish father. Brought up with one sister and two brothers. Left home to go to university, during which time my mother died. Writing has been a way of reconnecting with her. Now live in a women's house in London and teach in a girls' comprehensive. Have identified as lesbian since 1986. Writing this piece has been a painful but strengthening process – thanks to all the women who've supported me.

Dolores – Twenty-seven years old, my father was Indian, my mother is German, and I was born in London. Most of my school days were spent outside the old smoke, where I (and my family) suffered a lot of racial abuse. It wasn't until I got back to London that I started feeling good about my 'different' background. I work as a secretary and write in my spare time. I love dancing, country walks, reading, the sea and being with women.

Suzanne Doran – Thirty-seven, mother of one daughter, lesbian. Though now living in Wales, most of my adult life has been spent in either London or Dublin. I'm a 'pink' rather than 'red' feminist, a writer – have published a few poems, articles and short stories in minor magazines – and intend to write a novel that will make some of the world sit up and take notice. I am at the moment taking A-level English, and have been offered a place at university as a mature student.

Sharon Dunham – I am thirty, white and lesbian. My life from an early age was full of trauma and continual change, in and out of institutions. I blocked off my pain by becoming a nurse and channelling my needs into other people – I even tried to change my sexuality and go straight! Since writing poetry and publishing 'Sub-Animal Yells', I've been able to face my past and look forward in a more positive way.

Susan Evasdaughter – I'm thirty-six, from Yorkshire, and recently returned there. My mother's death at thirty-three – when I was six – has overshadowed my life. Left home at fifteen and, after a series of exploitative low-paid jobs including nursing, I qualified for university at twenty-one. After leaving the LSE, I got a high-powered job, but was so depressed I gave it up. It felt difficult to fit in. I'm now an art therapist, PT lecturer, sculptor and matriarchalist. I've written a book on Matriarchal Crete and feminist travel guides.

Eve Featherstone – I'm a lesbian, a mother, an equal opportunities officer in the building department of a local council, a writer and a poet. I can't spell, I have never worked out grammar; I write because I enjoy it and I want other women to have access to stories and poems written by working-class lesbian feminists.

Jane Fell – I am thirty-one years old and am married with a three-year-old son named Adam. I work in a factory – British Aerospace – dealing with incoming and outgoing raw material. When I was pregnant, I had a nervous breakdown, lasting until my son was three months old. One good thing about this experience was that it inspired me to write quite a few poems, and a short story.

Kitty Fitzgerald – Born in SW Ireland, brought up in Yorkshire where my father came over to work in the pits. My mother worked in the wool mills. I'm divorced, with a nineteen-year-old daughter. I've had a variety of jobs including shop work, waitressing, factory work, and at twenty-nine I went to college and taught for a few years afterwards. My first novel, *Marge*, was published by Sheba in 1985, and my second is almost complete. The belief that I grew up with, that working people have the power to transform society, is still with me.

Sally Flood – I am sixty years of age, with a family of seven and one grandson – the apple of my eye. I am an embroidery machinist. I have also taught creative writing, and am a member of the Federation of Worker Writers. I have read on radio and TV and am a long-time member of Basement Writers.

Caron Freeborn – Born in 1966, have lived all my life in Basildon. My mother is from a Jewish background, although none of my family practise any religion. Both my parents are Cockney. I am unemployed and study English literature part time. I suppose I would be called heterosexual, although I don't really believe in rigid definitions of sexuality.

Janice Galloway – Thirty-two, live in Glasgow. Mother from a mining family, in service till she was eighteen, became a clippie. Poor housing when she retired (as a school dinner lady) killed her. It's her strength and humour that recur, and motivate me in my work as a teacher in a comprehensive school, and as a writer. My piece, 'Two Fragments', was previously published by Polygon.

Lori Gatford – I was born in Leeds in 1963, and brought up by my mother on a council estate. At seventeen, I got a job in a printing co-op where I was introduced to feminism. I became ill with schizophrenia at eighteen and was admitted to psychiatric hospital, where I started writing lyrics, poems and short stories. I now live with a musician and my ambitions are to attend dancing school, release a record and write a book of poetry.

Joanna Gorner – Born 1961, in Lancs. Went to Ruskin school of drawing, Oxford, 1979–82. Since then, I've continued to do my own work, specializing in printmaking. Work primarily based on nature and my feelings for the earth. I was involved in co-founding and running a women's art group, and am currently working as a technician at the Oxford Printmakers Co-op.

Margaret Graham – I'm sixty-two years old and was born in the Midlands. My father was a metal worker. The war started when I was sixteen, then at eighteen I trained as a nurse. I married in my forties, causing a nine-day wonder, as he was ten years younger, and I became a step-mum. I have wanted to write since I was twelve years old, and the piece in this book is hopefully the first chapter of an eventual novel.

Sandra Grayson – Teacher, translator, medical secretary. Lived in Barcelona, worked briefly for Unesco in Paris and Geneva. Avid reader, keen foreign film buff and adventurous traveller. Married to a Hungarian refugee.

Alison Guinane – I was born in 1948 and went to school in Clayton, Manchester, where my parents lived and worked all their lives. Although I moved several times, I finally returned for good to the city where I feel my roots are. I have been writing poems since I was eight, but have never been able to write while away from Manchester. I was married for five years and had three babies. Two were born dead – an experience which often inspires my writing. I now live alone with my teenage daughter and teach English at a sixth-form college.

Kate Hall – Born 1945, white, physically able-bodied, but suffer from depression. I'm a lesbian mother of two grown-up sons and a teenage daughter. I've got an Open University degree in social science and a diploma in dance in the community. I write, paint when I have time, and dance a lot. I live in West London with various animals. My work in this book is for my mother with love and thanks.

Janet Hawkins – I am twenty-nine. I grew up in East London and have worked as a secretary, then nurse. I've only recently started writing for publication, but have always had the habit of writing as a way of sorting myself out. I love all forms of creativity and want to learn to paint. As I have an invisible disability, I am eager to see more representation of the lives of women with disabilities in art and in literature.

Mary Haylett – I'm forty-five and have brought up my four kids on my own. We've had good times and bad. I left school at fifteen, and all my jobs before having children were unskilled. About ten years ago I began to understand that I was some kind of feminist, and probably always had been. I write poems.

Jules Haywood – Born 1957, in London, and shared the first fourteen years of my life in three rooms with two sisters and a brother. My jobs have varied from shop work, waitressing, factory work, to child care, teaching keep-fit and community work. I have been active in the women's and peace movements. I have studied the visual and performing arts, and written and performed in a lesbian theatre group. My dreams are to get paid for my writing and performing work, to live in the sun, learn to scuba-dive, be deeply in love with myself, to have all my friends within walking distance, own a house and a Harley Davidson motorbike, heal my past pain, and see all women, especially working-class and less privileged women, get a bigger slice of the cake.

Margot Henderson – Born 1955 of an unmarried, Irish Catholic mother. Was adopted by Scottish Catholic parents. Brought up in Wishaw, a small steel town in the West of Scotland. I'm now thirty-three, a single parent, community education worker and I write, partly to pass on some of the stories I have inherited, and partly to make new ones.

Nannette Herbert – Born in 1965. At thirteen I was taken into care for not attending school. I spent six months in an adolescent unit – then a year in an assessment centre. I went to a convent boarding school and foster parents, but neither worked out and I returned home at seventeen. After six months' working in an office as part of a work experience scheme, I was unemployed for four years. I am now at Hillcroft College – Britain's only residential college for women, doing a CNAA combined studies course.

Marian Finan Hewitt – I grew up on a farm in the West of Ireland. After school, I joined the Civil Service in Dublin and also took a diploma in the Montessori method of education. I now live in Dublin with my husband and son. I joined a women's writing group when I lived in a high-rise flat, along with other women.

Helena Hinn – I am a twenty-nine-year-old woman from Newcastle-upon-Tyne, and I feel I have very strong roots in the area: a relative of mine was on the Jarrow march. I have had various jobs over the years, and now work in a bookshop.

Susan Hoult – White, single mum, aged thirty-three. Brought up in Hereford, and still spend a lot of time there visiting my dad, but now live in London with my daughter. We moved after my mum's suicide, three years ago. While out of work, I go to classes, including writing, which is a creative outlet and therapeutic. Thanks to my writing-class tutor, Brenda Beaghan, for giving me the confidence to write things down.

Billie Hunter – Thirty-three, white, mother of two-year-old son. Born in SE London, I've lived in London most of my life. Became involved in women's politics through the Association of Radical Midwives, and have fought to save the craft of midwifery. I've written sporadically since I was a child, and am involved in writing a book about childbirth in the 1920s–30s, based on oral history. As well as that, I've still got that novel going around in my head.

Sarah Hunter – Born in Wales in 1911. Moved to Oldham, where I was educated at a school for the blind. Poetry was in my heart from an early age. Wrote my first poem when I was twelve, and it was published in America. Later, I won a competition sponsored by an American magazine, which entitled me to free tuition at Hadley College for the blind, and I eventually got a scholarship with Chicago University. Later, I won four international contests for blind writers. I was a knitter at the workshop for the blind till I got married and had a son. I've been a lay preacher for twenty-five years.

Christine Hyde – Well, I can't believe I'm thirty-two – I still feel sixteen. I'm proud of my working-class roots. Born in Fulham, same as my dad, who was one of twelve. Left school at sixteen and got a typist's job, and I'm still typing for a living. I put a lot of energy into writing. I tend to smile a lot, tell jokes, and drink a lot of beer when I'm writing – it helps.

Jenneba Sie Jalloh – I am a black woman. I'm also many other things, but believe Malcolm X was right when he said that labels are dangerous and sometimes get in the way. I let my poems speak for me . . . They hold my experiences of life, which have shaped my beliefs, convictions, fears, confusions and my hopes. I'm a womanist, a survivor, a fighter and a West Londoner.

Pat Jourdan – Forty-eight, Liverpool, Irish-Roman Catholic. Went to Liverpool Art School. I write poetry and give readings, and paint and exhibit locally. I'm a typical Libran, idealistic and resilient.

Mary Legg – I am seventy-two years of age, a widow, and I exist on my weekly pension. I feel the powers that be do not realize the effect that war has had on women, and its long-term effect on families. Life is taken far too lightly, and personal experience is the only effective true education. I have always nursed a deep sense of injustice and feel that I have had very little return for what I gave.

Karen Liljenberg – Born 1957, Liverpool, in a working-class home. I had the privilege/misery of a university education at Cambridge. I've written poetry and one short (as yet unpublished) novel. I live in Wales, as a conscious cultural decision (having learnt Welsh), but am finding long periods without work very demoralizing. My other interest is traditional music – I play flute, whistle and Celtic harp. I have strong feminist sympathies, regard myself as working-class, although my education has made me feel alienated and rootless, in some sense.

Jesse Locke – Born 1906. A loner, not from choice. Little is known by me of my parentage; from the age of two years, I was brought up in an orphanage until I was fifteen. Thinking myself to be an orphan child, I had to rely on 'a living-in-job' as a servant (skivvy). Then married at twenty-seven. I've always been timid, lacked confidence in myself. Was told, 'tradesmen are not paid to stand at the back door chatting to my maid'. So I've always felt inferior, but know my rating is kindness. Don't judge a book by it's cover. Eighty years living I've contributed to this country – three daughters, and I've been a widow for twenty-two years.

Ann Lofthouse – I am twenty-two, an anarchist feminist. Grew up in the North, moved to Kent in 1984 and London in 1987. Started writing poetry after an abortion at sixteen. I love women and believe that through women a lot can be done to change the capitalist, patriarchal system.

Rozena Maart – Black, South African. Started writing to us several years ago. Now in York, England, doing an MA in women's studies.

Diane Mason – Married, eleven-year-old son, a vegetarian, committed to peace and living in harmony with the environment. Support CND, Greenpeace and the Labour Party, and am Methodist, hating all forms of prejudice and social inequality. I'm going back to college to get some GCSEs.

Maxine McCarthy – Twenty-two, an energetic Sagittarian, and I talk a lot. Grew up in East London and married at nineteen. Moved to Cornwall shortly before the birth of my second child, cut my hair and avoided men. I've recently begun to study communications arts and write poetry, whilst developing a positive outlook on life.

Heather McCracken – I was born in Lisburn, Co. Antrim, in 1958. I trained as a journalist, but disliked working for the establishment and emigrated to London, where I eventually made it to Fleet Street – plying the more honest trade of barmaid. In between bumming around Europe, I have been an actress, publicity agent, waitress and market trader. I now live in Portrush, Co. Antrim, with my baby daughter and partner. I run a vegetarian café and write whenever I can.

Marian McCraith – Brought up in Southall, West London, by Irish parents, both of whom have now died. I'm thirty-four, and have lived alone in Leicester since 1980. Wanted to be a writer all my life, and now combine writing stories, poems and radio plays with psychiatric nursing.

Heather Milne-Gordon – I am a survivor of foster homes, suicides, horrific deaths, and widespread alcohol addiction. I am now an old woman, living alone among the wreckage, and salvaging what I can from the broken pieces of my idealism, integrity, and self-esteem.

Sue Moules – Was born in 1957 in Sussex. Her grandfather was a Cockney, born within the sound of Bow bells. She has published three poetry collections: *Echoes* (Outcrop, 1981); *Patterns* (Outcrop, 1982); *Metaphors* (Spectrum, 1986). She lives with her husband and baby daughter in Wales. Her poems have appeared in England, Wales, Canada and USA in poetry and general magazines, including *Spare Rib* and *Women's Review*.

Pat Moy – With my two daughters established at school, I returned to employment at forty-three, came into contact with the women's movement, and in consequence gained a lot more confidence and understanding. At forty-nine, I find that I get 'easier' on myself as time goes by. I'm happily studying for exams which my secondary school couldn't offer, also I like reading because I'm curious about other people, and writing because I'm curious about myself.

Wilma Murray – I was born into the servant class on an estate deep in rural NE Scotland, almost within spitting distance of the big house. I have spent most of my life learning not to spit, and only the last few years enjoying it. My heroine is my grandmother who died younger than I am now, after bringing up sixteen children because she had no choice. I have two children and have chosen to write, mainly, in English, my first foreign language.

Gill Newsham – Twenty-four, a Northerner presently living in London, on the dole. Never realized my feminism – it was always part of my life, as was being working-class – sometimes helpful, sometimes harmful! It's reassuring to find women with similar backgrounds and experience to give you something to build from.

Julie Noble – I am a baby compared to the rest as I am only eighteen. I am a feminist, but have a lot of friends of both sexes. I'm studying A-levels and want to do something scientific in university, unsure what. My ambition is to write a good feminist book and I am in the process of having some work published in a collection of Girls' Experiences entitled 'True to Life'.

Maria Noble – I'm a Zami, aged thirty-three, living in Yorkshire, going through changes. I'm basking in the caring lavished on me by my lover and sistahs. I'm working for a time when women don't have to be casualties.

Bridget O'Connor – Twenty-six, second-generation Irish and heterosexual. Brought up in Harrow Wealdstone in a strong Catholic Irish community. I've been writing since a child, and now work for a community publisher in Hackney. My work concerns promoting and developing the writings of working-class people, 'Readers Wife' was first published by ARGO in 1988.

Marlene Packwood – No biographical details available.

Honor Patching – Living (now) in a middle-class environment. I hate it at dinner-parties when I hear myself adopting a poor parody of other people's posh accents. It's often a struggle to find my own voice. My nineteen-year-old daughter by my first marriage, thanks to my own lack of confidence in the past, has lived with her father for some years. Made up my mind to write at five but didn't start until thirty years later. I'm English, but live in Scotland and wouldn't want to leave. I'm thirty-nine and work in a vegetarian restaurant.

Barbara Ponton – Born in 1930 in Yorkshire. Tough, ambitious mother who struggled to give five children an education. Dreamy, introvert father I loved. Loving, supportive husband and family – three children, seven grandchildren. For many years chronically ill (renal failure). Find great comfort in my women's group.

Julie Rainey – I was born in 1970. I am white, Northern Irish Protestant. I went to a strict girls' grammar school and took up drama as an outlet. I am now very involved in the local theatre and arts centre. I am a recently converted vegetarian, a determined pacifist, a conservationist and a (sometimes naïve) idealist. Eventually, I want a career in the theatre (preferably on stage).

Ali Raven – I'm a twenty-five-year-old lesbian, and mother of my three-year-old daughter, Rowan. I mostly write about conflict, and it's only recently I've started to show my poems to anyone.

Jan Revell – Thirty-four, white, lesbian, disabled and a feminist. Born in London and lived here most of my life. Been mostly unemployed for last ten years, since becoming disabled. This is my first story and is meant to say something about the difficulty of expressing and sharing grief and accepting change. And about the way women seem to understand and share, without even speaking. Maybe writing the story was my way of expressing my own grief, as it's loosely based around a true event.

Nickie Roberts – Thirty-nine, married, one poodle. Born in Burnley, Lancs, into a weaving family. Left school at fifteen and worked the usual lousy, badly paid jobs – factory, waitressing, shopwork, etc. Went to London in 1969, became a stripper. First book, *The Front Line*, published by Grafton in 1986, documented my experience of working in the sex industry, and those of friends, black and white women – all working-class. Now working on a history of prostitution – the first to be written by a working-class woman.

Marie Roe – I am twenty-seven and recently married. I grew up in High Valleyfield. My father is a miner. Both my parents are from Dublin. I have three brothers and a sister. I have travelled a great deal and worked abroad. I work part-time now. I design and make my own clothes, so I am going to have a go at making them to sell.

Liza Rymer – I'm thirty, and for the past fifteen years I have devoted myself to the ultimate pleasure of writing, much to the disgust of my family, who would prefer it if I did the ironing occasionally. I have a husband and two sons, who are still learning the finer points of hoovering, a stuck-up cat and a budgie who are of no use at all, as they don't know one end of a sweeping brush from the other. I love my friends and family, the North of England, and people who make me laugh. I've been a non-conformist all my life and intend to remain so. I dislike narrow-minded people and love a good argument, which is just as well, really.

Krishna Sadhana – Thirty-four, lesbian feminist, mother of ten-year-old son. Mum was Irish, and Dad Greek-Cypriot. Brought up in Paddington, but spent about three months a year in the backstreets of Belfast or chasing rabbits around Newry. Spent several years travelling and am now a mature student aiming at a degree involving creativity, negative influences in children's literature and new ideas in children's books. I'm an incest survivor.

Clare Sambrook – Born 1964, Lincolnshire. Mother died 1972, father died 1982. Educated at a comprehensive school, then Jesus College, Cambridge, studying English and social and political science.

Olive Scott – Born Olive Josephine Earley on 30 June 1929, to a Tyneside mother and an Irish father. She was brought up a Catholic, although her family suffered excommunication when her father refused to see a priest before he died. Olive was still a child at this time. She married and had one child and worked as a dinner-lady and seamstress, wasting her brilliance in sweatshops. She was persuaded by her daughter to publish her writings.

Eileen Shaw – I'm forty, white, heterosexual and a tolerant feminist. I'm a member of a collective of Yorkshire writers, 'Left to Write', and writing has been vital to me for about five years. I'm doing a part-time humanities degree, and I work full-time for the Local Education Authority and part-time for the Workers Educational Association running a creative writing course. I won a Writer's Bursary Award from Arts Yorkshire. I have two sons, twenty-two and seventeen, and a daughter of sixteen. I left school at fifteen, married at seventeen and divorced at eighteen.

Carole Smith – Her piece is autobiographical.

Lauren Smith – White, heterosexual, single parent, two children aged twelve and six, and another on the way. Born 1957 – illegitimate, and brought up by my mother and grandmother in the Midlands. My mother suffered two nervous breakdowns. I left school, unqualified, at fifteen, enjoy reading, especially feminist books, and like painting and writing poetry. My ambition is to find a balance in my life, and the common thread which binds us all together, regardless of gender, colour and creed.

Edith Stanton – Born Salford, 1917. Father – dock labourer, self-educated. Left school at fourteen and studied at evening classes whilst working in offices. Qualified as shorthand typist and worked in co-operative movement and local government. Married a grocer and had three children, the first one dying at birth. Has been writing humorous articles for years. Moved to Derbyshire in 1956, fulfilling ambition to live in the country.

Maud Sulter – Born in Glasgow, Scotland, in 1960. Her mother Scots and her father Ghanaian. Following a tradition of her Scottish heritage, she is a writer. In the tradition of her African lineage, she is a storyteller and fighter for justice.

Lesley Summers – Born on 30 May 1966, in Staffordshire. The illegitimate child of an unmarried schoolgirl and a French-West African emigré miner. Her 'growing' years were spent in Australia with the English family that adopted her. She's currently living in Britain, working on her first novel, aided and abetted by two large dogs and the only cockatiel in Britain that does not talk.

Jane Toms – I was born in 1932 in the Channel Islands. During the war, my mother, my brother and myself were evacuated to Plymouth, where I now live with my youngest son in a 'trust' house. I have six children and eleven grandchildren and got divorced after twenty years of marriage. I am a Methodist, at the same church since I was sixteen. I have a deep faith in God, and am disillusioned with politics. I am grateful to my Aunt Irene who encouraged me to write.

Jan Turnbull – Thirty-two years old, single parent, two daughters. *Sun* reader till I was twenty-five. Started adult education after my marriage ended – it was a life-saver, and helped me to regain my self-esteem. Went to Greenham, joined a long occupation to stop a school closing and went on a miners' picket line. Read my first books since leaving school – *Hard Feelings*, which brought me to see women's oppression, and *Ragged Trousered Philanthropist*, which brought me to see the oppression of my class. Like this quote – 'Education teaches us how to spell experience'.

Theresa Verlaine – No biographical details provided.

Violet Verlaine – No biographical details provided.

Sue Vodden – Thirty-seven, born and brought up in Islington. I'm studying Jung, Brecht and Woolf at NE London Poly, for an HND in independent studies. In my practical work, I try to focus my studies and experience towards getting some kind of job at the end of the course – hopefully.

Tina Wildebeest – A Manchester-born Blackwoman, and founder member of 'Blackscribe', Manchester's first Blackwomen's creative writing group, set up in January 1987. Her work includes short stories, poetry, plays, song writing and cultural reviews. She runs creative writing workshops and carries out educational work in schools. She's been published in magazines and newspapers, and recently in an anthology of Blackwomen's writing entitled *Blackwomen Talk Poetry*.

Josephine Zara – Jewish, a feminist, a lesbian in politics, celibate in sexuality, now nearly sixty-five, still working, no intention of retiring or dying. Have seven grandchildren but don't care for Grandma role. Three clever, successful children whom I adore. Find life rich, over-full, satisfying but still striving for a better one. And I still have things to learn, and I'm learning them and growing up, too.

ZOE FAIRBAIRNS

Closing

Four women meet on a sales training course.

Gina: the highflyer who has it all – love, money, success and a career planned to the last detail. But who is doing the planning?

Ann: the mother who has always put her children first. In the bleak world of 80s unemployment, might there be something for her . . . Or someone?

Teresa: who finds that principles don't pay the bills and whose millionaire ex-lover has made her an offer she can't refuse.

And

Daphne: spellbinding, sinister, superb, whose mission is to turn women into sales women.

After a week in Daphne's grip, the women's lives are irrevocably changed . . .

'Witty and perceptive . . . funny and eminently readable'
Over 21

'Such a pleasure to read, such fun, so intelligent, so perspicacious, so well plotted, so unobtrusively moral, so elating, I find myself in danger of writing an extended quote rather than a proper review' Fay Weldon, *Books Magazine*

'A subtly feminist version of the power-sex-and-money sagas . . . highly enjoyable' *Spare Rib*

CLAUDIA KOONZ

Mothers in the Fatherland

Numerous books have appeared on the subject of Nazi Germany, yet half the Germans who helped to make dictatorship, war and genocide possible have largely escaped notice. Why was it that German women rallied round a man who promised to eliminate Jews from 'Aryan' society and to expel women from public influence, and flocked to support a party that declared the only true role of women to be 'the increase and preservation of the species of the race'?

From extensive research, including a remarkable interview with the unrepentant chief of Hitler's Women's Bureau, Claudia Koonz has traced the roles played by women – as followers, victims and resisters – in the rise of Nazism. Her book is an important contribution to the understanding of women's status, culpability, resistance and victimisation at all levels of German society, and a record of astonishing ironies and paradoxical morality, of compromise and courage, of submission and survival.

'A splendidly thorough analysis (though it often reads like a story) of an element of Nazism which has rarely been properly examined.' *Independent*

'A fascinating and intensely personal new study of women in Nazi Germany . . . a crucial insight into the role of women in that ruthless anti-feminist regime.' *Guardian*

'The first thorough treatment of women's collaboration in the madness and evil of Adolf Hitler's Germany . . . powerful, reflective and cathartic.' *Chicago Tribune*

MICHELLE ROBERTS

The Book of Mrs Noah

'A woman visiting Venice with her preoccupied husband fantasizes that she is Mrs Noah. The Ark is a vast library, a repository not only of creatures but of the entire knowledge and experience of the human race. She is its curator (or 'Arkivist'), and her fellow voyagers are a group of five Sibyls and a single man, the Gaffer, a bearded old party who once wrote a best-selling book and has now retired to a tax heaven in the sky. Each Sibyl tells a story and each story is about the way men have oppressed women down the centuries.

'I have not felt so uneasy and so guilty about my gender since I read Margaret Atwood's *The Handmaid's Tale*. To say that *The Book of Mrs Noah* is a superb novel sounds impertinent or patronizing. But it remains the case'
Kenneth McLeish, *Daily Telegraph*

'Sharply but sympathetically observed . . . both down to earth and visionary. Roberts' writing is rich, troubling and audacious . . . the female imagination at its best' *City Life*

'A feast of inventive imagery . . . it's not unusual for a woman writer to pitch for brave humour, but to strike the note as truly as Roberts does is a marvel' *Company*

'A strange and interesting book, pouring the subject matter of Virginia Woolf into a form designed by Boccaccio' *Independent*

'Like the best of new women's writing, takes a generous view of the widely different ways in which women find their salvation, and avoids feminist clichés . . . a poetic, visionary book, and humorous as well' *Cosmopolitan*

'A slow, rich read of pleasurable complexity' *Guardian*

NAWAL EL SAADAWI

The Fall of the Imam

'This is a tale of women suffering under harsh Islamic rule, but it could be about women anywhere there is cruelty and bullying. This novel is unlike any other I have read, more like a poem or a lamenting ballad, with something hypnotic about it, with its rhythmic, keening language, returning again and again to the same incident, a woman killed in the name of religion by the men who have used her.

'This is a wonderful book and I hope a great many people will read it' Doris Lessing

'A study of the psychology of power that goes far beyond slogans' *Books*

'Comparable to Marquez's *The Autumn of the Patriarch* for the way in which it finds vital metaphors to describe religions and political brutality, this is also a work which dares all in order to get important things said' *Literary Review*

'Clear and impassioned' *Times Literary Supplement*

'Brilliant . . . technically inventive, thematically stunning' *City Limits*

'Calls to mind the fundamentalist country of Margaret Atwood's *The Handmaid's Tale* . . . an intense and vivid book' Hilary Mantel, *Daily Telegraph*

VALERIE MINER

Blood Sisters

Blood Sisters tells the story of cousins, the daughters of Irish sisters. Liz is active in the women's liberation movement. Beth fights for Irish freedom as an activist in the Provisional wing of the IRA. The two young women are soon deeply engaged in attempting to understand each other's ideals, to cross the dangerous lines between them.

'Valerie Miner bravely handles a complex web of allegiances and loyalty systems – ties of blood, feminism and patriotism. Indeed, as the book scrutinizes the cousins' relationships with each other, with women, with mothers, with lovers, and the countries to which they're emotionally bound, all the questions seem to connect and all conflict. The demands and counter demands become intolerable. The end is disastrous. But *Blood Sisters* is highly intelligent and honest.' Hilary Bailey, *Guardian*

'Political fiction at its best . . . Miner offers no correct feminist "party line". What she offers instead is a thorough discussion of the issues . . . Miner reminds us that what ultimately binds women together are the shared experiences that transcend ideological doctrines' *New Women's Feminist Review*

'With understated humour, a crisp, terse and elegant literary style, Miner succeeds in creating a novel that explores with cliché the meaning of the now classic phrase "personal politics" . . . this is a rare and engaging novel' *Plexus*

VALERIE MINER

Movement

Movement captures ten years of changes in Susan Campbell's life. Expatriate, leftist activist, journalist, committed feminist – all these are part of her passage through the seventies. Travelling from the USA to Canada, Africa and Britain, we follow her search for self-knowledge in a decade of challenge and re-examination. Valerie Miner's skills as a storyteller and insights as a reflective feminist have never been stronger.

'I liked the form of *Movement* very much – it is indeed a novel of movement, political, personal movement from country to country and subculture to subculture . . . vignettes and stories out of Susan's life, but never episodic, always carrying her development as a person and as a political personage a step further' Marge Piercy

'This is a compelling book, invigorated by Susan's idealism and enthused with her deep passion for life' *Publishers Weekly*

ANTONIA FRASER

The Weaker Vessel

Antonia Fraser, one of our most popular and celebrated historians, here brings to life the women of seventeenth-century England. What was the effect on women's lives of the social disruption caused by the Civil War? Did women's education improve during the seventeenth century or was there some sinister degeneration? Was the lot of the heiress really so enviable compared to that of the dairymaid? Did anyone marry for love? Did divorce exist?

Above all, Antonia Fraser demonstrates through the life stories of particular women how, in an age when effective contraception was unknown and maternal mortality was high, childbirth dominated the life of every woman from the highest to the lowest. She considers these themes in terms of various female characters, both known and unknown, who include actresses, courtesans and whores, as well as educators, nuns, Quakers and businesswomen.

This brilliant, entertaining and moving book won the Wolfson Prize for History in 1984. By looking at women's lot between the death of one reigning queen and the accession of another, it draws attention to the many changes which have affected women's position in society since 1700. At the same time it illuminates those perennial issues about the fate of women which remain unchanged even today.

'A distinguished and graceful book, packed with interesting information' *Observer*

'Superbly readable' *Publishers Weekly*

A Selected List of Non-Fiction Available from Mandarin Books

The prices shown below were correct at the time of going to press.

☐	7493 0000 0	**Moonwalk**	Michael Jackson	£3.99
☐	7493 0004 3	**South Africa**	Graham Leach	£3.99
☐	7493 0010 8	**What Fresh Hell is This?**	Marion Meade	£3.99
☐	7493 0011 6	**War Games**	Thomas Allen	£3.99
☐	7493 0013 2	**The Crash**	Mihir Bose	£4.99
☐	7493 0014 0	**The Demon Drink**	Jancis Robinson	£4.99
☐	7493 0015 9	**The Health Scandal**	Vernon Coleman	£4.99
☐	7493 0016 7	**Vietnam – The 10,000 Day War**	Michael Maclear	£3.99
☐	7493 0049 3	**The Spycatcher Trial**	Malcolm Turnbull	£3.99
☐	7493 0022 1	**The Super Saleswoman**	Janet Macdonald	£4.99
☐	7493 0023 X	**What's Wrong With Your Rights?**	Cook/Tate	£4.99
☐	7493 0024 8	**Mary and Richard**	Michael Burn	£3.50
☐	7493 0061 2	**Voyager**	Yeager/Rutan	£3.99
☐	7493 0060 4	**The Fashion Conspiracy**	Nicholas Coleridge	£3.99
☐	7493 0027 2	**Journey Without End**	David Bolton	£3.99
☐	7493 0028 0	**The Common Thread**	Common Thread	£4.99

All these books are available at your bookshop or newsagent, or can be ordered direct from the publisher. Just tick the titles you want and fill in the form below.

Mandarin Paperbacks, Cash Sales Department, PO Box 11, Falmouth, Cornwall TR10 9EN.

Please send cheque or postal order, no currency, for purchase price quoted and allow the following for postage and packing:

UK	55p for the first book, 22p for the second book and 14p for each additional book ordered to a maximum charge of £1.75.
BFPO and Eire	55p for the first book, 22p for the second book and 14p for each of the next seven books, thereafter 8p per book.
Overseas Customers	£1.00 for the first book plus 25p per copy for each additional book.

NAME (Block Letters) ....

ADDRESS ....

....